Diving Deep

How to Find Truth in a
Sea of Lies, Bias, Spin, Scams, and Fraud

Frank J. Realin

Weymouth Press
Weymouth, Massachusetts
2013

For information contact: Weymouth Press, P.O. Box 16, Weymouth, MA 02191.

First Weymouth Press Edition 2013

Realin, Frank J.
Diving deep : how to find truth in a sea of lies, bias, spin, scams, and fraud
Includes bibliographical references and index / by Frank J. Realin
1. Truthfulness and falsehood. 2. Deception. 3. Fraud—prevention.

ISBN: 1469980681
ISBN-13: 9781469980683
Library of Congress Control Number: 2012901786
CreateSpace Independent Publishing Platform
North Charleston, South Carolina

Diving Deep

For Jaina Louise Farrington
May you always know the truth

CONTENTS

DISCLAIMER

The author and publisher have made every effort to provide accurate, useful information but make no representation or warranty about the book's accuracy, validity, or completeness. Some suggestions in the book may also not be appropriate for your circumstances. Thus the author and publisher cannot guarantee that you will achieve the desired outcome: avoiding the lies, bias, spin, scams, and fraud mentioned in the book's subtitle.

The book is not intended as a source of professional advice or services. For legal, medical, scientific, or other expert assistance, you should seek the services of qualified professionals.

The author has tried to include useful, up-to-date supplementary materials, but readers should use due diligence in consulting the websites and other recommended resources.

In short, the author has written this book in the hope that it will enrich readers' lives. But the author and publisher shall have no responsibility, risk, or liability for any errors or omissions in the book's contents or for any losses, injuries, or damages caused or alleged to have been caused, directly or indirectly, by the use of the book.

*"MK ulTRA" Interogations used by
CIA & FBI

mystery of UFO and USA air force
in connection with German Intelligent x
security.*

INTRODUCTION

When Richard M. Nixon resigned from the presidency in disgrace in 1974, thousands of people around the country thought poignantly of one person—not Vice President Gerald R. Ford, thrust unexpectedly into the White House because of the Watergate break-in, or Senator George S. McGovern, defeated by Nixon in a landslide two years earlier, but Helen Gahagan Douglas. Douglas was the former opera singer and Broadway star who became a three-term congresswoman and was defeated by Nixon in the 1950 California senatorial race, still remembered as one of the dirtiest elections ever. It was that election that made Nixon's ascent to the presidency possible.

Douglas worked tirelessly for social justice and has been lauded as "one of the grandest, most eloquent, deepest-thinking people we have had in American politics."[1] Yet as we'll see in Chapter 6, Nixon stopped at nothing to destroy Douglas's career and reputation, forcing her permanently from public office. His campaign against her became the prototype for all his subsequent campaigns, and opened the door to the kind of dirty politics that have become increasingly normative in the United States. Despite what Nixon had done to her, Douglas refused to be vindictive, explaining that "when I woke up the next morning [after the election] I felt free, uninjured, whole. Nixon had his victory but I had mine."[2] She went on to lead an extraordinarily productive life working on behalf of causes she cared deeply about, from the plight of farmworkers to environmental issues, from civil rights to disarmament.

Douglas is remembered as a model of courage and grace—as someone who found her own truth and remained loyal to it. After her death in 1980, hundreds of people and organizations paid tribute to her. A typical tribute came from a Sacramento newspaper, editorializing that "one of the several faces of courage is just being true to oneself in one's own place and in one's own time. Such was the courage of Helen Gahagan Douglas, the actress-turned-Congresswoman whose political career ended in a bitter clash with Richard M. Nixon in 1950."[3] We'll examine many kinds of truth and falsity in this book. Because the book is meant to provide you with useful, concrete information, the following chapters often focus on the minutiae of deception in everyday life—duplicitous advertising, sweepstakes scams, and the like. Underlying all the chapters, though, is the notion that like Douglas, we live the richest, most productive lives when we're truest to ourselves.

Deception in Contemporary Society

We're all bombarded on a daily basis by messages for the purpose of convincing us to make decisions or form opinions based on what we are being told is true. Statistics, poll results, and professional opinions may be cited to give credibility to these messages. Yet we've all had the experience of eventually finding out the messages were incorrect, misleading, and often outright lies. In the words of an *Advertising Age* editorial, "Whether it's about agency billings and income or high-stakes geopolitical strategy, disinformation is part of the communications arsenal. Efforts to confuse, misdirect, mislead, or confound a public are part of today's world."[4]

Some of this misinformation is so trivial or outlandish that it could be considered a minor annoyance, even a source of amusement—like the exaggerated claims some advertisers make to entice us to buy their products. But most misinformation isn't harmless, and sometimes it's profoundly destructive. Who can forget the Enron scandal, in which employees and investors lost millions? Enron was, for a time, the world's largest energy trader. Then it declared bankruptcy and thousands found themselves without a job. Many employees also lost their life savings when their 401(k) retirement plans were frozen and when the company's stock dropped from $90 to $1 a share. Among the tragedies was that of Cathy Peterson and her husband Bill, an Enron employee being treated for cancer when the company went under. "We really suffered. We suffered financially and emotionally," Cathy Peterson recalled. "We sold our home, our second car, anything we could live without we did without, cell phones, newspapers. I learned to buy the cheapest food we could buy. We moved in with my twin sister. My husband was not allowed the dignity of dying in his own home."[5]

The Madoff scandal also left a swath of destruction in its wake. Thousands of individuals lost everything and dozens of charities had to shut down as a result of financier Bernard Madoff's predatory practices. Referring to the disproportionate number of Jewish investors who had been victimized, one woman who lost "double-digit millions" said, "What Hitler didn't finish, he did!"[6] One of the most shocking aspects of the Madoff scheme was that he victimized Holocaust survivor and Nobel laureate Elie Wiesel, costing Wiesel and his wife Marion their life savings of $7 million and bilking the Elie Wiesel Foundation for Humanity out of $15.2 million.[7]

The Enron and Madoff examples show how high the stakes can be when we're fed misleading information. When we make decisions based on incorrect or deceptive information, we can not only lose money in a financial investment but can also opt for the wrong medical treatment, take out an inappropriate insurance policy, vote for the wrong political candidate, buy a house we shouldn't buy, or even marry the wrong person. More generally, a society in which a high level of deception prevails is a society that breeds disrespect and distrust among its citizens. *Diving Deep: How to Find Truth in a Sea of Lies, Bias, Spin, Scams, and Fraud* is intended to address these problems; it's about the deception surrounding all of us, and how you can dive through it to find truth.

Why This Book?

My parents were uneducated immigrants from Italy who didn't speak English. In my early childhood, we lived in a Boston attic with no bathroom. We survived on bread, milk, beans, and other staples dispensed by a federal program created under President Franklin D. Roosevelt's New Deal. My parents' dream was for me to attend parochial school, but to qualify, I had to be able to speak proper English. My parents couldn't teach me, so I mastered English pronunciation by listening to the radio.

At an early age I became aware of the prejudice and misinformation that existed about Italians, Jews, and blacks in the Boston area, which gave me a lifelong sensitivity to social injustice. Prejudice against Italians was often intense. Some of it had been stirred up by the Sacco and Vanzetti case, which people still talked about throughout my childhood.

The Sacco and Vanzetti case, profiled in Chapter 5, was one of the most notorious of the twentieth century. In 1920, a paymaster and guard transporting a factory payroll of just under $16,000 in South Braintree, Massachusetts, had been robbed and murdered. Two suspects were quickly rounded up and charged with the crime. Both were working-class Italian immigrants; Nicola Sacco was a shoemaker and Bartolomeo Vanzetti sold fish for a living. Based only on circumstantial evidence, they were convicted and sentenced to death in a trial lasting just a few weeks. Despite international outrage—demonstrators from Paris to Tokyo to Mexico City protested the unfairness of the trial—Sacco and Vanzetti were executed. Many still see their executions as a miscarriage of justice and blame anti-immigrant and anti-Italian prejudice.

With determination and hard work, I was able to overcome prejudice and realize another dream my parents had for me: to go to college. My interest in health issues and in social problems led me to choose a career path in hospital administration. My experience spanning many years as a hospital administrator, Public Health Advisor for the U.S. Public Health Service, and activist on behalf of judicial and political reform provides the backdrop for this book.

Much of my professional life as well as my community service has focused on helping clients and community members cut through the morass of deception and hype that ordinary Americans are confronted with every day—government bureaucracy, legal duplicity, deceptive advertising, financial scams, and the like. This experience has convinced me of the need for a succinct, readable book that surveys the major forms of deception people are likely to encounter and that offers strategies the average person can follow to minimize their risk.

In short, *Diving Deep* grew out of my experiences, research, much thought, and a strong desire to help others know how to find the truth. It's the culmination of my lifelong passion for social justice and is meant to fill a need not filled by any other book.

A Practical Guide

This book is not intended to be a discourse on philosophical truth or certitude. It's meant to be a practical guide on how to determine useful truths from the oral and written information presented to us. It's written for ordinary people like you who have to make decisions every day about politics, jobs, finances, personal relationships—in short, about every aspect of your life. In the following pages, you'll learn how to cut through the charade of words you hear and read in order to arrive at a basic stratum of truth. With this awareness, you'll have the clarity of mind to form opinions and make decisions that are right for you.

Diving Deep has ten chapters and an appendix. Chapter 1, "Finding Truth," lays the groundwork by providing basic definitions of truth, lies, spin, and other concepts. Chapter 2, "Propaganda: From Nazism to Soft-Drink Ads and Soft Porn," is also foundational because it shows how propaganda underlies many other forms of deception. (You might be surprised to know, for example, that *propaganda* was an early term for advertising—or maybe you're not surprised.) Chapter 3, "Big Brother, Brainwashing, and You," takes George Orwell's *Nineteen Eighty-Four* as a starting point and explores how brainwashing techniques are being used to deceive others in forums that go way beyond government interrogation sessions. Chapter 4, "The Brave New World of Advertising," looks at the incursion of advertising and public relations into our lives. Chapter 5, "Media Bias and What You Can Do about It," examines an ever-worsening problem in U.S. society and touches on some of the ways you can cut through it. Chapter 6, "Truth and Lies in Politics," covers honesty and deception in the political arena. Chapter 7, "Bigots and Demagogues," considers the extremes of hate and deception. Chapter 8, "The Legal Web," discusses how ordinary people can become ensnared in the legal system and suggests some things you can do to avoid this trap. Chapter 9, "Fighting Scams," focuses on recognizing and combating financial scams. Chapter 10, "Science: Not Always 'Scientific,'" alerts you to the problems of scientific bias and fraud. Finally, an appendix titled "Diving Deep and Thinking Critically" ties the threads of the previous chapters together by providing a quick-reference guide to the critical-thinking skills you'll need in your search for truth.

Supplementary materials in each chapter give you additional tools to help you achieve that goal. In the "Test Your Skills" boxes, you can apply what you've just learned to hypothetical cases of deception and fraud. At the end of each chapter, a "What You Can Do" section suggests actions you can take to address problems ranging from media bias to political deception to scientific fraud. "Further Reading" lists key works so you can follow up on topics you're interested in.

Conclusion

I hope this book will give you the awareness as well as the resources to help you know the truth—your truth. By becoming more aware of the myriad forms of deception in our society and taking concrete steps to minimize their impact, you can also help build a better, more just society for everyone, just as Helen Gahagan Douglas managed to do despite the campaign of lies and character assassination Richard Nixon waged against her.

Acknowledgments

My thanks to the following, who reviewed the manuscript and offered suggestions to make this a better book: Joan A. Beairsto, Lillian Brodie, Marilyn Gallivan, Janet P. Levasseur, Dorothy E. Morrell, Meridith Murray, Peggy Rosenberger, Mark A. Schlesinger, Robert Louis Sheehan, Richard E. Skinner, and Robert J. Wilson. I also wish to thank the many people I have met during my lifetime who intentionally or unintentionally made me aware of the sea of misinformation we live in and of the need for this book.

I. FINDING TRUTH

When I was involved in judicial reform, a judge once said to me that there aren't enough jails to put people in who lie in court. And surveys show a dramatic increase in dishonesty by young people, with more than 80 percent of high school students admitting they've cheated, lied, plagiarized, or stolen.[8] There's even a company that specializes in providing alibis and excuses for people trying to hide affairs or escape from their jobs.[9] We're surrounded by such a sea of deception that it's hard to know where to begin in discussing it. To get us started, this chapter provides a working definition of *truth*, then homes in on the five terms for deception in the subtitle of the book (*lies, bias, spin, scams,* and *fraud*).

What Is Truth?

To recognize truth we first have to know what truth is.

A glance at any reference work will show that defining truth is a daunting task. Many encyclopedias contain page after page of philosophical disputation, with no agreement in sight. For example, the online encyclopedia *Wikipedia* cautions that "there is no single definition of truth" about which most scholars agree and that "many theories of truth . . . continue to be debated." The *Wikipedia* article goes on to discuss truth under headings as diverse as "Aquinas and the Scholastics," "Biblical Inerrancy," "Truth in Eastern Thought," and "Truth in Mathematics."[10]

Luckily we don't have to get involved in these philosophical and theological disputes. For our purposes a simple dictionary definition will do. Many dictionaries define truth as "conformity with fact or reality" or something similar.[11]

Slippery Concepts and Paradigm Shifts

Of course, fact and reality are slippery concepts, too. Not everyone agrees on "the facts" or on what is "real." Our interpretations are often shaped by our education, experiences, memories, prior judgments, and prejudices. History abounds with famous examples. Consider the transition from the geocentric (earth-centered) to the heliocentric (sun-centered) theory of astronomy. The astronomer Ptolemy, who lived in Alexandria, Egypt, in the second century, worked out the version of the geocentric model that prevailed in Europe for more than a thousand years. According to this model, the sun, planets, and other celestial bodies revolve around the earth. Once the Ptolemaic model became embedded not only in scientific thinking but also in church doctrine, it became hard to dislodge.

Yet Copernicus, the influential Polish mathematician and astronomer, tried to do exactly that with his book *On the Revolutions of the Celestial Spheres*, completed just before his death in 1543. Copernicus argued for the heliocentric model, according to which the earth and other planets revolve around the sun. After the telescope was invented in 1609, scientists like the Italian astronomer and physicist Galileo provided more convincing data in support of the heliocentric model. Just as Protestants like Martin Luther voiced opposition to Copernicus's heliocentric theory in the sixteenth century, so also was the Catholic church hostile to Galileo's discoveries. His work was so threatening that he was tried for heresy by the Inquisition in 1633. Though he escaped the fate of being burned at the stake as others had been by the Inquisition, he was sentenced to house arrest for an indefinite period. The church didn't acknowledge the accuracy of his heliocentric model until 1992.[12]

The clash between these two profoundly different "truths" about the universe and the place of humans in it—the geocentric and heliocentric models—provides a vivid example of just how elusive concepts like truth and reality can be.

Another famous example is the introduction of Darwinian evolution in the nineteenth century. The idea that humans could be related to apes—let alone descended from them—was profoundly threatening. Numerous scientific and theological debates sprang up around these conflicting "truths" about evolution. At a famous meeting of the British Association at Oxford in June 1860, Darwin's views were put to the test. Representing the anti-evolutionary sentiment typical of the clergy, Samuel Wilberforce, Bishop of Oxford, lampooned Darwin's theories. Turning to Thomas Henry Huxley, who was a scientist and Darwin supporter, Wilberforce mockingly "begged to know, was it through his grandfather or his grandmother that he claimed his descent from a monkey?"[13] Not to be outdone, Huxley took Wilberforce to task for his scientific ignorance. Then he retorted that he would not be ashamed to be descended from a monkey, but would be "ashamed to be connected with a man who used great gifts to obscure the truth."[14]

To take an example of conflicting realities in the twentieth century, Rachel Carson—the biologist and author credited with setting the U.S. environmental movement in motion with her pathbreaking book *Silent Spring* (1962)—challenged majority opinion by warning of the dangers of pesticide use.[15] For her efforts "Carson was attacked by the chemical industry and some in government as an alarmist, but courageously spoke out to remind us that we are a vulnerable part of the natural world subject to the same damage as the rest of the ecosystem."[16] Over the last half century Carson's views have gradually spread through our society, but the battle is far from won.

The question of how one truth displaces another and becomes the prevailing view has fascinated generations of thinkers. Perhaps the best-known book on this subject is *The Structure of Scientific Revolutions* by Thomas S. Kuhn, a philosophy professor at MIT until his death in 1996.[17] Originally published in 1962, the book has gone through several editions because of its popularity. Kuhn traces the way "paradigm shifts" occur in science when old ideas give way to new ones, causing scientific revolutions like the ones I've just mentioned in astronomy, biology, and environmentalism. Of course, paradigm shifts can also occur in politics, spirituality, or any other area of our thinking.

A Working Definition of Truth

The early twenty-first century—like Darwin's era in the nineteenth century—is a time of social ferment, and it's impossible to overlook the paradigm shifts going on all around us. The "truths" people accept about the environment, the nature of animals, proper gender roles, the concept of race, and so on are changing all the time. Even in a practical guidebook of this nature we won't be able to completely sidestep these evolving understandings of "truth"; it would be unrealistic to claim otherwise. Yet for the most part we'll be concerned with how to recognize simpler, more straightforward truths—in the pronouncements of politicians, financial offers, ads, opinion polls, and the like. These are the situations in which you're called on every day to make decisions about the accuracy or inaccuracy of information. And as noted in the introduction, the stakes can be high—voting for an unqualified political candidate, entering into a disastrous financial deal, or making a dangerous healthcare choice, to list just a few examples.

So to answer the question posed by the first section heading in the chapter, in this book we'll avoid all the philosophical controversy about the meaning of truth and will use as our working definition the one given earlier: truth is conformity with fact or reality.

The preceding paragraphs have given us a foundation to build on by providing a basic definition of truth. I now turn to the other side of the coin: deception.

Lies, Bias, Spin, Scams, and Fraud: Some Definitions

A glance at a dictionary or thesaurus will turn up an endless list of synonyms for lies or dishonesty: *disinformation, dissimulation, duplicity, fabrication, falsehood, fib, mendacity, perjury, prevarication, untruth*, and many others. It's probably not an accident that we have such an extensive vocabulary for deception, because the world is full of deception.

It would take a work the size of a multivolume encyclopedia to adequately document the myriad forms of deception all around us. I can only touch on the highlights in the following chapters, so I've tried to discuss representative types of deception that you're likely to encounter. Five terms weave in and out of these chapters, the five terms in the book's subtitle: *lies, bias, spin, scams,* and *fraud.* A few comments will help to clarify their meaning.

Test Your Skills

Frank W. Abagnale—the former con artist whose exploits are described in the book, film, and play *Catch Me If You Can*—asserts that "we are living in an extremely unethical society. ...Until we are willing to face up to the importance of character and ethics, we can expect to see a lot more Enrons, corporate fraud, embezzlements."[1] David Callahan, author of *The Cheating Culture: Why More Americans Are Doing Wrong to Get Ahead*, agrees. Callahan says:

"Available evidence strongly suggests that Americans are not only cheating more in many areas but are also feeling less guilty about it. When 'everybody does it,' or imagines that everybody does it, a cheating culture has emerged.

Yet why all the cheating, and why now?"[2]

How would you answer those questions? What do you think can be done about the problem?

1. Frank W. Abagnale, with Stan Redding, *Catch Me If You Can: The Amazing True Story of the Youngest and Most Daring Con Man in the History of Fun and Profit!* (New York: Broadway Books, [1980] 2002), 291–292.
2. David Callahan, *The Cheating Culture: Why More Americans Are Doing Wrong to Get Ahead* (Orlando, FL: Harcourt, 2004), 12–13.

Lies and Those Who Tell Them

A lie, for our purposes in this book, is a statement deliberately made by someone who knows or should know that the statement is not true or not entirely true, is misleading for personal benefit, and may cause harm to someone. Lying typically involves falsification, but it can also involve concealment—as when President Richard M. Nixon and his aides misled congressional investigators during the Watergate hearings in the 1970s by claiming they "couldn't remember" key events.

Whether someone can be expected to know something is true depends on their knowledge of existing realities. Earlier I talked about paradigm shifts and the way certain ideas—like Rachel Carson's belief that many chemicals are hazardous to the environment—eventually become dominant in a society. So an individual or chemical company maintaining in the early twenty-first century that all chemicals are completely safe for the environment could be expected to know better. But statements that might be viewed as lies today could be seen merely as reflecting ignorance if they'd been made a century ago.

Some untruths shouldn't really be considered lies. "Little white lies," such as telling a child about Santa Claus coming down the chimney to deliver toys, or the hospital visitor who tells a gravely sick friend that he looks good when he really doesn't, are not lies by definition. These statements are made to give pleasure or hope to someone. The motive is not self-gain or the desire to harm someone. These are examples of statements that are not true but are not lies.

Then there are statements that appear to be true but are lies. These are called "mental reservations" by some philosophers. For example, A asks B if she could donate a dollar bill to a charity. B realizes that A doesn't literally mean a donation of a dollar bill and knows that she has several dollars in coins. But she doesn't want to donate, so she replies that she doesn't have a dollar bill. Her statement is intentionally misleading for her own benefit. The same would be the case if a worker told his boss he'd missed work the day before because he'd "been sick," while failing to mention that he was actually sick three months earlier.

Though I'll be focusing primarily on lies people tell to deceive others, self-deception can also be a problem. In fact, the German philosopher Friedrich Nietzsche said "the most common lie is the lie one tells to oneself."[18] Sometimes the circumstances are minor, such as when we convince ourselves that our singing voice or golf swing is better than it is. In other cases self-deception can have horrific consequences, as with the Space

Shuttle *Challenger* disaster on January 28, 1986. Only seventy-three seconds after liftoff, the *Challenger* exploded, killing all seven crewmembers. The tragedy was even more poignant than it might have been because one of those on board was Christa McAuliffe, a teacher whose students were watching the launch on television. Investigators traced the problem to the rubber O-ring seals on the solid rocket boosters, since the rubber tended to lose elasticity in cold weather. The hot gases released when the O-rings failed to seal properly were thought to have caused the huge adjacent fuel tank to explode. Though engineers at Morton Thiokol—the firm that manufactured the solid rocket boosters—recommended delaying the launch because cold weather was predicted, NASA officials failed to heed their advice. Apparently NASA managers were urged to view the issue through a "management" rather than an "engineering" lens. Since it was important to stay on schedule from a management standpoint—because NASA feared that more delays would mean a loss of congressional funding—the officials convinced themselves that the launch should occur as planned. Their self-deception, made possible by the larger culture that elevated management priorities over engineering concerns, cost seven lives and caused great suffering to their survivors and others.[19] President Ronald Reagan eulogized the astronauts the evening of the disaster with these memorable words: "We will never forget them, nor the last time we saw them, this morning, as they prepared for their journey and waved good-bye and 'slipped the surly bonds of earth' to 'touch the face of God.'"[20]

Who are the purveyors of lies? To begin, deceptive behavior is not limited to humans, because animals reveal extensive evidence of it. Scientists say incidents like the following are not uncommon: "A male [baboon], one who does not willingly share, caught an antelope. The female edged up to him and groomed him until he lulled under her attentions. She then snatched the antelope carcass and ran."[21] Perhaps in animals as in humans, the ability to deceive others rests on a sense of self and on the ability to see those others as separate.[22]

Certainly in humans, a long developmental process occurs in childhood and young adulthood, with almost everyone acquiring a capacity to lie. As Mark Twain quipped, "None of us could live with an habitual

Did You Know?

Some Psychologists Think Honesty May Be Correlated with Higher IQ

On one important study, according to psychologist Paul Ekman, "Below-average IQ was more common among liars than honest children. None of those kids with the highest IQs lied or cheated. Even in between these two extremes, the figures consistently show that the higher the IQ, the lower the percent of kids who lied. As with almost all of the studies of children's intelligence in the last fifty years, smarter kids lie less."[1]

Ekman suggests smarter kids may cheat less because they don't need to. But there are other possibilities. Some students may cheat to avoid hard work; if brighter students were given more challenging assignments and had to work harder, they might cheat at the same rate as poorer students. Or students with a high IQ may be motivated to cheat at the same rate as others but may be better at foreseeing the consequences of getting caught. Another possibility is that "smart kids may just be better liars, more clever cheaters."[2]

---

1   Paul Ekman, with Mary Ann Mason Ekman and Tom Ekman, *Why Kids Lie: How Parents Can Encourage Truthfulness* (New York: Scribner's, 1989), 39.
2   Ekman, Ekman, and Ekman, *Why Kids Lie,* 41.

truth-teller; but thank goodness none of us has to."[23] Some people—like con artists, top-level poker players, and certain mesmerizing politicians—become "advanced" liars. Some categories of liars are fascinating. You've probably encountered a few compulsive or habitual liars. These are people who can't stop lying even when it's not in their best interest.

Experts suggest compulsive lying is often an effort to compensate for low self-esteem and can be rooted in childhood trauma or dysfunctional family dynamics.

Another intriguing category of liars includes so-called impostors. Most impostors are men, except for a few women posing as men to escape the strictures of gender roles, like women who've passed as men in order to become soldiers or sailors. A well-known case of a woman impersonating a man is that of Dr. James Barry (about 1792–1865), who had a distinguished career as a British Army surgeon in Canada, Africa, India, and other locations.[24] Barry's identity as a woman only came to light during a postmortem exam in 1865. The army was never able to learn her identity, but she became a feminist hero for circumventing gender roles. After noting Barry's skill as a physician, one admirer said: "For high courage nothing could exceed the spirit of this woman who was so far ahead of her time that, to achieve her purpose, she renounced her sex."[25]

Ferdinand Waldo Demara Jr. (1921–1982) was a more typical and very famous impostor. Demara's exploits—which included successfully posing as a surgeon in the Royal Canadian Navy—became the subject of a bestselling biography by Robert Crichton titled *The Great Impostor* and of a 1960 film by the same name starring Tony Curtis.[26] Both mental health professionals and laypeople have puzzled over the motivation underlying this syndrome, because many impostors are highly intelligent, highly competent individuals who could easily have successful careers in their own names. When Demara was asked why he'd impersonated everything from a Trappist monk to a prison warden to a doctor, he said it was because he was a "rotten man."[27] Some impostors may overcome self-esteem problems and derive a feeling of superiority from duping others; some also say they no longer feel empty but become more alive or energized when carrying out deceptive acts.

The label "Great Impostor" has also been applied to a more recent impersonator, Frank W. Abagnale. A New York native, Abagnale (1948–) posed as a Pan Am pilot, pediatrician, attorney (for which he passed the bar exam despite being a high school dropout), college professor, and stockbroker. He also passed $2.5 million in bogus checks "scattered in earnest throughout all fifty states and twenty-six countries," making him one of the FBI's most wanted fugitives.[28] Incredibly, Abagnale did all this and more in a five-year period, between the ages of sixteen and twenty-one. His crimes eventually caught up with him. After serving six months in a harsh French prison and another six months in a luxurious Swedish one, he was extradited to the United States. After a brief escape—made by removing the toilet and squeezing through the hole onto the runway as his plane landed in New York—he was tried and received a lengthy prison sentence. Paroled after three years, he became a security consultant for the FBI, banks, and other organizations. Abagnale's story is the subject of a ghostwritten memoir, a 2002 film starring Leonardo DiCaprio, and a Broadway musical, all titled *Catch Me If You Can*.[29]

Another syndrome closely related to imposture (as the efforts of impostors are called) is Munchausen syndrome. In this bizarre condition, "patients" pretend to be sick and wander from hospital to hospital, sometimes subjecting themselves to unnecessary surgery (the medical record of one notorious "patient" includes more than 400 hospital stays!)[30] According to a psychiatrist, "The childhood experiences of the Munchausen patient frequently included a rejecting or sadistic parent, an association with death or chronic illness in the childhood home, bizarre or neurotic childhood behavior, and an episode of institutionalization or hospitalization. . . . Munchausen patients frequently regarded their childhood hospitalization as a positive experience because it rescued the child from an unhappy home situation, at least temporarily."[31] Other research suggests brain dysfunction may be at the root of some cases of Munchausen syndrome and related disorders.[32]

I won't be concerned with anything as dramatic as impostors or Munchausen patients in this book. The following chapters focus on the garden-variety liars you're unfortunately likely to encounter on a regular basis: politicians and their spinmasters, journalists and opinion makers, industry spokespeople, advertisers, and salespeople. This is not a blanket indictment of all of the above since many of them are honest, but just of those politicians, advertisers, and others who give their professions a bad name.

Liars shouldn't be confused with a different group. There's really no simple, polite name for them, so I'll call them what most people call them: bullshitters. An entire (though admittedly tiny) book has been written about them: Harry G. Frankfurt's sixty-seven-page *On Bullshit*.[33] After raising the issue of the gendered nature of the word *bull* in terms like *bullshit* and *bull session* (which he suggests is a "sanitized version" of *bullshit session*),[34] Frankfurt distinguishes bullshitters from liars. "A person who undertakes to bullshit his way through has much more freedom [than a liar]," Frankfurt notes, because "his focus is panoramic rather than particular."[35] There's another difference; interestingly, Frankfurt says, bullshitters have less regard for the truth:

> It is impossible for someone to lie unless he thinks he knows the truth. Producing bullshit requires no such conviction. A person who lies is thereby responding to the truth, and he is to that extent respectful of it. When an honest man speaks, he says only what he believes to be true; and for the liar, it is correspondingly indispensable that he considers his statements to be false. For the bullshitter, however, all these bets are off. . . . He does not care whether the things he says describe reality correctly. He just picks them out, or makes them up, to suit his purpose.[36]

Bullshit is especially common in certain contexts like politics, as we'll see in Chapter 6. Why do people lie? I'll explore this issue in more detail in later chapters, but as a preview, Table 1.1 lists five of the most common motives. As you can see, some motives, like exercising power, seem especially prevalent in the political and business arenas. More specific types of lies common in politics and business include aggressive

Table 1.1 Five common reasons for lying

Motive	Observations
Protect oneself	Surveys show the most common motive for lying in both childhood and adulthood is to avoid punishment. Lying may occur to protect against other forms of physical or psychological danger as well. To take a common example, a child could tell a stranger at the door that a parent will be back in five minutes when in fact the child is home alone. Some people also lie to block the intrusive and controlling behavior of others in order to maintain their psychological independence.
Enhance self-esteem	In this common type of deception, people with low self-esteem embellish the truth by exaggerating their accomplishments in sports, business, or some other arena. In extreme cases they may become a so-called impostor and impersonate an athlete, business tycoon, law enforcement official, or anyone else they aspire to be.
Exercise power	A common example involves lying in order to obtain something otherwise unobtainable. These lies could be intended to facilitate anything from a minor favor to a business deal or sex. More generally, power is obtained through reducing or distorting the information others possess; duping others through scams, practical jokes, or other deceptive acts also gives some people a sense of satisfaction and power. Some of these lies are trivial but others are vicious. Vicious lies can have many motives, ranging from hostility toward the target individual or group to displaced anger that is really meant for someone else, like an abusive parent or spouse.
Benefit others	Altruistic lies can range from the little white lies that preserve people's feelings to more serious lies that protect people's safety, as in the case of abolitionists who lied to protect fugitive slaves.
Aid self-deception	Self-deception takes many forms. As an example, if someone suspects a family member has committed a crime but the family member denies it, it may be tempting to accept the denials without question rather than face unpleasant truths. This could be seen both as one's own self-deception (refusing to acknowledge the criminal conduct) and as aiding the relative's self-deception (by failing to challenge their claims of innocence). The person could also reinforce their self-deception or that of the relative by lying to others.

or sadistic lies, usually told in order to inflict harm on opponents and/ or to shore up sagging self-esteem because of the satisfaction of putting something over on someone. If the liars are malevolent enough and their targets are gullible or vulnerable enough, these lies can have tragic consequences. A famous example from World War II involved the way Adolf Hitler—who was a pathological liar—duped British Prime Minister Neville Chamberlain into believing that Germany didn't intend to go to war. If Britain and other Allied countries hadn't let their guard down, millions of lives could have been saved. Closer to home, I'll touch on the duplicitous behavior of corporate executives in Chapter 9—behavior that has brought financial ruin on thousands of employees and investors.

Test Your Skills

The blurb on the back cover of a book called *A Treasury of Deception: Liars, Misleaders, Hoodwinkers, and the Extraordinary True Stories of History's Greatest Hoaxes, Fakes, and Frauds* includes this sentence: "We may *say* that honesty is the best policy, but history—to say nothing of business, politics, and the media—suggests otherwise."[1] What do you think the author means? Do you agree with his statement? Why or why not?

---

1   Michael Farquhar, *A Treasury of Deception: Liars, Misleaders, Hoodwinkers, and the Extraordinary True Stories of History's Greatest Hoaxes, Fakes, and Frauds* (New York: Penguin, 2005), back-cover blurb.

On a more positive note, as Table 1.1 shows, some lies are altruistic. Altruistic lies include the "little white lies" mentioned earlier that are intended to preserve someone's feelings, like a favorable comment on an unflattering hairdo. Interestingly, because young children lack the capacity to engage in this type of deception and it only develops with age, it's often considered a sign of maturity; many experts also feel it's correlated with good social skills or interpersonal sophistication.[37] In more serious cases altruistic lies can save lives, as with the Dutch and Danish citizens in World War II who lied to the Nazis to protect the Jewish families they were hiding.

If we're going to talk about our motives for lying to others, we should also talk about our motives for lying to ourselves. Self-deception is often rooted in self-justification—the urge to justify our actions, especially those that have been irresponsible, unethical, or harmful to others. The process of self-justification is the subject of Carol Tavris and Elliot Aronson's informative book *Mistakes Were Made (but Not by Me): Why We Justify Foolish Beliefs, Bad Decisions, and Hurtful Acts*.[38] They note that when they began working on the book, President George W. Bush was the "poster boy" for tenacity in refusing to let go of discredited beliefs because of his insistence that the Iraq War was justified despite intelligence failures and other mistakes and miscalculations by his administration. But he's not alone in engaging in self-justification: "Most of us will never be in a position to make decisions affecting the lives and deaths of millions of people, but whether the consequences of our mistakes are trivial or tragic, on a small scale or a national canvas, most of us find it difficult, if not impossible, to say, 'I was wrong; I made a terrible mistake.' The higher the stakes—emotional, financial, moral—the greater the difficulty."[39] Tavris and Aronson go on to caution that "self-justification is more powerful and more dangerous than the explicit lie. It allows people to convince themselves that what they did was the best thing they could have done. In fact, come to think of it, it was the right thing. 'There was nothing else I could have done.' 'Actually, it was a brilliant solution to the problem.' 'I was doing the best for the nation.' 'Those bastards deserved what they got.' 'I'm entitled.'"[40]

The impulse to engage in self-justification is often produced by cognitive dissonance, which occurs when we hold two conflicting beliefs at the same time. The dissonance causes discomfort or even agony, creating a need for a resolution. To take a common example, students who see themselves as ethical but who decide to cheat to get ahead may try to reduce the cognitive dissonance by reassuring themselves that "it's not really cheating because the professor is a jerk" or "it's okay because everyone's doing it." (The latter rationale has contributed to the exponential increase in student plagiarism, though this problem may diminish as plagiarism-detection software is more widely adopted in the educational system.)[41] Another common example involves smoking; someone who knows smoking is hazardous but can't stop may try to rationalize their behavior by claiming it helps them "lose weight." Government leaders who see themselves as fundamentally wise and just but who cause the deaths of thousands of innocent people in war have to find ways of reconciling these perceptions, perhaps by claiming they've prevented an even greater loss of life from some hypothetical future catastrophe. Scientists who have a self-image of being unbiased, yet who let their work be tainted by the drug industry that provides their funding, may try to reduce the dissonance by downplaying safety concerns. This is exactly what has happened in a long list of medical tragedies ranging from thalidomide to Vioxx (see Chapter 10).

Memoirists who falsify their life experience offer still another illustration of the connection between cognitive dissonance and self-justification. If they have a self-image of being ethical, they often try to eliminate the dissonance by claiming they've distorted the details of their experience to convey some larger truth. James Frey, who originally represented his controversial book *A Million Little Pieces* as a memoir, later admitted parts were fiction but justified the deception on the grounds that the fabricated account of his experiences would help others cope with alcohol and drug addiction.[42] A memoir titled *Angel at the Fence: A True Story of a Love That Survived* by a Holocaust survivor named Herman Rosenblat—scheduled for publication in 2009—was pulled from production when it was learned that key details had been fabricated. Rosenblat said he met his future wife while he was in a subcamp of Buchenwald and she threw apples over a fence to him, but this and other details were challenged by other Holocaust survivors. Confronted about his dishonesty, Rosenblat explained that "I wanted to bring happiness to people. . . . My motivation was to make good in this world."[43]

Cognitive dissonance can be especially painful when people's self-esteem is at stake; such individuals can be desperate to rationalize their behavior. A person who takes pride in being "progressive" but who feels guilt or shame about being prejudiced against particular groups may try to rationalize the prejudice as acceptable. Alternatively, a self-identified conservative who supports family values but has been caught in a sex scandal may feel compelled to justify their behavior. Perhaps Nietzsche summed it up best: "'I have done that,' says my memory. 'I cannot have done that,' says my pride and remains adamant—at last memory yields."[44]

Self-deception is bound up with ordinary lies in complex ways. The lies people tell others can reinforce self-deception. People can also be receptive to the lies of others if those lies aid the process of self-deception. For example, successful politicians are often good at reading the public's need for self-deception; they then campaign on slogans and promises that help to fulfill that need.

Some people are much better than others at detecting deception—studies have shown that U.S. Secret Service agents are unusually good at it—and this book is meant to help you sharpen those skills, too.[45]

The Problem of Bias

The dictionary defines *bias* as a personal inclination and often as a prejudice. Thus bias isn't quite the same as a lie, but it's interwoven with almost every form of deception. Bias motivates people to distort the truth, or what they see as the truth. When a spin doctor spins the poor debate performance of a political candidate into a stellar achievement, an advertiser hypes the virtues of a mediocre product, or a scientist distorts lab results so as to make false claims for a drug's safety or effectiveness, they're engaging in deception because of a bias in favor of their candidate, product, or drug, respectively.

Some forms of bias—like advertising hype—are usually trivial. But history provides many examples of bias with horrific consequences. Millions of "witches" were burned at the stake, hanged, or tortured in the Middle Ages and Renaissance because they were viewed through the filter of religious and cultural biases and were deemed heretics. A similar fate awaited many Native peoples in the wake of European expansionism. As the European colonists made their way across the North American continent, their bias against people they considered "primitive" provided a rationale for many forms of oppression. And only a century and a half ago, slaves in the United States were viewed as "chattel"—a word etymologically related to *cattle*—and sold at auction. Here again, destructive biases were at work.

But, you might argue, this is past history; what does it have to do with the way you make decisions today? We all have biases created by our education and life experience. Consciously or unconsciously these biases tend to make us believe what we want to believe. They prejudice our thought process and often prevent us from seeing things that it would be in our interest and society's interest to see. If you were born into poverty and lived in a shack with no running water, you would likely see a government poverty program differently from someone born into great wealth. Neither you nor the rich person would have walked in the other's shoes. You would never have experienced the comfort and financial independence of the rich person, and the rich person would never have experienced the pain and deprivation of poverty. These differences would influence the way the same government program is viewed. Hurricane Katrina provides another example. Many believe the inadequate response of the federal government to this hurricane, which struck Louisiana and Mississippi in August 2005, stemmed largely from the insensitivity of government officials to the plight of mostly poor, African-American evacuees. It was hard for these officials to perceive a level of desperation they'd never experienced. The same could be said for the inadequate government response to the Gulf oil spill in the same region in 2010. Many Louisiana residents found the federal government unresponsive to their safety concerns and concerns about the environment, as well as to the economic problems resulting from damage to industries like fishing and tourism.

To see the whole picture, therefore, we have to first be willing to identify and examine our biases. Recognizing the biases of others is equally important. If you can determine the biases of others, you can anticipate what they will say on a particular subject. For instance, if the subject is the impact of fossil fuel consumption on the global environment, you can pretty much predict the sentiments of a CEO of a large oil company versus those of an environmentalist. If the issue is toxins in baby food or plastic baby bottles, you can expect that the stance of a young mother will differ from that of a chemical-company executive.

Then there are people who will not discuss an issue when engaged. They may evade the issue or say "I don't want to talk about it." Watch out! This type of person isn't interested in knowing the truth at all. Their biases are so deeply ingrained that there is little chance they'll be open to other perspectives. They also generally see issues in black-and-white terms, not in shades of gray. What they believe becomes the truth, with little room for subtlety, complexity, or differing viewpoints. In the worst-case scenario, this approach can lead to the kind of demagoguery I discuss in Chapter 7.

Spin: A "Polite Word for Deception"

Another common term for deception is *spin*. The meaning of this word is hard to pin down, but I've included it in the subtitle of the book because it's so commonly used with reference to politics and the media. In their book *unSpun: Finding Facts in a World of Disinformation*, Brooks Jackson and Kathleen Hall Jamieson offer this definition: "'Spin' is a polite word for deception. Spinners mislead by means that range from subtle omissions to outright lies. Spin paints a false picture of reality by bending facts, mischaracterizing the words of others, ignoring or denying crucial evidence, or just 'spinning a yarn'—by making things up."[46] They note that spin is sometimes harmless but can include "outright dishonesty, misrepresentation, and a lack of respect for facts."[47] While it can evoke admiration, as a successful spin doctor might in a political campaign, spin should be seen as the destructive practice it usually is.

In short, *spin* encompasses many forms of dishonesty. It may be a synonym for *lie*; it also overlaps with *bias*, though not just in the sense of possessing a prejudice but of acting on it—say, as spin doctors do.

Scams: A Type of Fraud

Merriam-Webster's Collegiate Dictionary defines a scam as a "fraudulent or deceptive act or operation." In other words, scams are a subcategory of fraud. Though the two words are often used interchangeably, I've included both in the subtitle of this book because they can appear in different contexts. For example, people often speak of "sweepstakes scams" but of "scientific fraud." In keeping with popular usage, I've devoted one of the following chapters (Chapter 9) to sweepstakes scams, investment scams, and the like, and one chapter (Chapter 10) to scientific and medical fraud.

Fraud as Deceptive Behavior

Like the terms surveyed earlier, *fraud* can be a general term for deception. But it has other connotations, often involving actions taken to cheat or defraud someone, as in the sweepstakes scams and other financial scams just mentioned. The word *fraud* can apply to many other types of cheating as well. You glimpsed a couple of examples of literary fraud above (the allegedly fraudulent memoirs of James Frey and Herman Rosenblat), and as noted, *fraud* is also commonly used in the context of scientific and medical misconduct.

Conclusion

This chapter began with the metaphor of a sea of deception, because of the myriad forms of deception we have to plunge through to find truth (and to be rewarded by truth, to quote Simone de Beauvoir: "I tore myself away from the safe comfort of certainties through my love for the truth; and truth rewarded me"[48]). Now that we've set the stage, we're ready to turn to concrete examples of truth and lies in the world around us. The next chapter covers a type of deception that permeates our lives: propaganda.

What You Can Do

√*Address the problem of deception in children before it gets out of hand.* Most children lie.[49] There are no hard-and-fast rules for how to handle it, because appropriate solutions depend on parenting styles, the child's temperament, cultural values, and other factors. Severe punishment rarely helps and often makes things worse. With younger children, assisting them in sorting out truth from fantasy or falsity may be helpful. Parents can help older children understand the consequences of their actions. Pathological liars may need professional help, among other reasons because a pattern of lying is often correlated with other antisocial behavior. An extreme example is the Leopold and Loeb murder case, profiled in Chapter 8. Both Nathan Leopold and Richard Loeb were habitual liars, one of several warning signs that the two young men could be headed for more serious crime: the 1924 murder that came to be called the "crime of the century."[50]

√*Do your part to combat the materialism and obsession with status that often lead to cheating and other forms of dishonesty.* This applies to all of us, but it's particularly important to help young people develop a sense of self-worth separate from materialism and obsessive competition. Otherwise the results can be disastrous. As you'll see in Chapter 9, childhood friends of Bernard Madoff speculate that his investment scam that cheated investors out of billions was a compensation for his childhood sense of inadequacy, stemming from the humiliation he experienced because his parents couldn't afford to buy him the most fashionable clothes and toys.

√*Work toward creating a culture based on truth, not deception.* In his book *The Cheating Culture: Why More Americans Are Doing Wrong to Get Ahead*, David Callahan says that "taking on America's cheating culture requires taking on the societal forces that are driving this epidemic."[51] He recommends several measures to address the problem, including the establishment of a new "social contract": "We need to create a new social contract in America that gives people faith in a few simple principles:

Anyone who plays by the rules can get ahead. Everyone has some say in how the rules get made. Everyone who breaks the rules suffers the same penalties. And all of us are in the same boat, living in the same 'moral community' and striving together to build a society that confers respect on people based on a wide variety of accomplishments."[52] Callahan's vision of a society based on truth, not on cheating or lies, is much the same as the vision inspiring *Diving Deep*. None of us individually can banish the ocean of deception surrounding us, but together we can do it by adopting a different value system. Put differently, finding truth is not just an individual but a collective process, requiring the efforts of all of us in order to create an ethical, truthful society.

Further Reading

Paul Ekman is an expert on the subject of deception; see his *Telling Lies: Clues to Deceit in the Marketplace, Politics, and Marriage*, rev. ed. (New York: Norton, 2009). For a detailed treatment of lying and self-deception—with chapter titles ranging from "Everybody Lies" to "Pathological Lying" and "Therapeutic Approaches for the Deceitful Person"—see Charles V. Ford, *Lies! Lies!! Lies!!!: The Psychology of Deceit* (Washington, DC: American Psychiatric Press, 1996). For more on self-justification and cognitive dissonance, see Carol Tavris and Elliot Aronson, *Mistakes Were Made (but Not by Me): Why We Justify Foolish Beliefs, Bad Decisions, and Hurtful Acts* (Orlando, FL: Harcourt, 2007). On moral choices, see Sissela Bok, *Lying: Moral Choice in Public and Private Life*, rev. ed. (New York: Vintage, 1999). Also see Harry G. Frankfurt's pithy *On Bullshit* (Princeton, NJ: Princeton University Press, 2005).

On cheating, see David Callahan, *The Cheating Culture: Why More Americans Are Doing Wrong to Get Ahead* (Orlando, FL: Harcourt, 2004). A small but compelling book on one aspect of cheating is Richard A. Posner's *The Little Book of Plagiarism* (New York: Pantheon Books, 2007). Posner, a judge on the U.S. Seventh Circuit Court of Appeals, makes the complex subject of plagiarism accessible to readers by drawing on wide-ranging examples from literature, art, academia, and other fields.

For a real-life case study of truth and deception and of what can go wrong when the truth loses out, see Allan J. McDonald with James R. Hansen, *Truth, Lies, and O-Rings: Inside the Space Shuttle Challenger Disaster* (Gainesville: University Press of Florida, 2009). The Enron scandal provides another example of what can go wrong when the truth loses out; see Denis Collins, *Behaving Badly: Ethical Lessons from Enron* (Indianapolis: Dog Ear Publishing, 2006).

On the exploits of Ferdinand Waldo Demara Jr., see Robert Crichton's bestseller, *The Great Impostor* (New York: Random House, 1959). For more on Munchausen syndrome and related conditions, see Marc D.

Feldman and Charles V. Ford, with Toni Reinhold, *Patient or Pretender: Inside the Strange World of Factitious Disorders* (New York: Wiley, 1994).

The classic work on paradigm shifts is Thomas S. Kuhn's *The Structure of Scientific Revolutions*, 3rd ed. (Chicago: University of Chicago Press, 1996). Though an older book, William Irvine's *Apes, Angels, and Victorians: The Story of Darwin, Huxley, and Evolution* (New York: McGraw-Hill, 1955) is a well-known, readable account of the intellectual ferment in the nineteenth century as paradigms clashed and changed.

2. PROPAGANDA: FROM NAZISM TO SOFT-DRINK ADS AND SOFT PORN

On May 22, 1932, Leni Riefenstahl—then a twenty-nine-year-old German actress and later a notorious filmmaker—met Adolf Hitler for the first time. As they walked along a beach in a northern German fishing village, he expressed admiration for her films and said, "Once we come to power, you must make my films."[53] Hitler made good on his promise, hiring Riefenstahl to film the 1933 Nazi Party Congress in Nuremberg. Impressed by the results, he commissioned her to do the same for the 1934 party congress, being planned on a more grandiose scale in the same city. The resulting documentary—*Triumph of the Will* (1935)—became arguably the most successful propaganda film ever made.

Triumph of the Will exudes Nazism. Using footage of speeches by Hitler and other party officials, scenes of mass rallies, and a soundtrack featuring Wagnerian opera and the "Horst Wessel Lied" (the Nazi anthem), Riefenstahl produced exactly the kind of glorified, propagandistic interpretation of Nazism that Hitler sought. The messianic depiction of Hitler—his dramatic arrival in an airplane (unusual at the time), the adoring crowds, the inflammatory speeches—conveyed an image of unassailable strength. Other images or symbols of power and violence, like huge military formations, flags, eagles, and swastikas, pervade the film and were also meant to send an ominous message to the enemies of Nazism.

The film was an instant success, earning praise from the Nazi Party hierarchy and winning awards not only in Germany but also in France, Italy, and elsewhere. With the defeat of the Nazis in 1945, Riefenstahl's brilliant career was derailed. Though she was acquitted of war crimes, she was imprisoned by the Allies for four years as an alleged Nazi sympathizer, and her reputation remained tarnished for the rest of her long life (she didn't die until 2003, sixty-eight years after *Triumph of the Will* was released). Yet even today, her film continues to be regarded as a propaganda masterpiece. U.S. film director Frank Capra has observed that *Triumph of the Will* "fired no gun, dropped no bombs. But as a psychological weapon aimed at destroying the will to resist, it was just as lethal."[54]

In this chapter we'll look more closely at what propaganda like *Triumph of the Will* is and how it touches our lives.

What Is Propaganda?

Merriam-Webster's Collegiate Dictionary defines propaganda as "ideas, facts, or allegations spread deliberately to further one's cause or to damage an opposing cause." In their book *Age of Propaganda: The Everyday Use and Abuse of Persuasion*, Anthony Pratkanis and Elliot Aronson elaborate that propaganda involves the "use of images, slogans, and symbols that play on our prejudices and emotions; it is the communication of a point of view with the ultimate goal of having the recipient of the appeal come to 'voluntarily' accept this position as if it were his or her own."[55] The manipulative nature of propaganda deserves emphasis. As Josef Goebbels, the Nazi propaganda minister, said in 1933, "This is the secret of propaganda: Those who are to be persuaded by it should be completely immersed in the ideas of the propaganda, without ever noticing that they are being immersed in it."[56]

The word *propaganda* comes from the Latin verb *propagare*. In 1622, Pope Gregory XV created the Congregatio de Propaganda Fide (Congregation for the Propagation of the Faith), a Vatican department whose purpose was to oversee the spread of Catholicism by missionaries. *Propaganda* later acquired broader connotations, so that it now refers to any techniques—in literature, art, music, film, and other media—seeking to influence public opinion or behavior. The current connotation of propaganda as being intentionally misleading emerged relatively recently; that negative sense came into being in World War I, in connection with political and military propaganda.

The same negative sense of propaganda was prominent in World War II and its immediate aftermath and helped shape George Orwell's *Nineteen Eighty-Four*, published in 1949. Big Brother's use of propaganda to control the population is a central theme of the novel; an important strand is the propagandistic role of language. Thus in the totalitarian state Orwell depicts, Newspeak is introduced to channel thought along politically acceptable lines. An exchange in a cafeteria between Winston (the main character) and a colleague named Syme (a linguist compiling a Newspeak dictionary) makes this clear:

> "You haven't a real appreciation of Newspeak, Winston," [Syme] said almost sadly. . . . "You don't grasp the beauty of the destruction of words. Do you know that Newspeak is the only language in the world whose vocabulary gets smaller every year?"
>
> Winston did know that, of course. He smiled sympathetically he hoped, not trusting himself to speak. Syme bit off another fragment of the dark-colored bread, chewed it briefly, and went on:
>
> "Don't you see that the whole aim of Newspeak is to narrow the range of thought? In the end we shall make thoughtcrime literally impossible, because there will be no words in which to express it. Every concept that can ever be needed will be expressed by exactly *one* word, with its meaning rigidly defined and all its subsidiary meanings rubbed out and forgotten. . . . The Revolution will be complete when the language is perfect."[57]

Orwell's depiction of Newspeak may seem farfetched, but our society is not immune to the use of language to control thought. Think about terms like *sanitation engineer* (an alternative to "janitor"), *pro-choice* and *pro-life* (referring to abortion), *collateral damage* (a euphemism for "civilian casualties in a war"), or *man-caused disaster* (a synonym for "terrorist acts"); what message was each of these terms chosen to convey? Advertisers are even more notorious than policymakers for the manipulation of language to shape thought, as we'll see in Chapter 4.

Test Your Skills

List several other terms like *sanitation engineer* or *collateral damage* that seem to reflect a social or political viewpoint. In each case, what do the policymakers who coined the word want you to believe? How accurate do you think Orwell's depiction of Newspeak in *Nineteen Eighty-Four* is with respect to your own society?

Propaganda can play a role in almost any area of society—from the military to medicine, from advertising to sports—though it's most often associated with politics and war. I explore advertising and politics in Chapters 4 and 6, respectively; here I focus on what many people think of as the "classic" form of propaganda: propaganda used by the military in wartime. The reason it's important to begin with wartime propaganda techniques is that these techniques later found their way into many other fields, including advertising and public relations. Yes, we have wartime propaganda to thank for the ubiquitous media ads for everything from soft drinks to soft porn. Public-safety campaigns to buckle up and stop smoking also incorporate propaganda techniques that originated in the military.

Any medium can be adapted to propaganda purposes. Riefenstahl utilized film; the Nazis were also known for their oratory. Literature (ranging from novels to government reports to leaflets), music, art (including posters), "advertorials," TV and radio broadcasts, and a range of new media have all been utilized successfully to deliver propaganda messages.

Techniques of Mass Persuasion

Regardless of the medium, successful propagandists utilize certain common techniques of mass persuasion. They begin by creating conditions that will enable them to get their message across. An important first step is to establish the credibility or likability of the speaker or writer. Another preliminary step is what has been called *prepersuasion:* subtly influencing the terms of the discussion by framing or defining the issue in a way that is favorable to the propagandists' cause. This will allow them to stay on-message and will make it difficult for their opponent to rebut their arguments. Finally, the use of propaganda isn't just a rational process. Hitler and other Nazis were masterful propagandists because they knew how to tap into the emotions of their audiences, arousing just the right emotion to get their target audience to take the desired action.

Did You Know?

You Can Even Be Mesmerized by Propaganda in a Language You Don't Understand

It's true, at least if G. Gordon Liddy can be believed. Liddy, best known as one of the Watergate burglars who broke into the headquarters of the Democratic National Committee in 1972, says in his autobiography that he listened to Hitler's speeches on the radio in his youth. Liddy claims that though he knew almost no German, Hitler's propaganda had a profound effect on him: "Hitler's voice started out calmly, in low, dispassionate tones, but as he spoke of what his people would accomplish, his voice rose in pitch and tempo. Once united, the German people could do anything, surmount any obstacle, rout any enemy, achieve fulfillment. . . . He sent an electric current through my body and, as the massive audience thundered its absolute support and determination, the hair on the back of my neck rose and I realized suddenly that I had stopped breathing."[1]

---

1   *G. Gordon Liddy, Will, 3rd ed. (New York: St. Martin's Press, 1997), 11.*

Propagandists utilize many specific techniques to produce the desired effect. In a political and military context, these techniques can include

- *Demonizing the enemy.* Typical tactics include the use of ethnic slurs, stereotyping, or false accusations of barbaric behavior. These tactics are exemplified in the anti-German films churned out by Hollywood in World War I, like *The Claws of the Hun*, *The Prussian Cur*, and *The Kaiser: The Beast of Berlin*. The logic behind this strategy is that demonizing others provides a rationale for transgressing against them.

- *Appeals to fear.* This type of propaganda uses scare tactics, like the "domino theory" during the Vietnam War, which raised the specter of countries across the Pacific toppling like dominoes until communism reached the shores of the United States—unless the communist revolution was stopped in Southeast Asia. Appeals to fear also commonly play on ethnic, religious, or gender prejudice.
- *Flag-waving.* Flag-waving involves an appeal to patriotism or some other form of loyalty, elevating devotion to a cause over critical analysis of the issues.
- *Bandwagon appeal.* Here people are urged to take an action because "everyone else is doing it."
- *Direct order.* In this no-nonsense approach people are just told what to do, as with the famous World War I recruitment posters showing Uncle Sam pointing his finger at the viewer above the words "I Want You for U.S. Army."
- *Slogans.* Memorable examples include "No Taxation without Representation" from the American Revolution and "Liberty, Equality, and Fraternity" from the French Revolution.
- *Falsification of information.* An example of misinformation would be the George W. Bush administration's claim that Saddam Hussein had weapons of mass destruction, used as a rationale for attacking Iraq.

While some of these techniques were first applied in a military context, they were quickly harnessed for other purposes, as the next section suggests.

Propaganda: "Eloquence without Wisdom"?

The use of propaganda can be traced back to ancient times. Like many other heads of state and politicians down through the centuries,

Egyptian, Mesopotamian, and Mesoamerican rulers often tried to rewrite history in order to put a positive spin on their achievements. The Greeks did the same thing, but they also valued forms of persuasion other than propaganda. Many philosophers and statesmen as well as ordinary citizens saw rhetorical skills as a vital path to the truth, because these skills were essential to the kind of debate and discussion that could illuminate issues. The same emphasis on rhetoric existed in Rome, where a class of professional persuaders like politicians and lawyers emerged. This development in turn gave rise to concerns that still plague us in the twenty-first century. When the Roman statesman Cicero (106–43 BCE) was asked, "Has rhetoric produced more harm than good?", he gave an answer that seems as valid today as it was more than two thousand years ago: "Wisdom without eloquence has been of little help to the states, but eloquence without wisdom has often been a great obstacle and never an advantage."[58]

Cicero would have been shocked at the proliferation of "eloquence without wisdom"—the average American is exposed to more than seven million advertisements over a lifetime[59] — though this development would have to wait for certain technological innovations. Propaganda didn't become widespread until after the Industrial Revolution (mid-eighteenth through the nineteenth century). The evolution of printing made it possible to influence mass public opinion, and the introduction of radio, television, computers, and other media in the twentieth century accelerated the process. The emergence of nation-states and of large-scale war in the twentieth century also spurred the development of propaganda, because the warring nations in World Wars I and II as well as in other conflicts used propaganda to win support and undermine enemy morale.

During World War I, President Woodrow Wilson appointed psychologist Edward L. Bernays—an Austrian-born PR expert who was Sigmund Freud's nephew—to the Committee on Public Information (also called the Creel Committee).[60] Bernays (1891–1995) was an interesting character. Doubly related to Freud—Freud was his mother's brother and Freud's wife was his father's sister—he was an infant when his parents emigrated to the United States, but the U.S. and Austrian branches of the family stayed in touch, and Bernays absorbed his famous uncle's theories from an early age. Dubbed the "Father of Spin" by a biographer,[61] Bernays was one of the most influential proponents of social engineering in the early twentieth century. In some 15 books and 300 articles, he tirelessly promoted the role of PR specialists as a shadowy force making the important decisions in business, politics, and almost every other area of society. He described this invisible class as governing the collective mind with the use of propaganda: "We are governed, our minds molded, our tastes formed, our ideas suggested, largely by men we have never heard of. . . . As civilization has become more complex, and as the need for invisible government has been increasingly demonstrated, the technical means have been invented and developed by which opinion may be regimented [through propaganda]." [62]

Bernays's own membership in this "invisible class" got him involved in World War I. The Creel Committee's purpose was to whip up anti-German sentiment by means of speeches, newspaper ads, leaflets, newsreels, and other propaganda and to win support for the U.S. entry into the war on the side of the British. As in his later PR campaigns, Bernays used psychological techniques from Freud and other sources. He later said of these wartime propaganda efforts that "intellectual and emotional bombardment aroused Americans to a pitch of enthusiasm."[63] He went on to acknowledge that "critics charged that sometimes the [Creel] Committee's volunteers got hysterical, but, after all, hysteria was generally prevalent at the time. Reports that the Germans were beasts and Huns were generally accepted. The most fantastic atrocity stories were believed."[64] Almost as an afterthought, Bernays added that "after the war there was widespread disillusion with and reaction against propaganda. The American people resented their own wartime gullibility." [65]

Someone else whose name is often associated with the Creel Committee is Walter Lippmann, an influential journalist who acted as a consultant as President Wilson was setting up the committee in the spring of 1917.[66] Lippmann later served on a different propaganda commission based in Europe. Rather than churning out the crude anti-German propaganda the Creel Committee became known for, Lippmann and his colleagues tried to produce leaflets that touted the Allied cause more diplomatically and that encouraged German soldiers to desert. The most successful of these leaflets—the one that most often turned up in the possession of captured German soldiers—emphasized that POWs would be treated well. In it, Lippmann quotes a fictional POW as saying to the comrades he left behind, "Do not worry about me," adding that "I am out of the war. I am well fed. The American army gives its prisoners the same rations it gives its own soldiers: beef, white bread, potatoes, prunes, coffee, milk, butter."[67] More than a million copies of that leaflet were smuggled behind enemy lines or dropped by planes and unmanned balloons.

These propaganda efforts were so successful in creating anti-German hysteria and support for the American cause in only a few months that they permanently influenced U.S. business, which was quick to grasp the commercial potential of propaganda. The public relations industry grew out of the efforts of a few pioneers like Bernays and Lippmann, and as we'll see in Chapter 4, *propaganda* was in fact originally a synonym for *advertising*.

The same wartime propaganda achievements won Hitler's admiration. His first major propaganda effort was his book *Mein Kampf* (My Struggle), published in two volumes in the 1920s. As the introduction to an English translation of *Mein Kampf* notes, for years this book "stood as proof of the blindness and complacency of the world. For in its pages Hitler announced—long before he came to power—a program of blood and terror in a self-revelation of such overwhelming frankness that few among its readers had the courage to believe it."[68] The propaganda offensive sketched in *Mein Kampf* required a bureaucratic apparatus in order to be truly effective. The Creel Committee and similar wartime commissions and agencies provided a model. Hitler's admiration for the Allied use of propaganda in World War I was so intense that as soon as he came to power in 1933, he created a propaganda ministry and appointed Josef Goebbels to head it.

Though Goebbels failed to conform to the Aryan ideal of manliness (he was only 5 feet 5 inches or 165 centimeters tall and wore a metal brace on his shortened right leg) and had offended Nazi sensibilities by obtaining his doctorate at Heidelberg University under a Jewish dissertation advisor, Hitler was impressed by his intellectual and political acumen and delegated considerable authority to him. Goebbels was put in charge of journalism, radio, literature, theater, and film, and ruthlessly exploited these media—as well as mass demonstrations, parades, and oratory—to foment support for Nazism. His most vicious propaganda was anti-Semitic. On taking office he promptly had books by Jewish authors burned, and he orchestrated years of escalating anti-Semitic propaganda that culminated in Kristallnacht on November 9–10, 1938, the first large-scale Nazi pogrom. (*Kristallnacht* literally means "Crystal Night" and is sometimes called the "Night of Broken Glass." The term refers to the glass shattered as Nazi troops and civilians stormed Jewish homes, businesses, and synagogues all over Germany and in parts of Austria. Many Jewish people were killed outright and 30,000 were sent to concentration camps.) Until Goebbels committed suicide at the end of the war in 1945, he continued to marshal a wide range of propaganda tools to incite hatred, to justify the concentration camps and other atrocities, and to win the support of the German population for total war.

Scholars dispute the precise ways the Nazis drew on the work of Bernays and his U.S. colleagues, but the connection was obvious from the 1920s on because of Hitler's flattering comments in *Mein Kampf* on the Allied propaganda efforts in World War I.[69] In a 1945 review of a book by Bernays titled *Take Your Place at the Peace Table,* a critic accused Bernays of "cynical fascism," adding that "the author presumably intends only welfare and happiness for humanity, but his methods are largely identical with those portrayed in Chapters VI and XI of *Mein Kampf*."[70] Bernays himself had been dismayed to learn as early as 1933 from a journalist who had met Goebbels and toured his library that Goebbels was utilizing Bernays's book *Crystallizing Public Opinion*, published a decade earlier, as a foundation for his anti-Semitic propaganda campaign.[71] As Tye sums up this unsavory aspect of Bernays's legacy in his biography of Bernays, Goebbels used strategies almost identical to those Bernays advocated, "skillfully exploiting symbols by making Jews into scapegoats and Hitler into the embodiment of righteousness; manipulating the media by trumpeting Nazi triumphs on the battlefield and hiding their extermination campaigns; and vesting unheard-of power in state propagandists just as Bernays had advised in *Crystallizing*."[72]

Another country known for its skillful use of propaganda was the Soviet Union. After it came into being following the 1917 Russian Revolution, the Soviet Union waged a massive propaganda campaign in favor of communist ideals and against the capitalist West. It conducted similar propaganda campaigns in the Cold War era after World War II. This propaganda often demonized the West for its capitalist excesses, poverty, and racism.

A legendary propagandist from still another country was the sultry-voiced Tokyo Rose, said to have broadcast Japanese propaganda in English during World War II to demoralize Allied troops in the Pacific. Several women have been linked with the name Tokyo Rose, but no conclusive identification has been made. The legend may have originated or been embellished under stressful wartime conditions, with the misogynist imagery of seduction and betrayal projected onto Radio Tokyo's female broadcasters.

The United States has also been no stranger to the use of propaganda. Agencies like the Office of War Information (a government agency) and the Writers' War Board (a private organization that received government funding) carried out the same propaganda functions in World War II that their counterparts had in World War I, drumming up support for the war effort and demonizing the enemy.

An interesting chapter in the history of U.S. propaganda involves Walt Disney. Many people don't know that Disney played a major role as a World War II propagandist—in fact, 90 percent of Disney employees were mobilized for the war effort, churning out hundreds of thousands of feet of propaganda and educational films.[73] Many Disney cartoon characters were recruited for propaganda purposes. For example, Donald Duck starred in *Der Fuehrer's Face* (1942), an eight-minute animated film that takes place in a fictionalized Nazi town in which even the trees and clouds are shaped like swastikas. Donald is prodded awake in the morning, compelled to read part of *Mein Kampf,* and subjected to starvation rations (coffee brewed from a single contraband coffee bean and bread so hard it has to be sliced with a saw). Then he is marched off to a munitions factory where he is forced to toil under slave-labor conditions, alternately assembling artillery shells and giving the *Heil Hitler* salute to portraits of Hitler coming along the assembly line. Donald finally goes crazy, then wakes up and is relieved to realize it was all a nightmare. The cartoon ends as a tomato is thrown at a caricature of Hitler's face, providing the title of the film. *Der Fuehrer's Face* won an Academy Award and is considered one of the best cartoons ever made.

U.S. propaganda efforts continued during the Cold War. A key player was J. Edgar Hoover, director of the Federal Bureau of Investigation (FBI); Hoover made a personal contribution by writing a book titled *Masters of Deceit: The Story of Communism in America and How to Fight It.*[74] In 1953, during the Eisenhower administration, the United States Information Agency (USIA) was set up to disseminate pro-U.S. information abroad as well as to sponsor cultural exchange programs. This agency operated the Voice of America and Radio Free Europe, among other stations, to broadcast propaganda. Many propaganda efforts targeted Cuba to undermine the Castro regime.

The U.S. government continues to spend hundreds of millions of dollars per year on films, magazines, radio programming, and other media to burnish the U.S. image abroad. According to one tally, this amounts to "ninety films per year, twelve magazines in twenty-two languages, and 800 hours of Voice of America programming in thirty-seven languages with an estimated audience of 75 million listeners—all describing the virtues of the American way."[75] Many of these efforts are coordinated by the Broadcasting Board of Governors (BBG) and its administrative entity, the International Broadcasting Bureau (IBB), both of which were established as successors to the USIA in the 1990s.

Some U.S. propaganda takes the form of psychological operations or PSYOP, defined by the U.S. military as "planned operations to convey selected information and indicators to foreign audiences to influence the emotions, motives, objective reasoning, and ultimately the behavior of foreign governments, organizations, groups, and individuals."[76] The Smith-Mundt Act (1948) prohibits the use of such propaganda tactics on domestic audiences, but the line between foreign and domestic is becoming increasingly blurred in the global media era. This point was brought home by Army Col. James A. Treadwell, who directed the U.S. military PSYOP program in Iraq in 2003. When asked about the impact of PSYOP programs on U.S. audiences, Treadwell acknowledged that "there's always going to be a certain amount of bleed-over with the global information environment."[77]

U.S. propaganda isn't limited to the international sphere or to the "bleed-over" effect. I've emphasized that wartime propaganda techniques have found their way into many areas of society; obvious examples (discussed in later chapters) include advertising, political campaigns, and the efforts of corporate lobbyists. The widespread nature of domestic propaganda raises a final intriguing question: What is the difference between propaganda and education?

Propaganda and Education

The line between these two concepts doesn't always seem clear. For example, some parents of school-age children might feel sex education or a discussion of gay rights represents propaganda on behalf of a particular lifestyle, while others may regard these discussions as a normal, acceptable part of the educational curriculum. The same goes for coverage of a topic like environmental hazards or abortion on the network or cable news; reports that come across to one group of viewers as propaganda may seem straightforward to another group. Bernays gave a cynical answer to the question raised above: "The advocacy of what we believe in is education. The advocacy of what we don't believe in is propaganda."[78]

Is there a less cynical way out of this impasse? Though it's difficult to draw a hard-and-fast line between propaganda and education, the distinction seems to lie in the manipulative nature of propaganda versus the reliance of education on critical-thinking skills. Propaganda is meant to deceive (without the recipients' noticing they're being deceived, as Goebbels advocated). Ideally, education should rest on and foster good critical-thinking skills, so people become autonomous and form their own opinions on issues important to them. As one expert says, "Education, at its best, teaches more than just knowledge. It teaches critical thinking. . . . This is not thought control. It is the very reverse: mental liberation."[79] Because of the enormous importance of critical-thinking skills in helping us recognize and avoid propaganda and other forms of deception, the appendix to *Diving Deep* focuses on these skills and how to acquire them.

Test Your Skills

How would you distinguish between propaganda and education? Do you think the U.S. educational system (or that of another country of your choice) utilizes propaganda? If so, how?

Conclusion

This chapter has provided a brief overview of propaganda, the techniques it relies on, and its historical development. Even if propaganda is viewed in its narrowest sense, as political and military propaganda, it's all around us. There's no escaping it. If the term is interpreted more broadly to include its derivatives—like advertising—propaganda permeates the fabric of our lives in increasingly sophisticated ways. Bernays's assessment that PR professionals and others using propaganda form an "invisible government which is the true ruling power of our country" has perhaps become even more accurate than he could have imagined.[80] In the next chapter I turn to a closely related subject: brainwashing.

What You Can Do

√*Be vigilant to avoid being taken in by propaganda.* Cut through the doublespeak aimed at you by everyone from advertisers to government officials to cult leaders. Because nothing offers better protection than healthy skepticism and good critical-thinking skills, make it a habit to assess the credibility of the sources you encounter and the cogency of their arguments. Listen to any inner voices that warn you when someone is trying to manipulate your emotions, say, by playing on guilt or fear. Be wary of rhetoric that plays on prejudices. Do your homework before jumping on a political bandwagon or falling prey to dishonest campaign rhetoric.

√*In evaluating political candidates, look at how they walk the walk and not at how they talk the talk.* If they claim to support environmental causes, gay rights, tax cuts, or any other issue that's important to you, don't take their word for it. Look at their record. If you don't find relevant accomplishments to back up their claims, watch out!

√*Penalize candidates who utilize cheap propaganda attacks, and reward those who take the high road.* If we all followed this practice and refused to vote for politicians who conduct dirty campaigns, we'd send a strong signal that this conduct is unacceptable.

√*Consult diverse sources so as not to be manipulated by any monolithic line of thought.* By exploring alternatives to your favorite cable news channel or by sampling unfamiliar blogs outside your comfort zone, at a minimum you'll become more aware of others' views. You may end up changing some of your own as well.

√*Do your part to ensure that a wide range of communications outlets is available.* One of the best ways of preventing propaganda from taking hold in a society is to ensure that many types of communications outlets are available, reflecting a diversity of opinion. This diversity is increasingly endangered by the corporate consolidation of the media, so it's important to speak out and demand that a range of voices and viewpoints be heard.

√*Protect your children from propaganda.* If you have children, you're probably already aware of the importance of monitoring their TV viewing habits—for example, to limit the exploitative advertising they're exposed to or the violence and misogyny they're indoctrinated by. Try to instill good critical-thinking habits in them by teaching them to question the messages they receive and the motives for those messages in other areas of life besides TV.

√*Guard against personal attacks on individuals or groups.* These attacks can be extremely destructive; once disseminated online, for example, slurs and innuendos often acquire a life of their own and can destroy careers or lives. Such attacks can also mask a deeper political purpose. Ask yourself what the motivation underlying these attacks is. Is the individual or group perceived as too threatening to respond to through ordinary debate, and if so, why? You should hold the perpetrators accountable for their actions and try to steer the discussion back onto higher ground, because this kind of propaganda tactic profoundly undermines any democratic society. If carried to an extreme, it can reflect fanaticism and can be bound up with the kind of bigotry and demagoguery discussed in Chapter 7.

Further Reading

For an overview of propaganda with extensive references, see Anthony Pratkanis and Elliot Aronson, *Age of Propaganda: The Everyday Use and Abuse of Persuasion*, rev. ed. (New York: W. H. Freeman / Holt, 2001). Also see Philip M. Taylor, *Munitions of the Mind: A History of Propaganda*, 3rd ed. (Manchester: Manchester University Press, 2003). A thought-provoking book that challenges many common assumptions about propaganda is Jacques Ellul's *Propaganda: The Formation of Men's Attitudes*, trans. Konrad Kellen and Jean Lerner (New York: Vintage Books, [1962] 1973). Edward Bernays's classic work, *Propaganda* (Brooklyn, NY: Ig Publishing, [1928] 2005), is still suggestive after nearly a century.

On Nazi propaganda, see Susan Bachrach and Steven Luckert, *State of Deception: The Power of Nazi Propaganda* (New York: Norton, 2009), and David Welch, *The Third Reich: Politics and Propaganda*, 2nd ed. (London: Routledge, 2002). For more on Leni Riefenstahl and *Triumph of the Will*, see Leni Riefenstahl, *A Memoir* (New York: St. Martin's Press, 1992); Steven Bach, *Leni: The Life and Work of Leni Riefenstahl* (New York: Knopf, 2007); and Jürgen Trimborn, *Leni Riefenstahl: A Life*, trans. Edna McCown (New York: Faber & Faber, 2007). Also relevant are Anna Maria Sigmund, *Women of the Third Reich* (Richmond Hill, Ontario: NDE Publishing, [1998] 2000), and Guido Knopp, *Hitler's Women*, trans. Angus McGeoch (New York: Routledge, [2001] 2003). The Nazi film industry is the subject of David Welch, *Propaganda and the German Cinema, 1933–1945*, rev. ed. (London: I. B. Tauris, 2001).

For a biography of Walter Lippmann, see Ronald Steel, *Walter Lippmann and the American Century*, rev. ed. (New Brunswick, NJ: Transaction, 1999); on Edward Bernays, see Larry Tye's readable book, *The Father of Spin: Edward L. Bernays and the Birth of Public Relations* (New York: Crown, 1998). Besides Bernays's *Propaganda* (mentioned earlier), influential works by those two public relations pioneers include Walter Lippmann, *Public Opinion* (New York: Macmillan, [1922] 1960), and Edward Bernays, *Public Relations* (Norman: University of Oklahoma Press, 1952).

Classic fictional treatments of the role of propaganda in oppressive societies include George Orwell's novels; see his *Animal Farm*, foreword by Ann Patchett, preface by Russell Baker, introduction by C. M. Woodhouse, centennial ed. (New York: Plume [1946] 2003), and *Nineteen Eighty-Four*, foreword by Thomas Pynchon, afterword by Erich Fromm, centennial ed. (New York: Plume, [1949] 2003).

3. BIG BROTHER, BRAINWASHING, AND YOU

Mind control isn't just the stuff of science fiction and Soviet gulags— it's closer to home than you think. In this chapter I begin with George Orwell's powerful depiction of brainwashing in *Nineteen Eighty-Four*, then turn to the CIA's real-life search for a "Manchurian candidate," and finally glance at the role of brainwashing in religious cults. These dramatic illustrations of brainwashing offer a window into the more mundane forms of influence that pervade our lives in contemporary society.

From Big Brother to the Manchurian Candidate and Beyond

When it comes to brainwashing, fact and fiction can converge in chilling ways.

Brainwashing in Orwell's Nineteen Eighty-Four

Ironically, the best-known fictional treatment of mind control in English—George Orwell's dystopian novel *Nineteen Eighty-Four*—doesn't use the term *brainwashing*. Orwell's novel was published by Secker and Warburg in London in June 1949; the English word *brainwashing* didn't appear in print for the first time until September of the following year, when a journalist named Edward Hunter wrote an article titled "'Brain-Washing' Tactics Force Chinese into Ranks of Communist Party" for the *Miami Daily News*.[81] The term was a translation of the Chinese *xi-nao* or *hsi-nao* (literally meaning "to wash the brain" or "to cleanse the mind"), which Hunter said he heard from Chinese informants subjected to indoctrination techniques after the communists came to power in 1949. A longtime newspaper reporter and freelance writer, Hunter was later exposed as a covert CIA operative, and subsequent investigations have challenged his claims of extreme, systematic brainwashing by the Chinese communists of their own citizens as well as of foreign prisoners during the Korean War. Some have argued that by exaggerating the successes of the indoctrination techniques used by the Chinese, Hunter and others were trying to provide a rationale for the CIA's development of the same techniques. Others have suggested that in the wake of the U.S. bombing of Hiroshima and Nagasaki in 1945, the emphasis on Chinese indoctrination techniques diverted attention from the fact that Americans themselves were capable of extreme moral evil.[82]

Orwell may not have coined the word *brainwashing*, but he did give us many other words and slogans we now take for granted, like *doublethink, thought police,* and "Big Brother is watching you." Set against the background of Stalinist Russia, Nazi Germany, and the carnage of World War II, *Nineteen Eighty-Four* describes a totalitarian regime in a society called Oceania, incorporating the British Isles, the Americas, and parts of the Pacific. Orwell's depiction of brainwashing is chilling. One of Oceania's four ministries is the Ministry of Truth, which relentlessly controls all forms of mass media in the society. (Between 1941 and 1943 Orwell worked for the BBC producing propaganda as part of the war effort—a job he said made him feel like "an orange that's been trodden on by a very dirty boot."[83] The BBC was under the Ministry of Information, and Orwell acknowledged modeling the Ministry of Truth in *Nineteen Eighty-Four* on his former employer.) Those who report to Oceania's Ministry of Truth include the Thought Police, who use a network of informers, microphones, and telescreens in homes and public places to identify thought criminals. In an echo of Stalinist Russia and Nazi Germany, the informers include children, who have been trained since birth to report alleged thoughtcrimes—especially those of their parents.

The novel's main character, Winston Smith, works for the Records Department of the Ministry of Truth. His job is to doctor statistics, speeches, historical records, and other documents so they're always in line with Big Brother's latest version of history, ensuring that the Party always tells the truth. After all, "At all times the Party is in possession of absolute truth, and clearly the absolute can never have been different from what it is now."[84] Much of *Nineteen Eighty-Four* revolves around Winston's disillusionment with this system, heightened after he receives a book attacking the system reportedly written by a revolutionary named Emmanuel Goldstein (possibly a play on the name of the Lithuanian-born anarchist Emma Goldman). Goldstein's book captures the "doublethink" central to the brainwashing process:

> The key word here is *blackwhite*. Like so many Newspeak [the language of Oceania] words, this word has two mutually contradictory meanings. Applied to an opponent, it means the habit of impudently claiming that black is white, in contradiction of the plain facts. Applied to a Party member, it means a loyal willingness to say that black is white when Party discipline demands this. But it means also the ability to *believe* that black is white, and more, to *know* that black is white, and to forget that one has ever believed the contrary. This demands a continuous alteration of the past, made possible by the system of thought which really embraces all the rest, and which is known in Newspeak as *doublethink*. . . . *Doublethink* means the power of holding two contradictory beliefs in one's mind simultaneously, and accepting both of them.[85]

Scholars endlessly debate the meaning of *Nineteen Eighty-Four*.[86] Was the novel intended to be prophetic, warning of a future totalitarian world? Or was Orwell merely creating a work of fiction that didn't have much to do with the real world? He did seem to have very real fears of a future society in which brainwashing and doublethink would be the norm. He expressed these fears in a letter written in 1944, before the outcome of World War II was known:

> Hitler can say that the Jews started the war, and if he survives that will become official history. He can't say that two and two are five, because for the purposes of, say, ballistics, they have to make four. But if the sort of world that I am afraid of arrives, a world of two or three great superstates which are unable to conquer one another, two and two could become five if the fuehrer wished it. That, so far as I can see, is the direction in which we are actually moving, though, of course, the process is reversible.[87]

History has borne Orwell out in many ways. Though Hitler and Mussolini had died before *Nineteen Eighty-Four* was published, Stalin lived until 1953 and his legacy continued at least until the breakup of the Soviet Union in 1991. But as noted earlier, the term *brainwashing* came from a Chinese context and was associated not with World War II but with the Korean War.

Thought Reform in China

Originally a civil war, the Korean War (1950–1953) got underway when Chinese-backed North Korean troops invaded South Korea. The international ramifications of the conflict grew when the United Nations sent a multinational peacekeeping force made up mostly of U.S. troops. One of the tragic aspects of the "unknown war" or "forgotten war"—as the Korean War is sometimes called—was that thousands of combatants and civilians were taken prisoner on both sides, many never to be heard from again.[88] Of the 7,245 U.S. POWs, 2,806 died while captured, 21 refused repatriation, and 4,418 were repatriated after spending time in Chinese prison camps.[89] The U.S. government quickly noticed a worrisome development: even after the returning POWs were safely in American hands, some continued to swear allegiance to communist China and to denounce the American system. They appeared, in short, to have been the victims of exactly what Edward Hunter described in his articles and books: brainwashing.

Evidence came from other sources as well. As an Air Force psychiatrist, Robert Jay Lifton conducted psychiatric evaluations of the repatriated prisoners of war in Korea in 1953. Then, in what was to have been a brief stopover in Hong Kong on his way back to the United States, he learned from Western scholars and diplomats of what they considered shocking indoctrination efforts on the Chinese mainland. They told him "of Western missionaries who, after having made lurid 'espionage' confessions in prison, arrived in Hong Kong deeply confused about what they believed; of young Chinese students violating the most sacred precepts of their culture by publicly denouncing their parents; of distinguished mainland professors renouncing their 'evil' past, even rewriting their books from a Marxist standpoint."[90] Fascinated, Lifton decided to prolong his stay and spent 1954–1955 interviewing fifteen Chinese citizens and twenty-five Westerners who had experienced thought reform (Lifton's preferred term). The result was his *Thought Reform and the Psychology of Totalism: A Study of "Brainwashing" in China* (1961)—one of the most influential early investigations of mind-control techniques.

Though Lifton's account is more nuanced and less hysterical than Hunter's books and other Cold War–oriented publications, it confirms many of the general points made by others about indoctrination practices in communist China. The nature and goal of these practices can be inferred from an appendix to Lifton's book, containing a confession by a Chinese scholar after he had undergone thought reform.[91] Professor Chin Yüeh-lin, educated at Harvard and a distinguished authority on formal logic (a branch of philosophy) in China, made his confession in a Beijing publication in 1952. The following excerpts speak for themselves:

> Born of a bureaucratic landlord family, I have always led a life of ease and comfort. I went abroad at nineteen and stayed there for eleven years to absorb the way of life and the predilection for pleasure of the European and American bourgeoisie. The

principal source of my various pleasures lay in the decadent philosophy of the bourgeoisie, and for thirty years I played a game
of concepts. . . . To maintain my way of life, I had to have special privileges. I felt the need for these privileges, I enjoyed these
privileges, became obsessed by the ideology of special privileges,
and I became one of the privileged few of Tsinghua [University].
. . . When the regulation of departments and colleges started in
1950, I was dead against it. . . . For this I now hate myself beyond
measure.[92]

He blames his exposure to Americans and American culture for blind-
ing him to the evils of U.S. imperialism: "With regard to my attitude
toward American imperialism, as a result of long years of studying in
America, the evil influences of bourgeois education, my large number of
American friends, and my constant contact with Americans, I became
instilled with pro-American thoughts which prevented me from realiz-
ing American imperialism's plots of aggression against China during the
past hundred years, and turned me into an unconscious instrument of
American imperialistic cultural aggression."[93] Chin came to see the error
of his ways, noting that he was "a criminal for having sinned against the
people" but had realized the "scientific and truthful nature of Marxism-
Leninism" and "from now on . . . shall strive to become a new man."[94]

Lifton's *Thought Reform and the Psychology of Totalism* and other
publications established him as an authority on mind control. In 1976
he testified for the defense in the trial of newspaper heir Patty Hearst,
maintaining that she had been subjected to the same mind-control techniques by her kidnappers (the Symbionese Liberation Army) that the
Chinese government had used on Chinese citizens and U.S. POWs.[95]
Lifton went on to write a chilling and influential book on Nazi medical experiments, *The Nazi Doctors: Medical Killing and the Psychology of
Genocide*.[96]

Lifton wasn't alone in investigating the brainwashing phenomenon.
The Central Intelligence Agency (CIA)—founded just before the Korean
War—lost no time conducting its own investigation, with far-reaching
implications at home and abroad.

The CIA and the Hunt for the Manchurian Candidate

Determined to find out what was going on and paranoid about the national-security implications of Chinese and Soviet brainwashing practices, CIA Director Allen Dulles commissioned a secret study by two scientists, Harold Wolff and Lawrence Hinkle, late in 1953.[97] In his book *The Search for the "Manchurian Candidate": The CIA and Mind Control*, John Marks provides a fascinating look at this study, the paranoid Cold War environment that produced it, and unscrupulous CIA-sponsored research that it gave rise to.[98] Marks's book takes its title from the 1962 film *The Manchurian Candidate*, based on a 1959 novel by Richard Condon, describing the brainwashing of a U.S. soldier-turned-assassin by Chinese and Russian communists.[99] Two popular film versions of this novel have been made, the first starring Angela Lansbury, Frank Sinatra, and Laurence Harvey (as the brainwashed soldier) in 1962 and the second starring Denzel Washington and Meryl Streep in 2004.

In their study Wolff and Hinkle found plenty of evidence of communist reeducation programs, but no evidence of unusual brainwashing techniques. Neither drugs nor hypnosis played a significant role. Both the Chinese and Russians relied on standard techniques like enforced isolation, threats, and demeaning treatment to break down the resistance of prisoners and make them more suggestible. Interrogators then intervened and demanded a "confession." The confession was often extracted from prisoners in the context of an autobiographical sketch or personal history that they were required to produce (orally or in writing). As the interrogators went over the details of the prisoners' lives with them, they would coerce them into admitting their misdeeds. Within this general framework, there were some differences between the techniques used by the Russians and Chinese, apparently reflecting cultural differences: "The Soviet brainwashing system resembled a heavy-handed cop whose job was to isolate, break, and then subdue all the troublemakers in the neighborhood. The Chinese system was more like thousands of skilled acupuncturists, working on each other and relying on group pressure, ideology, and repetition."[100] In Stalinist Russia (1924–1953), prisoners who'd made a full confession were usually shot or sent to a labor camp. The Chinese frequently emphasized reeducation; the process by which they brought prisoners around to the correct ideology has sometimes been likened to a religious conversion.

Even if the communists didn't currently possess the "brainwashing equivalent of the atomic bomb,"[101] as the CIA feared, what was to prevent them from acquiring that bomb in the future? What was needed, of course, was for the United States to beat them to it. Thus "the CIA built up its own elaborate brainwashing program, which, like the Soviet and Chinese versions, took its own special twist from *our* national character. It was a tiny replica of the Manhattan Project, grounded in the conviction that the keys to brainwashing lay in technology. Agency officials hoped to use old-fashioned American knowhow to produce shortcuts and scientific breakthroughs."[102]

Though CIA Director Dulles claimed publicly in 1953 that the United States lacked the scientific apparatus with which to study brainwashing or the "human guinea pigs to try these extraordinary techniques," he knew better.[103] Founded in 1947, the CIA was an outgrowth of the wartime Office of Strategic Services (OSS), the U.S. government's first intelligence agency. In later years the CIA would come under fire for a long string of covert actions of questionable legality or ethics, including the Bay of Pigs fiasco in Cuba in 1961, military operations in Laos in the 1960s and 1970s, the Pentagon Papers case in the early 1970s, the assassination of President Salvador Allende of Chile in 1973, and the Iran-contra scandal in the 1980s, to name a few. The CIA acquired much of its brazenness during Dulles's tenure as director (1953–1961), and few efforts involved more brazenness than the agency's search for mind-control techniques:

In their attempts to find ways to manipulate people, Agency officials and their agents crossed many of the same ethical barriers [as Nazi scientists had]. They experimented with dangerous and unknown techniques on people who had no idea what was happening. They systematically violated the free will and mental dignity of their subjects, and, like the Germans, they chose to victimize special groups of people whose existence they considered, out of prejudice and convenience, less worthy than their own. Wherever their extreme experiments went, the CIA sponsors picked for subjects their own equivalents of the Nazis' Jews and gypsies: mental patients, prostitutes, foreigners, drug addicts, and prisoners, often from minority ethnic groups.[104]

Test Your Skills

In his widely read book *The Search for the "Manchurian Candidate": The CIA and Mind Control*, John Marks writes: "One former CIA psychologist, who still feels guilty about his participation in certain Agency operations, believes that the CIA's fixation on control and manipulation mirrors, in a more virulent form, the way Americans deal with each other generally. . . . This psychologist believes that the United States has become an extremely control-oriented society—from the classroom to politics to television advertising. Spying and [similar] techniques are unique only in that they are more systematic and secret."[1]

Do you think the psychologist is right that the CIA's "fixation on control and manipulation" mirrors similar tendencies in U.S. society as a whole? Why or why not? What kinds of control-oriented behaviors have you experienced or observed in the educational system, media, politics, or other areas of society?

---

1   John Marks, *The Search for the "Manchurian Candidate": The CIA and Mind Control*, rev. ed. (New York: Norton, 1991), 189.

Like ancient shamans and witches thought to be able to influence enemies' behavior through magic potions, the CIA was particularly obsessed with the potential uses of drugs in interrogations and other situations where they wanted to manipulate human behavior, not unlike what novelist and essayist Aldous Huxley describes: "It seems to me perfectly in the cards that there will be within the next generation or so a pharmacological method of making people love their servitude, and producing dictatorship without tears, so to speak. Producing a kind of painless concentration camp for entire societies, so that people will in fact have their liberties taken away from them but will rather enjoy it, because they will be distracted from any desire to rebel—by propaganda, brain washing, or brain washing enhanced by pharmacological methods."[105] LSD, discovered by the Swiss chemist Albert Hofmann in 1943, was of particular interest, and the CIA lost no time testing it after they found out about it in the late 1940s. Many subjects participated in these experiments by choice; college campuses were fertile recruiting grounds, with Harvard apparently contributing more than its share of recruits.[106] Some subjects were quasi-voluntary, like prison populations that could easily be coerced. Many other subjects were unwitting, because the CIA felt it could get the most authentic test results from subjects unaware they were being experimented on. Ironically, CIA staff and contractors were not exempt from these unwitting experiments. One of the most tragic outcomes involved a scientist named Frank Olson.

Olson was a biochemist whose area of expertise was the airborne delivery of disease. He'd been employed by the Special Operations Division (SOD) of the Army Chemical Corps, located at Fort Detrick in Frederick, Maryland, since the SOD was created in 1950. The SOD had a close working relationship with the Technical Services Staff (TSS), a unit of the CIA strongly interested in utilizing chemical and biological warfare agents in covert operations; in fact, "TSS was paying SOD about $200,000 a year in return for operational systems to infect foes with disease."[107] The joint army-CIA program for the development of chemical and biological weapons was called MKNAOMI, and in April 1953, it became part of a broader program of CIA-sponsored activities known as MKULTRA (also spelled MK-ULTRA).

Several times a year, CIA officials and SOD scientists held working retreats in secluded locations to discuss their joint ventures. In November 1953, they met for three days at a former Boy Scout camp overlooking Deep Creek Lake in western Maryland, near Camp David. The participants were understandably tight-lipped about their discussion topics. But these topics would have included the arsenal of diseases and toxins the SOD maintained for CIA use, ranging from strains of the staph infection and Venezuelan equine encephalitis virus to more deadly alternatives like anthrax; the delivery, detection, and treatment methods for these agents; and perhaps also their historical use, such as the anthrax and other biological agents allegedly used by the Japanese in China during World War II.[108]

The November 1953 meeting was more than an ordinary working retreat, because a CIA official had decided to make the SOD group the unwitting subjects in a drug experiment. On the evening of November 19, 1953—"the same day that a Washington *Post* editorial decried the use of dogs in chemical experiments"[109]—the official spiked a bottle of Cointreau with LSD just before it was shared by all but one SOD man who didn't drink and another who had health problems. Olson was among those who consumed the LSD-laced liqueur. Under the influence of the drug he became confused and agitated, and in the following days was overcome by a deep depression and sense of inadequacy. He was also overcome with paranoia, fearing that CIA agents were after him. Only a few days after consuming the LSD, Olson leapt to his death (some suspect he was pushed) from a New York hotel room.[110] The CIA mounted a cover-up, and it was not until twenty-two years later that Olson's family read a *Washington Post* story about a nameless individual matching Olson's description whose suicide had been triggered by a CIA-sponsored LSD experiment. His widow and three children threatened to sue; they received an apology from President Gerald Ford and dropped their suit after the government paid them a settlement of $750,000.

Olson wasn't the only victim. It's impossible to read about the CIA's biological and chemical warfare experiments without noting the horrific torture of animals that these experiments entailed. A typical example occurred in a CIA-sponsored project at a UCLA lab in the 1960s: "CIA Deputy Director for Intelligence Ray Clines recalled in a 1977 interview that in 1964 he traveled from CIA headquarters to a laboratory at University of California–Los Angeles where he was shown a group of sad-eyed, shaking chimpanzees who had had the tops of their heads removed so that a tangle of electrodes could be plugged into their brains. Clines listened attentively as proud UCLA researchers explained how they were able to control the chimps from afar."[111] Experiments at Fort Detrick produced so many thousands of "mutilated and dead" rhesus monkeys and chimpanzees that according to a former army scientist, a backhoe and dumptruck had to be used to scoop up their bodies so they could be hauled away and incinerated.[112]

Many of the experiments on animals were a precursor to experiments on humans. Some of the most chilling CIA experiments done in connection with the MKNAOMI germ-warfare program were done to African Americans beginning in 1955 and continuing at least until the early 1970s. In her book *Medical Apartheid: The Dark History of Medical Experimentation on Black Americans from Colonial Times to the Present*, Harriet A. Washington describes the deliberate release of disease-carrying mosquitoes in black communities: "Fort Detrick's Army Chemical Corps laboratory bred more than four million mosquitoes *per day* and released them in hordes around Florida, including near Carver Village [a black housing development in Miami]. This was an experiment to determine whether these droning syringes on the wing—disease vectors, in medical parlance—could be used as first-strike biological weapons to spread yellow fever and other infectious diseases, ostensibly among foreign troops during wartime. . . . By 1960, Carver Village residents had been plagued by a rash of mysterious illnesses, including the symptoms of dengue and yellow fever, and deaths."[113]

According to Washington, the CIA apparently "released various biological agents, from mosquitoes to bacteria, in hundreds of such dispersals," including in another black housing development named Carver Village in Georgia.[114] Among those affected was Savannah legislator and activist Dorothy Pelote, who later recalled that in 1955, young white men she assumed were from the Health Department had shown up at her home.

They told her and her husband they were doing a study on the spread of mosquitoes, then placed a box or trap in the backyard. After a spike in illnesses and deaths, people began to realize there was a correlation with the placement of the boxes by the "Health Department" workers, but the story that the victims had been used as guinea pigs didn't break until the 1980s.[115]

The unethical CIA experiments carried out under the auspices of the MKULTRA project also involved prostitution. A key player in this effort was an unsavory individual named George Hunter White. A former agent with the Federal Bureau of Narcotics, White had made national headlines in January 1949, when he raided the San Francisco hotel room of legendary jazz and blues singer Billie Holiday and arrested her for opium possession. Holiday was acquitted but continued to battle drug and alcohol problems. She was arrested for narcotics possession for the last time in a New York hospital, where she died in 1959 at the age of forty-four.

Holiday may have escaped White's clutches, but other, less influential people didn't. In 1953, the CIA hired White to set up a "safehouse" in Greenwich Village; he expanded the operation to San Francisco two years later. Additional safehouses were established in other locations, some under the direction of other agents. These houses were anything but safe for the prostitutes and other vulnerable people lured into them, unwittingly plied with drugs, and coerced into engaging in sex acts observed by CIA employees through two-way mirrors and other surveillance devices. The ostensible aim of the CIA experiments was to learn more about the use of prostitutes for intelligence-gathering purposes, and also to test LSD and myriad other drugs on the unsuspecting safehouse "guests." The safehouses were closed in the mid-1960s, and most records attesting to this sordid chapter in the CIA's history were destroyed in the early 1970s to preclude lawsuits by victims. White, however, left behind a letter to his former CIA boss in which he exulted: "I toiled wholeheartedly in the vineyards because it was fun, fun, fun. Where else could a red-blooded American boy lie, kill, cheat, steal, rape, and pillage with the sanction and blessing of the All-Highest?"[116]

Many others besides White "toiled wholeheartedly in the vineyards" as the CIA hunted for the Manchurian candidate. Marks notes that "some of their experiments would wander so far across the ethical borders of exper-imental psychiatry (which are hazy in their own right) that Agency offi-cials thought it prudent to have much of the work done outside the United States."[117] "Outside the United States" didn't mean that far away. Decades later, victims were still taking legal action as the result of CIA-funded research done by Dr. D. Ewen Cameron at the Allan Memorial Institute in Montreal between 1957 and 1960.[118] Incredibly, the Scottish-born Cam-eron (who'd become a U.S. citizen) had served on the Nuremberg medical tribunal after World War II, charging Nazi doctors with some of the very crimes he himself had been or would be guilty of.[119] Using a range of tech-niques including powerful electroshock treatments (thirty to forty times the normal strength), LSD, paralytic drugs like curare, sensory depriva-tion, and drug-induced coma, Cameron and his staff did mind-control experiments on mostly female patients, who had come to the hospital unwittingly for treatment of conditions like postpartum depression and menopause. The idea was to wipe their minds clean through depatterning, then to repattern or brainwash them, "as coffee will leave a stain upon a fresh, snowy tablecloth," to borrow an unsettling metaphor for brainwash-ing from Condon's novel *The Manchurian Candidate*.[120] Cameron's experi-ments in Montreal accomplished nothing other than to leave many of the victims with amnesia or other forms of mental impairment.

Some members of philanthropic organizations and other groups assess-ing Cameron's work, both while he was head of the Allan Memorial Insti-tute and subsequently, offered scathing descriptions of his conduct, but they carried little weight because of Cameron's professional stature and political power. (Regarded as the "godfather of Canadian psychiatry,"[121] Cameron was an internationally known psychiatrist who became head of the American Psychiatric Association in 1953 and also served as the first president of the World Psychiatric Association.) A representative of the Rockefeller Founda-tion, which had helped establish the Allan Memorial Institute in 1943 and continued to fund it, commented that Cameron "appears to suffer from deep insecurity and has a need for power which he nourishes by maintaining an extraordinary aloofness from his associates."[122] After Cameron's retirement in 1964, his successor took the unusual step of commissioning a study of his work. One member of the evaluation committee spoke bitterly of the memory loss suffered by some of Cameron's patients, noting that one woman had to write detailed instructions to herself to be able to do even the most routine housework. "'I probably shouldn't talk about this,' the investigator added, 'but Cameron—for him to do what he did—he was a very schizophrenic guy, who totally detached himself from the human implications of his work . . . God, we talk about concentration camps. I don't want to make this comparison, but God, you talk about "we didn't know it was happening," and it was—right in our back yard.'"[123] Cameron died in a hiking accident at the age of sixty-five in 1967, so he didn't live to see the furor his work would cause.

Other Forms of Brainwashing

Not all claims of brainwashing have involved such dramatic events. An arena where more subtle brainwashing plays a pervasive role is advertising, discussed in Chapter 4. In his book *A Terrible Mistake: The Murder of Frank Olson and the CIA's Secret Cold War Experiments*, H. P. Albarelli Jr. notes that ironically, in the same period in which the CIA was investigating brainwashing abroad, "The American techniques for consumer advertising and mass marketing had already taken on many of the principal characteristics of brainwashing."[124] Subtle influence tactics aren't limited to advertising; they're also common in politics. Celebrity endorsements represent a well-known example. A less well-known but interesting influence tactic is the use of food to win votes. Studies have shown that plying people with good food is an effective way of winning their liking and support, so it's no accident that you've often heard of legislators being summoned to the White House for a lavish meal before a contentious vote. This is basically the same tactic the Russian scientist Pavlov used when he taught a dog to transfer its normal response to food—salivation—to a different stimulus, the ringing of a bell.[125]

Alternatively, brainwashing may be dramatic but very close to home, as in the case of domestic violence (see the accompanying box). Another dramatic example involves brainwashing in the context of religious cults, sometimes leading to tragic consequences.

Did You Know?

Domestic Abuse May Involve an Extreme Form of Brainwashing

Brainwashing doesn't just involve political institutions but may also involve the family. As Kathleen Taylor says in her book *Brainwashing: The Science of Thought Control*, domestic abuse can be "one of the most intense and damaging" forms of social interaction: "A skilled abuser can use every trick in the influence technician's repertoire, from authority to commitment traps to sheer brute force, building up even an initially small inequality in power into an imbalance so huge that the abused partner in effect becomes a slave. Such abusers achieve a degree of control over their victims which is closer to the traditional idea of brainwashing than [almost any other] situation . . . , with the possible exception of the most extreme cults."[1]

Taylor goes on to note similarities between abusers' behavior and characteristics of totalitarian regimes identified by psychiatrist Robert Jay Lifton and others. One key similarity is the presence of an all-encompassing ideology. The ideologies of totalitarian states are well known. But "what, then, is the abuser's ideology? Like all ideologies, it is a set of beliefs, in this case centred on the abuser's superiority. The abuser will act to reinforce these beliefs, partly by maximizing the contrast between his power and his victim's helplessness, partly by demonstrating his control over her, by force if need be."[2]

In domestic violence, as in totalitarian societies, the ideology is imposed so mercilessly on the victim that it breaks down resistance and does other damage. This is of little concern to the abuser, because what is at stake is the "abuser's fragile ego."[3] In short, "Issues of self and self-image . . . are at the heart of any discussion of mind control techniques."[4] Just as brainwashing can be a powerful weapon in the arsenal of an oppressive state, so too can it be a destructive force in the context of an abusive family.

1   Kathleen Taylor, *Brainwashing: The Science of Thought Control* (Oxford: Oxford University Press, 2004), 86.
2   Taylor, *Brainwashing*, 88.
3   Taylor, *Brainwashing*, 89.
4   Taylor, *Brainwashing*, 90.

Cults

The word *cult* is hard to define. Some people have a tendency to label any group or movement a cult that they find bizarre or unappealing, but we should avoid this practice because it can infringe on religious or intellectual freedom. Most groups regarded as cults have a distinctive pattern of social relations emphasizing dependency—the dependency of the followers on the group and especially on its leader. Typically, the leader is a charismatic individual who maintains absolute control of the group; the members become largely reliant on him (it's almost always a him) for housing, food, and other essentials. The leader and other top officials regulate every aspect of the members' lives and do not tolerate dissent.

The loyalty and cohesion of the group are maintained through unusually stringent brainwashing techniques. Members are subjected to both physical and emotional isolation. Cults are often located in remote areas, like the Branch Davidians in the compound in Waco, Texas, that was destroyed in a shoot-out and fire during a raid by the federal government in 1993. (The federal agents were investigating allegations of child abuse and other illegal activity; tragically, eighty-four people—including twenty-one children—died in the raid.) Cult followers are often allowed little or no contact with their family or others in the outside world, a practice that not only deprives them of information that might undermine their loyalty to the cult but that also makes them emotionally dependent on the leader and group. This dependency relation is reinforced by a range of persuasion tactics that indoctrinate the members with a belief in the messianic qualities of both the leader and the cult. Contrary to popular belief, those attracted to cults usually have a normal middle-class educational and economic background; they don't tend to have mental problems, though cults sometimes target people who are emotionally vulnerable like those who have recently lost a family member.[126]

One of the best known examples of cult brainwashing resulting in violence and death is the Jonestown massacre. In 1977, following accusations of tax evasion and other scandals, the Reverend Jim Jones moved his Peoples Temple organization from San Francisco to a remote jungle in Guyana, a small country on the Atlantic coast of South America. The commune was beset by growing internal strife and was under increasing attack from defectors and relatives of commune members, who claimed Jones was abusive and was using brainwashing techniques on his followers. In November 1978, after a delegation of government officials, family members, and journalists headed by Congressman Leo Ryan (D-CA) arrived in Jonestown and was attacked (and Ryan and others were killed), Jones resorted to an apocalyptic solution: mass suicide. After drinking grape Flavor Aid (similar to Kool-Aid) laced with cyanide and Valium, more than 900 people died.

Test Your Skills

How would you distinguish between propaganda and education? Do you think the U.S. educational system (or that of another country of your choice) utilizes propaganda? If so, how?

Conclusion

This chapter has given you a capsule view of brainwashing or mind control. Many of the activities profiled in the chapter represent the outer limits of human conduct; they are the most morally corrupt area of the sea of deception and so require extreme vigilance to prevent their recurrence.

The fact that the chapter has featured dramatic examples of brainwashing ranging from CIA experiments to the Jonestown massacre shouldn't blind you to the reality that you're subject to lesser forms of mind control on a daily basis. The next chapter turns to a prime example: advertising.

What You Can Do

As with all the forms of deception and manipulation surveyed in this book, the first step in combating brainwashing is to recognize the problem. Then you can take other steps. Here are a few guidelines.

√*Be alert and aware and practice critical thinking.* In her book *Brainwashing: The Science of Thought Control,* Kathleen Taylor calls these "stop-and-think reactions" and describes them as a prerequisite to other forms of action.[127]

√*Offer personal resistance.* Interestingly, highly dogmatic individuals are often better able to resist influence attempts because of their rigid belief structure. If you're a low-dogmatism type of person who's creative and open to new ideas, you may need to make an extra effort to resist influence attempts.[128] Personal resistance to brainwashing can take many forms. An obvious strategy is simply removing yourself from the situation if you feel mind control is being exercised—for example, in certain cults or religious groups. But removing yourself from the situation isn't always possible. We glimpsed a different form of resistance earlier in discussing the behavior of U.S. POWs during the Korean War. Many POWs swore allegiance to communism temporarily, believing that this short-term compliance would lead to better treatment while in prison or would even save their lives. Finally, even the types of brainwashing that involve violence can sometimes be resisted by means of techniques like dissociation—an adaptive response in which traumatic memories, thoughts, perceptions, or sensations are walled off or compartmentalized so as to make them less painful to the conscious mind.

√*Help create a climate in which society as a whole is resistant to the use of mind-control techniques.* Being able to protect yourself against brainwashing techniques is only a superficial measure. As Marks points out in his book *The Search for the "Manchurian Candidate,"* a deeper solution is to make most of these techniques socially and legally unacceptable, a strategy that depends on a high level of public awareness: "A free society's best defense against unethical behavior modification is public disclosure and awareness. The more people understand consciousness-altering technology, the more likely they are to recognize its application, and the less likely it will be used."[129] Just how indifferent certain segments of society can be to the ethical questions surrounding this technology can be seen from the fact that even after D. Ewen Cameron presented papers describing his depatterning experiments before audiences of psychiatrists, "his fellow psychiatrists . . . elected him their president."[130] Marks concludes his book with these words: "The more vigilant we and our representatives are, the less chance we will be unwitting victims."[131]

√*Create lasting solutions by working for social justice.* On the deepest level, you can try to head off the problems of totalitarianism and brainwashing by working toward a free and open society in which all groups have equal rights and in which intellectual freedom and public debate are high priorities. In other words, unlike the dystopian world Orwell portrays in *Nineteen Eighty-Four*, this would be a society in which there's no room for Big Brother, for the Thought Police, or for doublethink and doublespeak.

Further Reading

For an introduction to brainwashing, see Kathleen Taylor, *Brainwashing: The Science of Thought Control* (Oxford: Oxford University Press, 2004). On influence more generally, see Robert B. Cialdini, *Influence: Science and Practice*, 5th ed. (Boston: Pearson/Allyn and Bacon, 2009).

For a useful edition of Orwell's classic novel, see George Orwell, *Nineteen Eighty-Four*, foreword by Thomas Pynchon, afterword by Erich Fromm, centennial ed. (New York: Plume, [1949] 2003). For a biography of Orwell, see Gordon Bowker, *George Orwell* (London: Little, Brown, 2003).

On the CIA's mind-control research, see John Marks, *The Search for the "Manchurian Candidate": The CIA and Mind Control*, rev. ed. (New York: Norton, 1979] 1991). (The 1979 edition is available at http://www.druglibrary.org/schaffer/lsd/marks.htm.) Also see Anne Collins's perceptive book, *In the Sleep Room: The Story of the CIA Brainwashing Experiments in Canada* (Toronto: Lester & Orpen Dennys, 1988). For a shorter account, see the chapter titled "The Torture Lab: Ewen Cameron, the CIA and the Maniacal Quest to Erase and Remake the Human Mind" in Naomi Klein's *The Shock Doctrine: The Rise of Disaster Capitalism* (New York: Metropolitan Books / Henry Holt, 2007), 25–48. The Frank Olson case is the subject of the compelling, 800-page investigative study by H. P. Albarelli Jr., *A Terrible Mistake: The Murder of Frank Olson and the CIA's Secret Cold War Experiments* (Walterville, OR: Trine Day, 2009). On the CIA more generally, see Tim Weiner's highly regarded *Legacy of Ashes: The History of the CIA* (New York: Doubleday, 2007).

For influential early works on Chinese brainwashing, see Robert Jay Lifton, *Thought Reform and the Psychology of Totalism: A Study of "Brainwashing" in China* (New York: Norton, 1961; reprint with a new preface, Chapel Hill: University of North Carolina Press, 1989); Edward Hunter, *Brain-Washing in Red China: The Calculated Destruction of Men's Minds* (New York: Vanguard Press, 1951; 2nd ed., 1953); and Edward Hunter, *Brainwashing: The Story of Men Who Defied It* (New York, Farrar, Straus and Cudahy, 1956). For fascinating insight into the Cold War environment in which Hunter was operating, see the transcript of his 1958 appearance before the House Un-American Activities Committee: Committee on Un-American Activities, House of Representatives, *Communist Psychological Warfare (Brainwashing), Consultation with Edward Hunter, Author and Foreign Correspondent,* March 13, 1958 (Washington, DC: Government Printing Office, 1958), http://www.crossroad.to/Quotes/globalism/Congress.htm.

On cults, see Steven Hassan, *Combatting Cult Mind Control* (Rochester, VT: Park Street Press, 1990); Janja Lalich and Madeleine Tobias, *Take Back Your Life: Recovering from Cults and Abusive Relationships,* 2nd ed. (Berkeley, CA: Bay Street Publishing, 2006); and Margaret Thaler Singer, *Cults in Our Midst,* rev. ed. (San Francisco: Jossey-Bass, 2003). For a survivor's moving account of the Jonestown tragedy, see Deborah Layton, *Seductive Poison: A Jonestown Survivor's Story of Life and Death in the Peoples Temple* (New York: Anchor, 1998).

4. THE BRAVE NEW WORLD OF ADVERTISING

In 1957, Vance Packard—a journalist and cultural critic—published a book titled *The Hidden Persuaders*, which went on to sell over a million copies and made Packard famous.[132] A half century ago, advertising barely touched the life of the average American. Television was still in its infancy, junk mail didn't exist, and telemarketing was hardly feasible in an era in which many people didn't have phones. True, newspapers and magazines featured ads for everything from Studebakers and Edsels, to "stereophonic record playing instruments," to Singer sewing machines and Toni home permanent kits. These ads were greeted with curiosity or amusement, or occasionally provided a useful basis for purchasing decisions. But most people would have described them as peripheral to their lives.

That was about to change. Packard warned of a brave new world in which people would be manipulated into buying things they didn't need, into doing things against their will, even into thinking unwelcome thoughts. In fact, he wrote in the opening paragraph of *The Hidden Persuaders*, "professional persuaders" were already at work utilizing psychiatric techniques to influence people's attitudes and behavior: "This book is an attempt to explore a strange and rather exotic new area of American life. It is about the large-scale efforts being made, often with impressive success, to channel our unthinking habits, our purchasing decisions, and our thought processes by the use of insights gleaned from psychiatry and the social sciences." He elaborated: "Typically these efforts take place beneath our level of awareness; so that the appeals which move us are often, in a sense, 'hidden.' The result is that many of us are being influenced and manipulated, far more than we realize, in the patterns of our everyday lives."[133]

Packard's words seem almost quaint today, yet they're a useful reminder that the psychological manipulation we now take for granted hasn't always existed: "Seemingly, in the probing and manipulating nothing is immune or sacred. . . . Public-relations experts are advising churchmen how they can become more effective manipulators of their congregations. In some cases these persuaders even choose our friends for us, as at a large 'community of tomorrow' in Florida. Friends are furnished along with the linen by the management in offering the homes for sale. Everything comes in one big, glossy package."[134] We may not be able to put the genie back in the bottle, but we don't have to let deceptive advertising rule our lives. In this chapter you'll learn more about how Packard's "hidden persuaders" work and what you can do about it.

Advertising: From Papyrus to Text Messages

Evidence of advertising—on media ranging from papyrus to rocks and walls—has been found in Egypt, India, Greece, Rome, and other ancient cultures. But advertising in the sense of mass marketing had to wait for the invention of printing in the fifteenth century. Further impetus came from the Industrial Revolution in the eighteenth and nineteenth centuries, because industrialization made the large-scale production of material goods possible. It also provided an incentive to entrepreneurs to profit from the sale of those goods, in part with the aid of advertising.

One of the most successful nineteenth-century mass marketers was not an industrialist but a patent medicine manufacturer named Lydia Pinkham (1819–1883). From 1875 on, she mass-marketed Lydia E. Pinkham's Vegetable Compound—a tonic for women that contained herbs used in Native American and Chinese medicine. It is still available (in a different form) today. Pinkham is considered a pioneer in the women's health movement because of her efforts to improve healthcare for women, though her company was not immune to deceptive practices. Advertisements encouraged women to write to Pinkham for advice, but for years this advice was dispensed under suspicious circumstances. A 1905 issue of the *Ladies Home*

Journal featured a photo of Pinkham's tombstone and exposed the fact that she'd been dead since 1883. Without the knowledge of Pinkham's loyal customers, her correspondence was actually being handled by a paid secretarial staff; a 1907 photo came to light showing a large number of women sitting at desks and answering letters in the Pinkham firm's "correspondence room."[135]

If Pinkham built her empire with patent medicines, Madam C. J. Walker (1867–1919) did the same with hair-care products. The daughter of slaves, Madam Walker was born on a Louisiana plantation and orphaned at seven. After two decades eking out a living as a washerwoman, she devised a popular hair-care product for black women and laid the foundation for a fabulously successful business. Through word of mouth and eventually with the aid of skillful advertising campaigns, she built a beauty empire and amassed unprecedented wealth, becoming one of the first prominent African-American entrepreneurs. She also left her mark as a social activist and philanthropist, moving in circles that included W. E. B. Du Bois and Booker T. Washington and supporting causes ranging from NAACP antilynching campaigns to the creation of schools in West Africa.

Entrepreneurs like Pinkham and Walker made good use of the advertising resources available to them in earlier periods, but advertising as we know it is often traced back to the spectacular successes of propaganda in World War I. Chapter 2 touched on the role of psychologist Edward L. Bernays and journalist Walter Lippmann as public relations pioneers during the First World War. Bernays is considered the first theorist of advertising, which he often referred to as "propaganda."[136] As a nephew of Freud, he was well acquainted with Freud's theories of the unconscious, and quickly grasped the commercial potential of the theory that we're all governed by irrational, unconscious motives.[137] Bernays's own PR successes are legendary. One of the best-known involved soap sculpture. Procter & Gamble (P&G) was one of Bernays's major clients. Unfortunately a key demographic group proved resistant to the use of P&G's main product, Ivory soap. Deciding that "children, the enemies of soap, would be conditioned to enjoy using Ivory,"[138] Bernays came up with an ingenious solution: a soap-sculpture contest. He had gotten the idea after a sculptor contacted P&G to order large blocks of Ivory that could be carved like clay. So in 1924, Bernays set in motion a National Soap Sculpture Contest. Extensive media coverage and cash prizes guaranteed it would catch on. From the beginning, entrants included sculptors and other artists, but the contest organizers increasingly reached out to children, distributing brochures on how kids could use a pocketknife or paring knife and a few other simple items to produce winning sculptures. By the time the contest was ended in 1961, a million soap bars a year were being carved into every conceivable form and Bernays had achieved his goal of making Ivory soap a familiar household item—including among kids.

Bernays also put his theories to good use on behalf of the tobacco industry. In 1929, he orchestrated a legendary PR stunt aimed at encouraging women to smoke. His biographer, Larry Tye, sets the stage:

> U.S. tobacco tycoons scored nearly as stunning a triumph as did U.S. troops during World War I. When America joined the war, cigarettes were considered unsavory, if not unmanly; most men preferred cigars, pipes, or chewing tobacco. But cigarettes proved more convenient in the trenches, new blended tobaccos produced a milder and more appealing product, and Uncle Sam began putting cigarettes in soldiers' rations, with the result that many doughboys changed their smoking habits. Cigarettes were manly things now, the stuff of warriors. And as their use among men soared, so did the profits of the companies making them. All of which convinced cigarette makers that the time was ripe to open a second front, this time targeting females.[139]

Since smoking was stigmatized as unfeminine, Bernays had to find a way of making it appealing to women. Psychiatrist A. A. Brill convinced him that cigarettes were a phallic symbol, and that many women would take up smoking if they could be persuaded it was a way of rebelling against the male establishment. So Bernays talked a contingent of cigarette-smoking New York debutantes into marching in the 1929 Easter parade as a feminist statement. He sent photos of what he called the "Torches of Liberty Brigade" to newspapers and played up the connection between smoking and women's rights. Women readers—like the defiant debutantes themselves— were unaware they were being manipulated as part of an ad campaign.[140]

Did You Know?

A PR Expert Helped Topple a Government

One of Edward L. Bernays's most controversial successes as a PR expert was on behalf of United Fruit Company—a Boston-based company with massive landholdings and political influence in Central America—in the 1950s. Bernays's role started out innocently enough in the 1940s: promoting United Fruit's primary product, bananas, among U.S. consumers. But United Fruit came to be seen as a symbol of Yankee imperialism, and in the early 1950s the Guatemalan government under President Jacobo Arbenz Guzmán began to expropriate the company's landholdings. Bernays went from promoting bananas to warning of communist incursions in Central America, and he orchestrated a propaganda campaign in major U.S. newspapers and magazines in favor of U.S. intervention in Guatemala. The time was ripe for such intervention because of the anticommunist paranoia of the Cold War era. Things came to a head in June 1954, when the CIA engineered a coup against Guzmán and replaced him with a president of their choice, an army officer named Carlos Castillo Armas.

Bernays's formula, according to his biographer, had an "explosive potential": "Add a wealthy and self-interested private sponsor to sympathetic U.S. operatives, then let a masterful propagandist stir the pot by firing up public opinion, and even toppling foreign governments seemed possible. Or so it seemed to policy makers who would repeat the recipe in Cuba, Nicaragua, and elsewhere across Latin America and around the globe."[1]

---

1   Larry Tye, *The Father of Spin: Edward L. Bernays and the Birth of Public Relations* (New York: Crown, 1998), 178. Tye devotes a chapter (pp. 155–184) to Bernays and United Fruit. On the CIA coup in Guatemala, also see Tim Weiner, *Legacy of Ashes: The History of the CIA* (New York: Doubleday, 2007), 93–104.

Advertising has increasingly encroached on our public space and is now ubiquitous. It appears on everything from bus-stop benches and the sides of subway trains to web banners and skywriting to supermarket receipts and concert tickets. More familiar venues include radio and television ads, magazines, newspapers, billboards, and posters. Of these formats, television commercials are viewed as the most effective, which explains their high price. During the annual Super Bowl football championship in January or February, a single thirty-second commercial can cost several million dollars.

Technological advances have made new marketing approaches possible. These approaches include online advertising (a growing competitor for TV commercials as the Internet siphons more viewers from television), bulk email marketing (spam), and commercial text messages. Because of their intrusiveness in our lives, these new media add to the problem of *viral marketing*—marketing that encourages us to buy or acquire ever more products or services we don't need or want. The impersonal, informal nature of viral marketing also lends itself to deceptive practices, because we've come a long way from the days when you could demand that the Fuller Brush man or Avon lady get out their brushes or cosmetics and demonstrate the truthfulness of their claims in your living room.

To an extent that the Fuller Brush man or Avon lady couldn't have envisioned, the corporatization of society is leading to ever more intrusive and deceptive advertising practices. As consumerism seeps into more and more areas of life that were previously sacrosanct—in other words, as "corporate power is woven so deeply into the culture that it becomes invisible, unquestionable"[141]— it's becoming harder and harder to distinguish fact from marketing spin. In this era of hypercommercialism, content and commercialism are frequently indistinguishable, with advertisers determining editorial content and integrating marketing messages with print, broadcast, film, and other media. Thus "the traditional distinction between editorial or creative work and advertising—the separation of church and state—is being toppled by commercial pressures."[142] In this blurring of church and state, the most obvious casualty is the truth.

Test Your Skills

In their book *Unreliable Sources: A Guide to Detecting Bias in News Media*, Martin A. Lee and Norman Solomon outline the guidelines followed by TV censors in the United States. Lee and Solomon say these guidelines are "explicitly spelled out by big-league sponsors":

- **Make sure nothing in a script undermines the sales pitch for the advertised product.** For example, a gas company sponsoring a TV version of *Judgment at Nuremberg* demanded that the producers delete references to "gas chambers" from accounts of Nazi concentration camps. Pharmaceutical firms won't tolerate scenes in which someone commits suicide by overdosing on pills. . . .
- **Portray Big Business in a flattering light.** Sponsors are adamant about this. Procter & Gamble, which spends over a billion dollars a year on advertising, once decreed in a memo on broadcast policy: "There will be no material that will give offense, either directly or indirectly to any commercial organization of any sort." Ditto for Prudential Insurance: "A positive image of business and finance is important to sustain on the air." If a businessman is cast as the bad guy, it must be clear that he is an exception, and the script must also include benevolent business folk so as not to leave the wrong impression. Corporate sponsors are unlikely to underwrite programs that engage in serious criticism of environmental pollution, occupational hazards or other problems attributable to corporate malfeasance. . . .
- **Cater to the upper crust.** Sponsors don't want just any audience; they want affluent viewers with buying power. To impress potential sponsors, ABC once prepared a booklet with a section called, "Some people are more valuable

---

Test Your Skills

than others." If the elderly and low-income counted for more in the advertising department, their particular concerns would figure more prominently in the tone and content of TV programming. . . .

- **Steer clear of overly serious or complex subjects and bleach out controversy wherever possible.** DuPont, a major advertiser, told the FCC that commercials are more effective on "lighter, happier" programs. Comedy, adventure, and escapism are standard fare, as advertisers push mass media toward socially insignificant content that offends as few viewers as possible.[1]

In light of these guidelines, speculate on the role advertisers have played in shaping U.S. society in the decades in which television has been a major cultural force. How would your guidelines differ from the ones Lee and Solomon list?

---

1   Martin A. Lee and Norman Solomon, *Unreliable Sources: A Guide to Detecting Bias in News Media* (New York: Lyle Stuart / Carol Publishing Group, 1998), 61–63.

Deceptive Advertising Tactics

This section looks at the deceptive tactics advertisers employ, ranging from psychological manipulation to outright lies.

Psychological Manipulation

Since its inception, almost all advertising has utilized some degree of audience manipulation. This, of course, is the subject of Packard's *Hidden Persuaders*. It's worth taking a closer look at his discussion, because it was prescient in tackling problems that would later come to plague us.

According to Packard, psychologists had helped marketers identify eight "hidden needs" that could shape purchasing decisions if ads promised fulfillment of those needs:

- *Selling emotional security.* "Womb-seekers," as Packard calls them, can be persuaded to buy anything from freezers to air conditioners to tools. For example, he reports that advertisers were advised to sell tools to men by selling them security: "A man concentrating on his tools or his machinery is in a closed world. He is free from the strains of interpersonal relationships. He is engaged in a peaceful dialogue with himself."[143]
- *Selling reassurance of worth.* Advertisers were told that "many housewives feel they are engaged in unrewarded and unappreciated drudgery when they clean," so cleaning products should be marketed in a way that boosts housewives' self-esteem.
- *Selling ego gratification.* Advertisers found that selling ego gratification—by promising fame and fortune—was more profitable than merely selling a product on its merits.
- *Selling creative outlets.* You might be surprised to learn that when they first went on the market in the 1950s, cake mixes and other food mixes included the milk and eggs in dried form. Then General Mills and other companies made an interesting discovery: women did not respond well to the instructions "Do not add milk, just add water." The manufacturers, Packard says, "found themselves trying to cope with negative and guilt feelings on the part of women who felt that use of ready mixes was a sign of poor housekeeping and threatened to deprive them of a traditional

source of praise."[144] So the milk and eggs were removed from the mixes to allow women to add a creative touch.

- *Selling love objects.* Entertainers could be promoted or products sold more successfully if ads appealed to emotional needs. For example, Liberace—the television pianist—was deliberately marketed to older women by stressing his boyish qualities. Pictures of his real-life mother were often flashed on the screen to show her doting on her son, hopefully encouraging other women to do the same.
- *Selling a sense of power.* Especially for men, ad agencies found the word *power* had great magic. Stressing this aspect of a car, a boat, or even a cigarette could be counted on to boost sales.
- *Selling a sense of roots.* Imagery associated with family and "home sweet home" also boosts sales.
- *Selling immortality.* "Perhaps the most astounding of all the efforts to merchandise hidden needs was that proposed to a conference of Midwestern life-insurance men," Packard reports.[145] Attendees who made a living selling life insurance to men were advised to stop emphasizing the comfort the family would enjoy after the man's death and instead emphasize his *immortality*— that is, the way he'd continue to control the family's destiny (their standard of living, the children's educational opportunities, and so on) from beyond the grave.

In chapters like "The Built-In Sexual Overtone" and "Back to the Breast, and Beyond," Packard shows how advertisers have utilized the above insights to market everything from Plymouths to political candidates. Many marketing campaigns have been based on perceived gender differences. A well-known example involves Marlboro cigarettes, originally lipstick red and marketed to women. Faced with the fact that male smokers outnumbered women two to one, Philip Morris revamped their Marlboro ads from the mid-1950s on to emphasize cowboys and other virile-looking men (the "Marlboro Man"). Since Marlboros were pitched as "A man's cigarette that women like too," many women remained loyal to the brand. The new campaign won praise from experts for its ability to "express powerful meanings indirectly," beyond the conscious awareness of the consumer.[146]

As with the Marlboro campaign, products often have to be sold to both women and men though they may have different tastes or preferences. Packard describes a housing development near Chicago that had to sell a thousand homes as fast as possible. An ad agency consulted several psychiatrists, who recommended strategies to reach both genders:

> The task of selling the houses was complicated, the probers found, by the fact that men saw home in quite a different light from women. Man sees home as a symbolic Mother, a calm place of refuge for him after he has spent an abrasive day in the competitive outside world, often taking directions from a boss. He hopes wistfully to find in his idealized home the kind of solace and comfort he used to find as a child when at his mother's side.
>
> Women on the other hand see home as something quite different since they already are symbolic Mothers. A woman sees home as an expression of herself and often literally as an extension of her own personality. In a new home she can plant herself and grow, re-create herself, express herself freely. As a result of these insights the agency devised several hard-hitting themes to reach both men and women. One ad that was drawn up to appeal especially to men showed a small home with two feminine arms stretching out, seemingly beckoning the troubled male reader to the bosom of her hearth. Mom would take care of him![147]

Class differences also provide fodder for covert advertising strategies. Packard discusses a book titled *Social Class in America* (1948) by a University of Chicago professor named Lloyd Warner, noting that the book "create[d] an even greater stir in merchandising circles" than in scholarly circles. Warner divided the U.S. social structure into six classes; two—the "lower middle" and "upper lower"—were of special interest to marketers. Warner drew a composite picture of the women in these groups as "Mrs. Middle Majority" and urged advertisers to focus their efforts on her because of her purchasing power. This wouldn't be easy; according to Packard, Warner took a dim view of "Mrs. Middle Majority":

> Warner sums her up . . . graphically by telling ad men: "This middle majority woman is the target you are supposed to hit," and goes on to explain that she lives in an extremely restricted world. She works harder than other women, her life has very narrow routines, she likes to deal only with familiar things and tends to view anything outside her narrow world as dangerous and threatening. He adds: "Her imaginative resources are highly limited," and she finds it difficult to manipulate ideas in an original way and is not very adventurous. Finally, he points out: "And this is very important. Her emotional life is highly restricted and repressed, spontaneity is very low, she has a strong moral code that presses in on her most of the time, and she feels a deep sense of guilt when she deviates from it." For these women the safe world is there in the home. If you put these women out in the outer world, it is quite frightening to them. "That," he said, "is what soap opera is all about . . . and fundamentally it is always true of an ad. You can get anxiety in response to an ad because it does have that threatening aspect. These women fear anything to do with uncontrolled impulse and emotional life where the sexuality theme gets too high." Some ads, he continued, are poison to these women for that reason.[148]

This account makes you wonder about the extent to which gender roles, class assumptions, and other fundamental aspects of U.S. society have been engineered by marketing executives. The theme of the intrusive, manipulative nature of advertising runs throughout Packard's book. He concludes *The Hidden Persuaders* with this advice: "The most serious offense many of the depth manipulators commit, it seems to me, is that they try to invade the privacy of our minds. It is this right to privacy in our minds—privacy to be either rational or irrational—that I believe we must strive to protect."[149]

Test Your Skills

Many discussions of problematic ads focus on the denigration of women by the advertising industry, such as through sexualized images. But ads also devalue men. How many negative stereotypes of men can you find in ads? What impact do you think these stereotypes have on men in real life?

Other Deceptive Tactics

The explicitly psychoanalytic approach of many of the advertisers profiled by Packard in the 1950s may have gone out of fashion, but that doesn't mean psychological manipulation by advertisers isn't alive and well—or that they aren't using a range of other deceptive tactics, too. Subtle manipulation is widespread. Language is carefully chosen for maximum effect, so that, for example, ads employing words like *quick, easy, new, improved,* and *amazing* sell more products. Ads featuring babies or animals or utilizing sex appeal (say, an ad for a convertible showing a glamorous woman next to the car) also sell more products. Consumers can be manipulated by personal appeals from celebrities or "experts" as well.

Another common advertising strategy uses the principle that scarcity sells (these ads persuade customers that a product is valuable because it's part of a "limited edition" or is only available "while supplies last"). Many consumers are also easily manipulated by sales gimmicks like bundle pricing; they respond better to an ad offering two products for $5 than one for $2.50. Similar gimmicks involve the "Buy one, get one free" or the "75% off" approach. Consumers are often duped by this approach because they feel they're getting a bargain; they fail to notice that the original price of the item has been jacked up, so the final price is anything but a bargain.

Other deceptive marketing strategies include bait-and-switch tactics, in which the "bait" is an inexpensive product on sale, which is "switched" with a more expensive product when customers get to the store and are told the original version is sold out or inferior.

Finally, of course, some ads exaggerate or misrepresent the virtues of a product, or simply lie outright.

Negative Impact of Advertising

The spread of advertising in our lives has led to mounting criticism. This criticism has focused on several overlapping problems. One is the psychological manipulation of consumers, discussed above.

A second set of problems involve intellectual freedom issues. If a publication or TV show receives most of its revenue from advertisers, how likely is it to air information critical of those advertisers? Suppose Drug Company XYZ is the major sponsor of an investigative TV program. What are the chances that an exposé documenting the lethal effects of one of XYZ's drugs will make it on the air? Because of their financial vulnerability, the TV executives will probably exercise self-censorship and block the exposé even before it comes to the attention of Drug Company XYZ.

A third group of criticisms of advertising pertain to its social impact. For example, mass marketing is increasingly targeting children. Studies suggest the marketing of junk food is contributing to childhood obesity, just as the marketing of sexualized images leads to precocious sexuality and the marketing of violent toys and video games encourages violence. In her eye-opening book *Buy, Buy Baby: How Consumer Culture Manipulates Parents and Harms Young Minds*, Susan Gregory Thomas exposes the growing corporate manipulation of parents, who may be inadvertently harming their children when they succumb to corporate pressure to buy so-called educational products.[150] Other chilling investigations explore the targeting of teenagers, who are easily manipulated by marketers because, in the words of an ad executive, "they don't smell the sell."[151] By focusing on this vulnerable group, teen advertising strives to instill consumer preferences—even for products teenagers aren't old enough to purchase yet, like alcohol and cigarettes—that will persist for years.

A fourth, overarching criticism or set of criticisms is that the advertising industry fosters a kind of phony happiness that rests on counterproductive behaviors or belief patterns like immediate gratification, materialism, and consumerism. Critics argue that these behaviors in turn contribute to everything from crime to environmental destruction to the breakdown of democracy. As one author summarizes, "The message is constant: all our most treasured values—democracy, freedom, individuality, equality, education, community, love, and health—are reduced in one way or another to commodities provided by the market. Social problems either cannot be solved or can be solved only through individual material consumption. Likewise, human happiness derives from material consumption."[152] Or in Bernays's blunt words, "The American way of life is soap, tooth paste, automobiles, or breakfast food and can be sold like them."[153] He wrote those words more than a half century ago; what would he say today?

Citizens Fight Back

Though the advertising industry is a force to be contended with in U.S. society, some efforts to regulate advertising and protect the public interest have been successful. Perhaps best known is the ban on cigarette ads on television and radio. In the 1950s and 1960s, tobacco companies were a major presence on television, sponsoring popular shows like *I've Got a Secret* and *To Tell the Truth* and delivering catchy slogans like "Winston tastes good like a cigarette should!" But in 1970, Congress passed the Public Health Cigarette Smoking Act, which took effect on January 2, 1971. A commercial for Virginia Slims cigarettes—marketed to women and known for the slogan "You've come a long way, baby!"—was the last cigarette commercial shown on U.S. television. This ban was the culmination of years of efforts by the Federal Trade Commission and other organizations and individuals to protect the public from the harmful effects of cigarettes—and cigarette advertising.

Incredibly, for example, war had broken out in the 1920s between tobacco companies and candy manufacturers because the tobacco companies claimed cigarettes were a more healthful treat than candy. The American Tobacco Company promoted its Lucky Strikes with the slogan "Reach for a Lucky instead of a sweet," which provoked the following counterattack from the candy sellers: "Do not let anyone tell you that a cigarette can take the place of a piece of candy. The cigarette will inflame your tonsils, poison with nicotine every organ of your body, and dry up your blood—nails in your coffin."[154] Despite attacks like this and growing medical evidence on the adverse effects of smoking, tobacco products continue to be marketed as a lifestyle choice.

Activist organizations also try to serve the public interest by calling attention to deceptive or otherwise problematic advertising. One well-known example is Adbusters Media Organization (www.adbusters.org), founded in Vancouver, British Columbia, in 1989 to combat consumerism and related problems. Adbusters encourages tactics like culture jamming (such as the defacing of billboards and other ads) and google bombing (manipulating the ranking of a web page). Adbusters is also known for its spoof ads, satirizing liquor, tobacco, and other products it deems harmful. Another anticonsumerist group is Media Watch (www.mediawatch.com), a feminist organization founded in 1984 to challenge misogyny, racism, and other forms of prejudice and violence in the media.

Conclusion

Creating better-informed consumers of the media is also one of this book's goals. This chapter has provided a thumbnail sketch of the advertising industry and of some of its tactics. You've seen that psychological manipulation is key to most advertising campaigns. It's hard to avoid these campaigns; like political propaganda, they're everywhere. So it's up to you to be vigilant and avoid making choices not in your best interest. It's especially crucial to avoid being seduced into making "lifestyle" choices—for example, by adopting harmful habits like smoking or by purchasing electronic devices you don't need or can't afford—merely on the basis of an advertising campaign. Remember, advertisers know the vulnerabilities of their target audiences and will take advantage of them. It's up to you to fight back by educating yourself and resisting temptation.

The next chapter takes up the subject of media bias.

What You Can Do

√*Say no to commercialism by turning off the TV or watching it selectively, registering your phone number with a do-not-call list, removing your name from mailing lists, and generally simplifying your life.* Advertisers can't influence you if they can't reach you. To list personal phone numbers (landline or cellphone or both) with the National Do Not Call Registry, go to www.donotcall.gov or call 1-888-382-1222 from a number you plan to register. You can also do a web search to see if your state has a similar registry.

√*If you find an ad especially inaccurate or misleading, contact the advertiser and demand evidence to back up the claims made.* If enough people do this, many offenders will be embarrassed into cleaning up their act. This is not a trivial issue, because certain types of deceptive ads—for example, regarding drug safety or food additives—can seriously damage people's lives.

√*If you receive a mailer, catalog, or other piece of direct-marketing material that offends you, take action.* Businesses are always trying to hone their message to make it as effective as possible; if they find out a piece of direct mail is a turnoff to potential customers, they may be willing to revise or eliminate it. Call the toll-free number in the mailer or catalog to voice your complaints. You can report serious infractions like fraudulent business practices to the Federal Trade Commission (1-877-382-4357 or www.ftc.gov) and/or to the attorney general's office in your state.

√*Organize protests against companies whose ads demean women, and boycott their products.* Misogynist ads, such as those depicting sexual violence, have become common and should be met with strong action. One ad expert says "advertisers were more afraid of offending women . . . when feminists were more unified and quicker to protest."[155] Besides complaining to advertisers and boycotting their products, you can complain to publications and TV stations that display the ads. You can also get involved with organizations combating ads that exploit women, like Media Watch (www.mediawatch.com), mentioned earlier.

√*Both at home and in school, educate children to be critical consumers of ads.* Teach them to recognize advertising hype as well as exploitative or demeaning ads. The website of psychologist Susan Linn (author of *Consuming Kids*) lists many links to "resources for raising commercial-free children"; see www.consumingkids.com/resources/organizations. htm. Other educational resources are available from the Center for Media Literacy (www.medialit.org).

√*Push for better regulation of advertising, as well as for the law-enforcement resources and stiff penalties necessary to hold advertisers accountable.* Not all advertisers will respond to gentle persuasion; consumer protection requires that adequate legal safeguards and enforcement mechanisms be available.

√*Join organizations fighting the negative impact of advertising and other forms of consumerism.* An example is the Campaign for a Commercial-Free Childhood (www.commercialfreechildhood.org); a web search will turn up many other examples, depending on your interests.

Further Reading

On the development of advertising, see Roland Marchand, *Advertising the American Dream: Making Way for Modernity, 1920–1940* (Berkeley: University of California Press, 1985); Jackson Lears, *Fables of Abundance: A Cultural History of Advertising in America* (New York: Basic Books, 1995); Stephen Fox, *The Mirror Makers: A History of American Advertising and Its Creators* (New York: Morrow, 1984); Paul Rutherford, *Endless Propaganda: The Advertising of Public Goods* (Toronto: University of Toronto Press, 2000); and Michael Schudson, *Advertising, The Uneasy Persuasion: Its Dubious Impact on American Society* (New York: Basic Books, 1984).

Though published more than a half century ago, Vance Packard's classic work *The Hidden Persuaders* (New York: David McKay Company, 1957) is still all too relevant. For a biography of Packard, see Daniel Horowitz, *Vance Packard and American Social Criticism* (Chapel Hill: University of North Carolina Press, 1994).

For an entertaining and informative book on Lydia Pinkham, see Sarah Stage, *Female Complaints: Lydia Pinkham and the Business of Women's Medicine* (New York: Norton, 1979). A fascinating book on Madam C. J. Walker and the larger cultural milieu in which she built her empire is A'Lelia Bundles, *On Her Own Ground: The Life and Times of Madam C. J. Walker* (New York: Scribner, 2001). (Bundles, a former network news bureau chief and producer, is Walker's great-great-granddaughter.)

For a hard-hitting attack on consumerism and the deceptive advertising bound up with it, see Michael F. Jacobson and Laurie Ann Mazur, *Marketing Madness: A Survival Guide for a Consumer Society* (Boulder, CO: Westview Press, 1995). On the impact of consumerism on children, see Susan Linn, *Consuming Kids: The Hostile Takeover of Childhood* (New York: New Press, 2004; published in 2005 with the subtitle *Protecting Our Children from the Onslaught of Marketing & Advertising*), as well as Susan Gregory Thomas, *Buy, Buy Baby: How Consumer Culture Manipulates Parents and Harms Young Minds* (Boston: Houghton Mifflin, 2007), and Juliet B. Schor, *Born to Buy: The Commercialized Child and the New Consumer Culture* (New York: Scribner, 2004). Teen advertising is the subject of Alissa Quart's book *Branded: The Buying and Selling of Teenagers* (Cambridge, MA: Perseus Publishing, 2003). On the sexualization of childhood, see Diane E. Levin and Jean Kilbourne, *So Sexy So Soon: The New Sexualized Childhood and What Parents Can Do to Protect Their Kids* (New York: Ballantine Books, 2008). Also see Jean Kilbourne's *Can't Buy My Love: How Advertising Changes the Way We Think and Feel* (New York: Free Press, 2000; originally published as *Deadly Persuasion*).

For insightful and sometimes amusing commentary on a topic inseparable from the topic of this chapter, see Rachel Bowlby, *Carried Away: The Invention of Modern Shopping* (New York: Columbia University Press, 2001), as well as Susan Strasser, *Satisfaction Guaranteed: The Making of the American Mass Market*, rev. ed. (Washington, DC: Smithsonian Books, 2004).

5. MEDIA BIAS AND WHAT YOU CAN DO ABOUT IT

The first to be televised, the 1960 presidential debates between John F. Kennedy and Richard M. Nixon ushered in the media era in politics. Though Nixon was judged the loser in the all-important first debate and went on to lose the 1960 election, he became savvier at the use of the media and won the 1968 election in part by staging carefully controlled TV discussions featuring preplanned questions and answers. One advertising expert speculated that "this is the way they'll be elected forevermore," adding presciently that "the next guys up will be performers."[156] He couldn't have known that one of the "next guys up," elected only twelve years later—Ronald Reagan—would in fact be a movie actor.

More than a half century after the historic Kennedy-Nixon debates, the manipulation of the media has become a fact of life in U.S. politics. Thus there's often an uncomfortably fine line between the media and the topics of our earlier chapters—propaganda, brainwashing, and advertising. Take propaganda, for example. You saw in Chapter 2 that propaganda involves "ideas, facts, or allegations spread deliberately to further one's cause or to damage an opposing cause." What's the difference, say, between propaganda and the kind of partisan political reporting and commentary we've come to expect in election campaigns? The answer: not much.

This chapter explores these issues, by looking first at the corporatization and loss of diversity in the media, then at the most common types of media bias like gender and racial bias, next at the question of whether media "objectivity" is at an end under the impact of the blogosphere and other developments, and finally at the growing media-reform movement.

Corporate Control of the Media

Recent presidential elections have played a pivotal role in the mainstream media's turn toward partisanship—a development facilitated by the increasing presence of online news sources and blogs. The impact of the media on John Kerry's unsuccessful presidential bid in 2004 is instructive.

Test Your Skills

On October 24, 2008, just before election day, a columnist named Michael S. Malone wrote:

"The traditional media are playing a very, very dangerous game—with their readers, with the Constitution and with their own fates.

The sheer bias in the print and television coverage of this election campaign is not just bewildering, but appalling. And over the last few months I've found myself slowly moving from shaking my head at the obvious one-sided reporting, to actually shouting at the screen of my television and my laptop computer.

But worst of all, for the last couple of weeks, I've begun— for the first time in my adult life—to be embarrassed to admit what I do for a living. A few days ago, when asked by a new acquaintance what I did for a living, I replied that I was 'a writer,' because I couldn't bring myself to admit to a stranger that I'm a journalist."[1]

Do you agree with Malone's assessment that media bias was unusually severe in the presidential election he's describing? Why or why not? What do you think the average citizen can do about the problem of media bias as it affects politics?

---

1   Michael S. Malone, "Media's Presidential Bias and Decline," *ABC News*, October 24, 2008, http://abcnews.go.com/print?id=6099188.

Many believe changes in the media—or rather, Kerry's lack of awareness of those changes—led to his defeat. He was far more tech savvy than George W. Bush, so it wasn't that he failed to understand the way the Internet worked and could be harnessed for political purposes. Instead, as John Nichols and Robert W. McChesney suggest in their book *Tragedy and Farce: How the American Media Sell Wars, Spin Elections, and Destroy Democracy,* "Kerry had never adapted to the radical changes in how a consolidated, formatted, and rigorously bottom-line oriented media covers politics. He did not understand that in most cases issues no longer mattered, that prevailing again and again in debates was inconsequential, and that having the truth on his side when he was attacked was about as useful as having a horse-and-buggy at the ready for a final campaign swing through the Midwest."[157] To Kerry, it was inconceivable that the media (or the public) would give any credence to the smears about his Vietnam War record spread by the Swift Boat Veterans for Truth and other groups. Nichols and McChesney say bluntly that Kerry "lost the presidency because he clung throughout the campaign to the romantic notion that the media were still some sort of watchdog guarding against abuses of the political process rather than the vehicle by which the worst abuses were executed."[158] George W. Bush was under no such illusions. He had a healthy contempt for the mainstream media and had learned that the bottom-line orientation of media outlets made most of them susceptible to political pressure.

At issue here is the corporate control of the media, reinforced by a symbiotic connection between politicians and the media. As two media critics say bluntly, "The intersection of Madison Avenue, Wall Street and Pennsylvania Avenue is a heavily-trafficked zone, where lies and facts cohabitate as convenience and opportunism dictate."[159] While the "cohabitation of lies and facts"—in other words, media bias—has a long history, almost everyone blames the consolidation and corporatization of the media for making the problem worse.

These trends got underway in earlier centuries. Newspapers and other periodicals represented the first mass media, but they were originally confined to local markets. With the growth of capitalism, they evolved into larger enterprises, often expanding into other related or unrelated industries and eventually into international markets. A similar process led to the development of wire services like Reuters, the Associated Press, and the United Press (later United Press International), made possible by the telephone, telegraph, and other nineteenth-century technological innovations. Until the late twentieth century, these news agencies were the most important global media, though they had some competition from radio after World War I and from television and the film industry after World War II.

Did You Know?

The Owners of All the Major U.S. Media Corporations Could Fit in a Phone Booth

An astonishing consolidation and corporatization of the media has taken place in recent decades. The heads of the fifty corporations controlling the U.S. media in 1983 "could have fit comfortably in a modest hotel ballroom."[1] By the early 1990s the number of corporations had shrunk to less than two dozen. And by 2003, "five men controlled all these media once run by the fifty corporations of twenty years earlier. These five ... could fit in a generous phone booth."[2] The five megacorporations are Time Warner, the Walt Disney Company, the Murdoch News Corporation (an Australian firm), Bertelsmann (a German corporation), and Viacom (formerly CBS).

These corporations have become major political players. Politicians across the political spectrum, in turn, have promoted the interests of the media cartel. They routinely enact favorable legislation or extend special favors like access to the White House, knowing their political success depends on their ability to influence the media

---

1   Ben H. Bagdikian, *The New Media Monopoly*, rev. ed. (Boston: Beacon Press, 2004), 27.
2   Bagdikian, *The New Media Monopoly*, 27.

The trends toward media corporatization and globalization came to fruition in the 1980s, as a wave of privatization and deregulation swept through the United States and other countries and fueled global corporate capitalism. Since the 1980s, these changes have accelerated, leading to a profound loss of diversity as hundreds of individual media outlets have been consolidated into a handful of global media giants. A casualty has been any pretense toward journalistic objectivity. Media bias tends to be exacerbated by the corporate control of the media because sensitivity to the needs of advertisers and other power brokers takes precedence and dissenting voices are silenced.

Media Bias: From Social Prejudice to Sensationalism

Media bias can take many forms; I'll discuss three here. First, biases often reflect social prejudice like gender or racial prejudice and may be exacerbated by the uneven representation of various groups among media professionals and the experts they consult. In Chapter 10 you'll encounter a major example of racial bias when you read about the Tuskegee Syphilis Study, the study that began in the early 1930s and went on for forty years, allowing hundreds of African-American men with syphilis to go untreated. The experiment not only reflected the bias of the medical profession but also of the media; journalists could have exposed the experiment and called a halt to it years earlier but did not.

Second, news biases may reflect a desire to protect citizens from an awareness of their country's ethical wrongdoing. Examples could include German publications that played down the impact of Nazism, or U.S. publications that minimized the impact of the bombings at Hiroshima and Nagasaki. Similar examples could be found in almost any country, because an acknowledgment of wrongdoing creates cognitive dissonance for the large numbers of people who prefer to see themselves and their culture in a positive light.

Third, you don't have to be told that there is a pervasive bias in the U.S. media in favor of sensationalism. Lurid or quirky details take precedence over what is truly important: "If millions of children are bullied in schools every day and suffer lifelong damage from that experience, that probably will not be considered news. If millions of children go to bed hungry every night all over the globe, that is not news. But if one school serves caviar during the school lunch, that is news. If women and children are sold every day in an international slave trade, that is not news. But if a solitary teacher has a sexual relationship with a student, that is news."[160]

To give you a better idea of how complex and pervasive the problem of media bias is, I provide detailed examples in the rest of this section that illustrate the three problems just mentioned. The first example, dealing with the Sacco and Vanzetti case from the 1920s, illustrates ethnic (anti-Italian) prejudice. The second, discussing the use of chemical warfare in Vietnam, illustrates a desire to protect Americans from knowledge of their mistreatment of the Vietnamese people and their ecosystem. The third, on the adoption by U.S. parents of troubled orphans from Romania and Russia, illustrates a bias toward sensationalism.

The Infamous Sacco and Vanzetti Case

The Sacco and Vanzetti case was one of the most notorious in twentieth-century America.[161] The afternoon of April 15, 1920, a paymaster and security guard were transporting 500 or so envelopes containing $15,776.51—the weekly payroll of the Slater & Morrill Shoe Company— down a street in South Braintree, a small town south of Boston. Two gunmen ambushed them, killing both men and seizing the payroll, then jumped into a waiting Buick and escaped. Three weeks later, Nicola Sacco (a shoemaker) and Bartolomeo Vanzetti (a fishmonger) were charged with the crime despite inadequate evidence. After a seven-week trial, Sacco and Vanzetti were convicted on the basis of circumstantial evidence and sentenced to death. The verdict sparked outrage around the world, with demonstrators from London to Tokyo to Buenos Aires protesting the injustice of the trial. Many prominent individuals, including future Supreme Court Justice Felix Frankfurter, poet Edna St. Vincent Millay, novelist Upton Sinclair, and philosopher Bertrand Russell, sided with Sacco and Vanzetti. Yet after seven years of appeals, the two men were executed on August 23, 1927.

Ironically, Sacco and Vanzetti may have had the last laugh. Three months before he was electrocuted, Vanzetti gave an interview to the *New York World*. His English was flawed but moving, and his soliloquy has long outlasted him:

> If it had not been for these thing, I might have live out of my life, talking at street corners to scorning men. I might have die, unmarked, unknown, a failure. Now we are not a failure. This is our career and our triumph. Never in our full life can we hope to do such work for tolerance, for justice, for man's understanding of man as we now do by dying. Our words, our lives, our pains—nothing! The taking of our lives—lives of a good shoemaker and a poor fish peddler—all! That last moment belongs to us—that agony is our triumph![162]

To this day, the innocence or guilt of Sacco and Vanzetti has never been conclusively established, but many are convinced that their conviction and execution represented a serious miscarriage of justice. The case is still officially open and the evidence continues to be reexamined. Whatever the truth of the matter, virtually no one thinks they got a fair trial, and media bias was partly to blame.

Sacco and Vanzetti had two major strikes against them: they were Italian immigrants at a time of virulent anti-immigrant and anti-Italian prejudice, and they were militant anarchists at a time of severe political repression. In the early twentieth century, as immigrants flocked to the land of opportunity, many U.S.-born citizens felt the "American way of life" was being eroded and were quick to scapegoat Sacco and Vanzetti and others like them. Many Americans were also threatened by the radical ideals manifested in the Russian Revolution of 1917, and saw Sacco and Vanzetti's involvement in the anarchist movement, labor strikes, and other forms of political agitation as dangerous—an understandable fear because President William McKinley had been assassinated by an anarchist in 1901. Widespread government raids called the "Palmer

Raids" (after A. Mitchell Palmer, the U.S. attorney general) were targeting suspected radicals in that period and contributed to the paranoia surrounding anarchists like Sacco and Vanzetti. Some of the most draconian Palmer Raids were orchestrated by J. Edgar Hoover, who got his start in government as Palmer's assistant between 1919 and 1921 and would serve as FBI director from 1924 until his death in 1972.[163]

Where was the press in all of this? Ben Bagdikian, a well-known media critic, provides an interesting account. "I was seven years old when the two men were electrocuted at Charlestown Prison in Boston," he says, adding that "I never heard anything except certitude that the two Italians were murderers and that when the switch was thrown on their electric chair there was such a powerful flow of electricity that in my hometown of Stoneham, fifteen miles away, the electric lights blinked."[164] Years later as a reporter, Bagdikian investigated the case. He learned that the lights had never blinked when Sacco and Vanzetti were executed. He also learned that the media had failed to do the job of safeguarding the truth because of "biases in favor of the status quo"—biases that "protect corporate power and consequently weaken the public's ability to understand forces that create the American scene."[165]

Bagdikian elaborates:

> At the time of the arrests, most newspapers supported the Palmer Raids and, despite the overwhelming evidence of gross improprieties of justice, were enthusiastic about convicting Sacco and Vanzetti. . . . By the time Sacco and Vanzetti were to be electrocuted in 1927, most of the serious press had changed its mind. Reporters confirmed that the state had been dishonest and suppressed evidence. Editors had become convinced that there had been a grave miscarriage of justice. It was too late. By that time the pride of the Commonwealth of Massachusetts had become attached to its need to electrocute the two defendants. The state, frozen in its attitude, resisted a commutation because, in the words of Herbert Ehrmann, an admirable lawyer in the case, it would have "signaled a weakness within our social order."

In the United States we depend on our mass media to signal, among other things, "weakness in our social order." In 1921, when Sacco and Vanzetti were tried, the newspapers failed to send that signal, though there was ample evidence to support one. By 1927, when the men were electrocuted, a significant portion of the press had changed its mind. The change did not save the two men, but it said something about the media.[166]

Not all media bias leads to questionable convictions and executions, as in the Sacco and Vanzetti case. But this case is a reminder of just how high the stakes can be.

Chemical Warfare in Southeast Asia

During World War II, Admiral William Leahy strongly opposed a proposal to destroy Japanese rice crops, arguing that this action would "violate every Christian ethic I have ever heard of and all known laws of war."[167] By the 1960s the military saw things differently. In their book *Manufacturing Consent: The Political Economy of the Mass Media*, Edward S. Herman and Noam Chomsky provide this horrifying summary of U.S. chemical attacks on South Vietnam:

> Between 1961 and 1971 . . . the U.S Air Force sprayed 20 million gallons of concentrated arsenic-based and dioxin-laden herbicides (mainly Agent Orange) on 6 million acres of crops and trees, besides using large quantities of the "super tear gas" CS and vast amounts of napalm and phosphorous bombs. An estimated 13 percent of South Vietnam's land was subjected to chemical attacks. This included 30 percent of its rubber plantations and 36 percent of its mangrove forests, along with other large forest areas, destroyed by toxic chemicals in programs that included multiple "large-scale intentional effort[s] combining defoliation with incendiaries to produce a forest fire in South Vietnam." A 1967 study prepared by the head of the Agronomy Section of the Japanese Science Council concluded that U.S. anticrop warfare had already ruined more than

3.8 million acres of arable land in South Vietnam, killing almost 1,000 peasants and over 13,000 livestock.[168]

Interestingly, the United States subjected only its ally (South Vietnam) to these large-scale chemical attacks, not its enemy (North Vietnam). "One reason for this," Herman and Chomsky say, "was that North Vietnam had a government with links to other countries, so that the use of these barbarous and illegal weapons against it would have been widely publicized. South Vietnam was occupied by the United States and its client regime, so that the victimized people of the South were voiceless and could be treated with unlimited savagery."[169]

The contradiction just mentioned—the fact that we attacked the country we were purporting to save from communist aggression—was only one of many underreported aspects of the story. After some initial attention when the use of chemical warfare first came to light in the mid-1960s, media coverage essentially ceased, except for a few articles like Orville Schell Jr.'s 1971 *Look* magazine piece "Silent Vietnam: How We Invented Ecocide and Killed a Country."[170]

After the end of the Vietnam War in 1975, the subject was reopened, but almost always in the context of the health effects of Agent Orange on the U.S. soldiers who'd been exposed to it. The statistics speak for themselves:

> Of 522 articles in the *New York Times*, the *Washington Post*, the *Los Angeles Times*, *Newsweek*, and *Time* during the 1990s that mentioned Agent Orange and Vietnam together, the vast majority focused on the harm done to U.S. service personnel; only nine articles acknowledged the targeting of food crops (thirty-nine mentioned forest cover alone as the target); only eleven discussed in any detail the impact on Vietnamese and the Vietnamese environment; only three characterized the use of Agent Orange as a "chemical weapon" or "chemical warfare;" and in only two articles was it suggested that its use might constitute a war crime.[171]

The Vietnam War and other wars provide dramatic examples of media bias. Other kinds of bias occur on the home front, as the next example shows.

Selling Fear to Mothers of Small Children

Not long ago, disturbing stories cropped up in the news media about adoptions gone horribly wrong. Among the thousands of children adopted from overseas were some who'd been so badly damaged that they suffered from severe attachment disorder. Symptoms included "the absence of conscience, an inability to give or receive love, learning disabilities, self-mutilation, cruelty to siblings and animals, morbid fascinations with fire and violence and overt sexuality."[172]

Most of the troubled children were from two countries, Romania and Russia. When state-run orphanages were opened up after the fall of communism, Americans and other foreigners rushed to adopt extraordinarily needy orphans. Countless Romanian and Russian children have been placed in U.S. homes, and most are doing fine.

One who did not do fine was the adopted son of Mike and Sharon Venhaus of Albuquerque, New Mexico, who came from a Russian orphanage. The adoption experience turned into a nightmare and the boy was placed in foster care. The Venhauses were charged with child abandonment for putting him there after he tried to kill his adoptive sister and a dog and attacked Sharon Venhaus's parents. Unable to handle the situation, Mike Venhaus left the family and the couple got a divorce.

Another child who did not do fine was the teenage Russian daughter of Priscilla and Neal Whatcott of Washington state. The Whatcotts, too, confronted child-abandonment charges for placing their child in foster care—a step they say they took only after she sexually assaulted children and adults, set fire to her bedroom, and kept running away. The girl was eventually put in a mental ward in Michigan.

Adoption experts caution that while parents like the Venhauses and Whatcotts may be severely criticized for giving up their adopted children, the children in question are often disturbed beyond anything normally seen in the U.S. adoption system. One expert emphasizes the recurrent problem of the Russian or Romanian adoptee endangering the safety of younger children in the family—often by attempting to kill a younger child.[173]

You would think this chilling story would attract a wide readership on its own merits, but in her book *Selling Anxiety: How the News Media Scare Women*, Caryl Rivers gives a compelling example of the media bias used to sell even more newspapers.[174] In May 1998, the *New York Times Magazine* devoted a cover story to the problems faced by parents like the Venhauses and Whatcotts.[175] How did the *Times* spin the story? Instead of merely representing it as a problem involving troubled orphans and their adoptive parents, the article extrapolated to the mother-child separations resulting when U.S. mothers place their children in day care! The following passage is typical: "Mother-child separations are part of the warp and woof of life these days, and so are our worries about them. The research on Eastern European adoptees matters not only to them and their parents but also to many of the rest of us as well."[176] Only later does the author reverse course:

> Suddenly, after all the *sturm* and *drang*, the backpedal appears. Just as we are prepared to believe that, yes, there is a link between these orphans and the children of working mothers, the story abruptly changes direction. After the flashy, foreboding graphics, the coverline hinting darkly at harm, the theme paragraph graph hinting at connections between orphans and ordinary kids, the author starts to backpedal like mad, citing [a] major federal study of day care . . . : "While there are some negative effects of child care, they are quite small—statistical flutters . . . [T]here were *not* significant differences in attachment related to child care participation." (Italics added)[177]

Rivers's analysis of the story about the troubled orphans is a cautionary tale, but only one of many. In a section on "Women's Rights and Media Wrongs" in their book *Unreliable Sources*, Lee and Solomon note that "between the lines and between the transmitters is an invisible shrug about the status of women in America. We are told that it's improving but usually without reference to how bad the situation remains. The mass media, ill-equipped to play a constructive role, are key contributors to the problems facing women. That's not surprising, since news media companies are bastions of male supremacy themselves."[178]

The three examples you've just glimpsed reflect the failure of the media to live up to the traditional standard of objectivity guiding generations of journalists. Obviously, complete objectivity is an unrealistic goal, because we're all shaped by our culture and life experience, and news writers and broadcast journalists are no exception. But most reputable journalists have assumed in the past that there is, or should be, a line between a minor coloring of the news and the major distortion or suppression of a story.

What if the media rejects that standard? The next section touches on that question.

The End of Media "Objectivity"?

The "consolidated, formatted, and rigorously bottom-line oriented media" has increasingly lost any pretense toward objectivity in its political coverage. This turn toward partisanship has been spurred by the growth of the blogosphere, which emerged from 1997 on and is now a political force to be reckoned with.[179] In his book *Bloggers on the Bus*—which takes its name from Timothy Crouse's book *The Boys on the Bus*, on the role of the press in the 1972 election—Eric Boehlert chronicles the intense, unapologetic partisanship of many bloggers and their disdain for the ideal of objectivity traditionally guiding journalists: "Collectively, bloggers expanded well beyond the traditional role of journalist or commentator; they tossed aside the mantle of objectivity that the boys on the bus had worn for decades. Instead, bloggers raised money, trained leaders, forged vibrant online communities, picked candidates, fostered participation, forged coalitions among existing special interest groups, launched policy initiatives, produced original reporting, called bullshit out on the press, and occasionally, and out of sheer force of will, attached a spine to the Democratic Party."[180]

Those words appear in the introduction to Boehlert's book; later chapters provide a more unsettling picture of the impact of bloggers on politics. At a minimum, these chapters suggest that despite the image of the blogosphere as a grassroots alternative to the corporate media, bloggers often harbor the same biases found in the corporate sources they disparage. At worst, because of the ubiquitousness, anonymity, and lack of regulation of the Internet, bloggers have a greater megaphone for prejudice and hatred—and greater ability to alter the course of elections—than the mainstream media have traditionally had.

Test Your Skills

Discuss the role of personal attacks in the media in a recent election. Do you think these attacks influenced the outcome of the election? If so, how?

Boehlert devotes several chapters to the harassment and hatred directed at Hillary Clinton and Sarah Palin, as well as at their supporters, in the 2008 election. On the anti-Clinton hostility, he says:

> Some neutral netroots writers became concerned about the anti-Clinton hate speech being promoted online (i.e., "We know that Hillary Clinton will do or say *anything* in her mad pursuit of power," wrote Markos at Daily Kos) and what the drawbacks were for the progressive movement as a whole. The anger "really is indistinguishable from how the right hates her," noted the influential liberal writer Glenn Greenwald, who blogged at Unclaimed Territory. "If you go over to Daily Kos, you would think you were reading Ann Coulter or Rush Limbaugh. The level of hatred towards Hillary by a lot of pro-Obama bloggers is really extreme and even kind of disturbing and creepy."[181]

Illustrating the intensity of this hostility, Boehlert quotes a Daily Kos diarist called jarhead 5536, who said he was leaving the site because of the treatment of Clinton: "'I fold. You win, Obama wins, my candidate has not, cannot, and will not get a fair hearing here, and I'm done. . . . For you people, it is not enough that Barack wins, Hillary must lose, and lose completely, crushingly, and humiliatingly badly. . . . I cannot describe what I read on these posts as anything other than pure hatred.'"[182] A blogger named Armando Llorens-Sar— an attorney in Puerto Rico who also left the Daily Kos because of its trashing of Hillary Clinton—noted that he actually thought Obama had a better chance of winning the general election because of the more favorable media coverage he could expect. But Llorens-Sar was severely critical of the treatment of Clinton by bloggers, pointing out that they had become what they purported to detest in the mainstream media: obsessed with personality and image and uninterested in policy issues. He ridiculed the netroots, proclaiming that "The progressive blogosphere is dead!" and "Long live the 'progressive' blogosphere!"[183]

Many netroots commentators, especially women, ascribed the anti-Clinton hostility to the demographics of the blogosphere. Despite the netroots' self-image as a grassroots, democratic, and inclusive phenomenon, the prevailing demographic was "white men in their thirties and forties who didn't like Hillary. With so many of them tapping away online, their viewpoint was bound to dominate."[184] These biases parallel those in the mainstream media and probably reflect the demographic similarities between bloggers and mainstream journalists (overwhelmingly white and male).[185]

The same situation affected Sarah Palin's candidacy. Legitimate political debate was overshadowed by personal smears and attacks. A typical example was the fake-pregnancy scandal picked up by many left-leaning blogs beginning the day John McCain announced Palin as his vice presidential running mate. In a Daily Kos diary that night, a blogger named Inky99 speculated that Palin's four-month-old son, Trig, was actually the son of Bristol Palin (Sarah Palin's teenage daughter). Andrew Sullivan, an influential *Atlantic* blogger, gave the story legitimacy a few days later by claiming it deserved serious investigation. The story was debunked when a photo of an obviously pregnant Palin—taken during a

TV interview just before Trig's birth—was posted online. But the rumors had not only damaged Palin's candidacy; many critics across the political spectrum felt they damaged the credibility of the netroots by highlighting tendencies toward misogyny and sensationalism.[186]

The partisanship and mean-spiritedness of the media have continued unabated in more recent elections, raising growing concerns among media analysts. Gene Weingarten, a staff writer for the *Washington Post Magazine*, conducted a revealing experiment that he reported on in a piece titled "Cruel and Unusual Punishment."[187] Wondering about the impact of the 24/7 information barrage on today's citizens, Weingarten decided to subject himself to media overload by holing up in a windowless room for twenty-four hours where he would be surrounded by a nonstop flood of political news and commentary coming from six television sets, two radios, and a laptop. (The laptop went with him when he went to the restroom.) The results of the experiment were sobering. Weingarten was initially impressed by the realness and immediacy of the cable shows and blogs, but his optimism soured. "I cannot tell you how horrible it is," he said in giving his final assessment of the new media culture. He explained: "It rattles the very center of your being. If you care about the state of humankind, it fills you with despair. We are as a people bleak and hostile and suspicious, filled with senseless partisanship and willing to believe anything and everything about anyone. We are full of ourselves and we hate. And we do it 24-7."[188]

Others concur. Dan Balz (the lead political reporter for the *Washington Post*) and Haynes Johnson (a Pulitzer Prize–winning author) write that "Weingarten was correct in characterizing the background of public discourse during the [2008] election as being bleak, hostile, filled with senseless partisanship and hate."[189] While acknowledging that there is no simple solution, they emphasize that "the public, from political leaders to ordinary citizens, needs to challenge the haters and reassert the values of tolerance, civility, and respect for differences of opinion."[190] This in turn "requires an educational system that stresses teaching citizens these basic elements about a democratic society, and their responsibility to participate, be informed, and appreciate all sides of an argument before rendering a political judgment."[191] Balz and Johnson call, among other things, for better critical-thinking skills on the part of Americans; I agree, which is why I've included a guide to critical thinking as an appendix to this book.

The jury is still out on whether the current loss of media objectivity will become permanent, and if so, what its long-range impact will be. One thing's for sure: the public doesn't seem to like the trend. Surveys show that the public perception of accuracy and fairness in the media is at an all-time low. A Pew Research Center study indicated that the public evaluation of accuracy in the media has dipped to the lowest level ever.[192] The public is similarly disenchanted with news organizations' political bias; the Pew survey showed that the public assessment of media bias and independence—the degree to which the media are free of corporate and other powerful influences—is as low as it has ever been. The only saving grace, though a dubious one because it highlights other problematic areas of our society, is that the public trusts the government and business even less than it does the media.

Media Reform

Growing public concern over media bias and other problems has fueled a vibrant media-reform movement. Some media-reform efforts have focused on media criticism and literacy campaigns. Many organizations—for example, the Center for Media and Public Affairs (www.cmpa.com)—have an educational component of this nature.

Other efforts have led to the creation of alternative media like blogs, but this development has had mixed results, as discussed above. Critics caution that "the technology has not proved sufficient to break up the market power of the giants. Indeed, this market power is allowing for convergence, for a digital media system to emerge where the traditional media giants remain dominant."[193]

This situation has led to a third focus of the media-reform movement: political activism aimed at bringing about substantial policy reform. Though the policy issues are complex, John Nichols and Robert W. McChesney—both influential media critics—identify two overarching themes shaping proposals for media reform: "1) to the extent the media system is commercial, it should be as competitive as possible; and, to the extent technology and economics permit, there should be a priority given to locally owned and operated media. In short, policies should attempt to make it easier for people to start their own commercial outlet; and 2) a purely commercial media system has distinct limitations, generating what economists call negative externalities. Therefore, it is imperative to establish a vibrant and heterogeneous nonprofit and noncommercial media sector."[194]

Conclusion

By exploring the issue of media bias, this chapter has touched on an increasingly problematic source of untruths and distortions in our society. Like deceptive advertising, media bias is everywhere. The more attuned you are to this problem, the better equipped you'll be to combat it.

What You Can Do

√*Be informed.* Learn to be an active rather than a passive consumer of the news. One of the first steps in detecting media bias is to be aware of the sources of the news. If you find out a news show is sponsored by a drug manufacturer, you'll almost certainly have to go elsewhere for objective coverage of health and safety issues involving their products or similar ones. If the network is owned by a producer of nuclear power plants or a weapons manufacturer, you may want to take their coverage of energy and military issues, respectively, with a grain of salt.

Watch carefully for telltale signs of spin. Even small forms of manipulation can be problematic, like giving a story a misleading headline. Have you ever started reading an article, only to wonder if they'd put the wrong headline on it? That may not have been an accident. Some people never read beyond the headline, so the misleading title may be enough to create a false impression of a topic. Another common form of bias involves generalizing from a few statistics, a small unrepresentative study, or a trivial anecdote. Spin may also be created by backpedaling. This common tactic involves making slanted or sweeping assertions, then backing off later in the story—too late for readers who only read the first few paragraphs.

To summarize, caveat emptor ("let the buyer beware!") is a good rule for any media consumer to follow. Put differently, being a critical thinker is essential. Critical thinkers are able to safely make their way through the sea of media spin inundating them because

- They study alternative perspectives and worldviews, learning how to interpret events from multiple viewpoints.
- They seek understanding and insight through multiple sources of thought and information, not simply those of the mass media.
- They learn how to identify the viewpoints embedded in news stories.
- They assess news stories for their clarity, accuracy, relevance, depth, breadth, and significance.

- They notice contradictions and inconsistencies in the news (often in the same story).
- They notice the agenda and interests served by a story.
- They notice the facts covered and the facts ignored.
- They notice what implications are ignored and what implications are emphasized.
- They mentally correct stories reflecting bias toward the unusual, the dramatic, and the sensational by putting them into perspective or discounting them.
- They question the social conventions and taboos being used to define issues and problems.[195]

√*Speak out.* If people of color are consistently underrepresented as panelists on a Sunday morning political show, contact the show's producers to complain. If a newspaper rarely prints op-ed pieces by women, challenge the editor to do better. If an online news site is dominated by a single political faction, provide feedback urging them to be more inclusive. The same goes for specific causes you advocate. If you support educational reform, or conservation, or programs to curb child abuse, and you don't feel those efforts are adequately reflected in the media, make your concerns known to the appropriate media outlets. Yes, your voice counts, especially if your criticisms are thoughtful and are expressed in a constructive way. Your letter will have more impact if it's short, to the point, factually accurate, and conforms to the website or newspaper's formatting guidelines.

You can also speak out by expressing your concerns to political candidates or elected officials, such as your members of Congress.

A useful, sixty-eight-page "Action Guide" to media reform is included in Robert W. McChesney, Russell Newman, and Ben Scott's *The Future of Media: Resistance and Reform in the 21st Century*.[196] This special section provides detailed instructions on actions the average person can take, even including a sample letter to the editor, op-ed piece, and newsletter article you can use as models in drafting your letter or article. It also offers tips on contacting elected officials.

√*Join media-reform groups.* Another option is to join groups that monitor and challenge media bias. A few examples:

- Center for Media and Public Affairs (www.cmpa.com)
- FactCheck.org (www.factcheck.org)
- Free Press (www.freepress.net)
- Pew Research Center's Project for Excellence in Journalism (www.journalism.org)
- Women's Media Center (www.womensmediacenter.com)

For other resources, see the Media Reform Information Center's website (www.corporations.org/media/), which provides links on media reform and related topics. Another resource is the ipl2: Information You Can Trust site (www.ipl.org), offering links to thousands of websites deemed reliable by information science professionals.

Further Reading

Growing concerns about the media crisis have fueled an enormous literature on media bias and related topics. The books listed here are only a starting point; they'll point you toward other useful resources on subjects that interest you.

For comprehensive histories of the media, see Asa Briggs and Peter Burke, *A Social History of the Media: From Gutenberg to the Internet*, 3rd ed. (Cambridge: Polity Press, 2009), as well as *The Creation of the Media: Political Origins of Modern Communications* (New York: Basic Books, 2004) by the Pulitzer Prize–winning author Paul Starr. An influential work on corporate consolidation and its impact on the media is Ben H. Bagdikian, *The New Media Monopoly*, rev. ed. (Boston: Beacon Press, 2004). For more international coverage of the same topic, see Edward S. Herman and Robert W. McChesney, *The Global Media: The New Missionaries of Corporate Capitalism* (London: Cassell, 1997). On the deteriorating quality of journalism under the impact of corporatization, see *News Flash: Journalism, Infotainment, and the Bottom-Line Business of Broadcast News* (San Francisco: Jossey-Bass, 2004) by Bonnie M. Anderson, a former print reporter, broadcast reporter, and network executive.

For an older but still useful survey of media bias, see Martin A. Lee and Norman Solomon, *Unreliable Sources: A Guide to Detecting Bias in News Media* (New York: Lyle Stuart / Carol Publishing Group, 1998). Many of the books cited in this chapter rest on the influential work of Noam Chomsky and his colleagues. A classic example is Edward S. Herman and Noam Chomsky, *Manufacturing Consent: The Political Economy of the Mass Media*, rev. ed. (New York: Pantheon Books, 2002).

Accounts of media spin in relation to recent U.S. history and politics include Brooks Jackson and Kathleen Hall Jamieson, *unSpun: Finding Facts in a World of Disinformation* (New York: Random House, 2007); Nancy Snow, *Information War: American Propaganda, Free Speech, and Opinion Control Since 9/11* (New York: Seven Stories Press, 2003); Stephen J. Farnsworth and S. Robert Lichter, *The Nightly News Nightmare: Media Coverage of U.S. Presidential Elections, 1988–2008*, 3rd ed. (Lanham, MD: Rowman & Littlefield, 2011); and John Nichols and Robert W. McChesney, *Tragedy and Farce: How the American Media Sell Wars, Spin Elections, and Destroy Democracy* (New York: New Press, 2005). On the increasing partisanship of the mainstream media, see Tim Groseclose, *Left Turn: How Liberal Media Bias Distorts the American Mind* (New York: St. Martin's Press, 2011), and Bernard Goldberg, *A Slobbering Love Affair: The True (and Pathetic) Story of the Torrid Romance between Barack Obama and the Mainstream Media* (Washington, DC: Regnery, 2009). For a different political perspective, see Eric Boehlert, *Bloggers on the Bus: How the Internet Changed Politics and the Press* (New York: Free Press, 2009). Boehlert provides a lengthy discussion of the online gender war in the 2008 election; see especially pp. 91–158, 223–243. In her book *Women for President: Media Bias in Nine Campaigns*, 2nd ed. (Urbana: University of Illinois Press, 2010), Erika Falk explores the biased coverage of eight women presidential candidates, ranging from Victoria Woodhull in the 1872 election to Hillary Clinton in 2008. Caryl Rivers focuses more generally on biased coverage of women and women's issues in her *Selling Anxiety: How the News Media Scare Women* (Hanover, NH: University Press of New England, 2007).

For an overview of media reform, see Nichols and McChesney's *Tragedy and Farce* (cited above), 178–203. A more in-depth treatment is provided by the contributions to Robert W. McChesney, Russell Newman, and Ben Scott, eds., *The Future of Media: Resistance and Reform in the 21st Century* (New York: Seven Stories Press, 2005).

For a detailed retelling of the Saco and Vanzetti case, see Bruce Watson, *Sacco and Vanzetti: The Men, the Murders, and the Judgment of Mankind* (New York: Viking, 2007).

6. TRUTH AND LIES IN POLITICS

When George Orwell's *Nineteen Eighty-Four* was first published in 1949, the flap copy said the book "leaves the reader with the shocked feeling that there is no single horrible feature in the world of 1984—only two generations away—which is not present, in embryo, today."[197] Well, 1984 has come and gone, and Orwell's original readers would surely have been even more shocked if they'd foreseen today's politics, with its dishonest campaigning, manipulative advertising, and mean-spiritedness evocative of Orwell's Two Minutes Hate.[198] And then of course there are the dubious fundraising practices, corrupt lobbyists, even—in the opinion of some—overtones of totalitarianism.[199]

This chapter explores deceptive politics and its consequences.

Deceptive Politics: An Overview

Deceptive politics takes many forms, ranging from campaign smears to false promises to ballot tampering and more.

Negative Campaigning

Many of the best-known examples of deceptive politics in U.S. presidential elections have involved negative campaigning. Given the ubiquitousness and lavishness of campaigning in current presidential elections, you may be surprised to learn that campaigning was considered unseemly in presidential elections before the twentieth century. Some earlier politicians, like

Andrew Jackson, campaigned energetically behind the scenes, but the first to campaign openly was Stephen A. Douglas, Lincoln's challenger in 1860. Douglas was severely criticized for his actions; the *Jonesboro Gazette*—an Illinois newspaper—reflected the public's distaste for campaigning when it wrote: "Douglas is going about peddling his opinions as a tin man peddles his ware. The only excuse for him is that as he is a small man, he has a right to be engaged in small business; and small business it is for a candidate for the Presidency to be strolling around the country begging for votes like a town constable."[200] Lincoln not only wouldn't campaign but wouldn't even vote for himself; he agreed to vote for the others in his party only after cutting his name off the ballot.[201]

By the early twentieth century attitudes had changed. Woodrow Wilson was the first candidate to be elected president after engaging in the speechmaking and other forms of electioneering we now take for granted.[202] A Democrat, Wilson served between 1913 and 1921. Since that period included the World War I years, Wilson was closely involved with the propaganda efforts described in Chapter 2. He was quick to grasp the value of publicity not only for military purposes but for political purposes; as a result, "pitiless publicity" became one of his key policies. In a related development, he was the first president to hold press conferences on a regular basis.[203] His immediate successors followed suit in making use of sloganeering and other public relations techniques, campaigning on slogans like Harding's "Back to Normalcy" and Coolidge's "Keep Cool with Coolidge." It's hard to imagine what Harding or Coolidge—let alone Lincoln—would say if they could witness an election in the early twenty-first century, because electioneering in all of its senses is now front and center. For example, candidate Barack Obama once beat out Apple, Nike, the online shoe seller Zappos, Coors beer, and other marketers in winning the "Marketer of the Year" award from a major U.S. marketing association.[204]

Of course, publicity can be used for good or ill, which brings us back to the main subject of this section: dirty politics. Dirty politics frequently involves guilt by association; the objective is to slander opponents by linking them with people or policies that are out of favor. Imagine for a moment that you think highly of a candidate and want others to as well; a logical strategy would be to try to link them in the eyes of the public with a revered figure like Martin Luther King Jr. or Mother Teresa. The same tactic works in reverse. Hint at associations between your opponent and, say, a communist, criminal, or racist, and you're on your way to winning the election. In negative campaigning, candidates are often linked not only with reviled individuals but with failed policies. Since the Great Depression in the late 1920s and early 1930s—often blamed on the failed economic policies of President Herbert Hoover—even a whiff of "Hooverism" has sufficed to tar a politician with an image of having disastrous economic policies.

In earlier centuries these attempts to pair politicians with disreputable individuals or policies were usually verbal, but with the advent of photography, television, and other media technologies, attack tactics have increasingly taken visual forms. A powerful image used by the Democratic candidate in both the 1964 and 1988 presidential elections was a torn Social Security card. In 1964, the TV commercial most often run by Lyndon Johnson's campaign showed a Social Security card torn in half, suggesting the election of Arizona Senator Barry Goldwater would threaten the program. In 1988, an ad aired by Michael Dukakis's campaign showed a card torn until it was a fraction of its normal size, implying (falsely) that George H. W. Bush was in favor of "cutting" almost all Social Security benefits.

The most famous visual image from U.S. presidential campaigns is perhaps the so-called daisy commercial produced by the Doyle Dane Bernbach advertising agency for the Johnson campaign in 1964. Goldwater had already earned a reputation as an extremist—he'd backed the use of nuclear weapons by NATO commanders and had proposed using low-level nuclear devices as defoliants in Vietnam—so the Johnson campaign had rich material to work with. To discredit Goldwater as a warmonger, the Democrats contrasted the image of a child plucking the petals of a flower with the image of a bomb exploding. As one media expert describes it,

> A young girl is picking daisies in a field. "Four, five, six, seven,"
> she says. An announcer's voice (actually the voice used to count

down the space launches at Cape Canaveral) begins an ominous count. "Ten, nine, eight . . ." At zero the camera has closed on the child's eye. A nuclear bomb explodes. Lyndon Johnson's voice is heard: "These are the stakes. To make a world in which all of God's children can live. Or to go into the darkness. We must either love each other. Or we must die." Until the tag line appears, that ad has no explicit partisan content. "Vote for President Johnson on November 3. The stakes are too high for you to stay at home."[205]

Because this commercial is so famous, most people don't realize it was only shown once—during the CBS program *Monday Night at the Movies* on September 7, 1964. That single airing was so explosive that the ad did its job. Its effects were magnified by the extensive news coverage it got (all three network news programs aired and discussed the commercial the next night), as well as by the firestorm of protest from the Goldwater campaign and Republicans more generally. The daisy ad was the first major TV attack ad in the United States, so Lyndon Johnson deserves credit (or blame, depending on your perspective) for setting this type of campaigning in motion.

The potential uses of visual imagery today are greater than ever. It's chilling to imagine how certain earlier politicians—Richard Nixon is a prime example—might have utilized Internet resources like YouTube videos in smearing their opponents. The negative buzz about an opponent that took months of dirty tactics to accomplish in Nixon's era, can now be created in a matter of hours with a YouTube clip that goes viral.

Regardless of the technology involved, attempts at guilt by association rely on innuendo to plant the idea that the candidate being attacked is more sinister or more inept than meets the eye. These attacks also rely on the complicity of viewers or readers, who are called on to suspend critical-thinking skills and make decisions not necessarily in their own best interest or that of the country. These attacks should be viewed as propaganda no different from other kinds of propaganda surveyed in Chapter 2, and with similar results: "When a propagandist unscrupulously plays on our feelings of insecurity, or exploits our darkest fears, or offers fake hope, exploration and inquiry stop. . . . The goal is to prove yourself superior and right no matter what. We become dependent on those who will support our masquerade. Our emotions overwhelm our critical abilities. And we take actions that we might not otherwise consider wise to take."[206] As we'll see, many of the most egregious smear campaigns in U.S. history have involved religious prejudice, racism, or misogyny, because political campaigns are often a microcosm of larger forces at work in society and can tap into deep-rooted fears as different groups jockey for power.

It's worth noting that skilled politicians or others can deflect attacks or smears by reframing the issue. Reframing is a process of changing the meaning of the attack or smear by altering the frame or perspective through which it's viewed. This process empowers the target of the attack by allowing him or her to take control of the situation.

Test Your Skills

As you watch interviews or debates involving politicians, look for situations where they are under attack and successfully reframe the issue to their advantage. Now try the same tactic in your own life when someone tries to attack or insult you in an argument. Can you see how this tactic empowers the target of the attack?

A good example occurred in the Texas gubernatorial battle in 1990 between Ann Richards (the Democratic candidate) and Clayton Williams (her Republican opponent). At a forum on crime, Williams called Richards a liar. After Richards said she was sorry he felt that way, she extended her hand, but Williams refused to shake it. Instead of letting Williams's charge of dishonesty dominate the news, the Richards campaign reframed the situation by featuring the rejected handshake in an ad.[207] This was especially effective because it reinforced Williams's reputation as condescending and misogynist. Richards won the election but was unseated by George W. Bush four years later.

Misleading Campaign Statements and False Promises

I've focused so far on campaign smears because they're colorful and easy to trace, but of course there are many other kinds of deceptive politics, like misleading or inaccurate campaign statements (for instance, made by politicians about their own record) or false promises about actions politicians will take if elected. Many politicians have been known to embellish their academic or military record; you'll glimpse an example of the latter in the next chapter, in regard to Senator Joseph McCarthy's questionable claims about his World War II heroics. A famous false promise was George H. W. Bush's pledge—made as he accepted the nomination at the 1988 Republican National Convention—not to raise taxes. His phrase "Read my lips: no new taxes" came back to haunt him after he raised taxes in order to reduce the deficit. In the 1992 election both Pat Buchanan and Bill Clinton called attention to Bush's duplicity, which contributed to his defeat.

Election Fraud

Then there is election fraud, of the type alleged in the last several presidential elections. This can include voter-registration fraud, in which ineligible voters—including dead people—are registered; voter fraud, in which ineligible people vote or legitimate voters are disenfranchised; threats or acts of violence against voters or election monitors in polling places or caucus locations; ballot tampering, including voting-machine irregularities; and other dishonest practices in recording the vote. I cite a few examples of these practices later, when I touch on recent presidential elections.

Deception in Government

Getting a candidate into office doesn't necessarily bring the problem of deception to an end. It may only be the beginning, because of course government officials—like candidates—have been known to lie. For that matter, entire governments can be deceptive. A shameful example from earlier stages of U.S. history would be the "forked tongue" with which the federal government often negotiated with Native Americans. Again and again, the government made promises to or signed treaties with Native American nations, only to go back on its word when waves of white settlers swept across the country and the promises or treaties were no longer feasible. Of course, the problem of government deception didn't stop in earlier centuries. One of the more important examples from recent history would be the claims of Vice President Dick Cheney and other Bush administration officials that Saddam Hussein had weapons of mass destruction. These claims provided a rationale for the U.S. invasion of Iraq beginning in 2003, leading to the death of thousands of U.S. military personnel as well as Iraqi civilians.

Government officials can be the targets as well as the perpetrators of dirty politics. Their families are also often targeted by smears. Some attacks are amusing, like the attacks on the music career of Margaret Truman, the only child of President Harry S. Truman and his wife Bess. One incident stands out. In December 1950—after the twenty-six-year-old Truman had been singing professionally for several years—she was invited to perform at Constitution Hall in Washington, D.C. A *Washington Post* music critic named Paul Hume panned her performance, eliciting a scathing note from President Truman. The note said in part: "Some day I hope to meet you. When that happens you'll need a new nose, a lot of beefsteak for black eyes, and perhaps a supporter below!"[208] Chivalry also played a role in a well-known incident involving a different politician two years later. In his famous "Checkers" speech on September 23, 1952, Richard Nixon defended himself against the charge of financial improprieties. He bristled at the insinuation that his wife, Pat, had worn a mink coat, insisting that she merely had a "respectable Republican cloth coat."[209]

The attacks on First Lady Hillary Rodham Clinton in the 1990s were more serious. It's hard to disentangle several factors: the widespread opposition of the health insurance industry and the general public in the 1990s to changes in the healthcare system, the determination of House Speaker Newt Gingrich and other Republicans to block reform so as to undermine Bill Clinton's chances of reelection, and the prejudice directed at Hillary Clinton as an outspoken first lady who had a career in her own right. But the result was relentless personal attacks.

The Role of Technology

Technological innovations have made it easier for politicians and government officials to engage in deceptive practices. There are precedents in earlier periods for the deceptive use of technology. James A. Farley, who chaired the Democratic National Committee when Franklin D. Roosevelt first ran for president in 1932, played a key role in getting Roosevelt elected, in part with the ingenious use of technology. Grasping the potential of mass mailings before they became common, Farley obtained a check-writing machine—the ancestor of the automated autographer used by politicians, celebrities, authors, and other public figures today—and sent what appeared to be personalized letters to all 3,000 Democratic county chairs in the United States. The effort paid off handsomely. Farley later boasted to Edward L. Bernays, the master propagandist and PR expert you met in Chapter 2, that "by the time I got through [with] this correspondence his nomination was in the bag."[210] Subsequent technological developments have opened the door to a much greater array of deceptive practices than Farley could have envisioned. The spread of telephone technology made many of these practices possible. In the dirty 1950 California senatorial campaign between Richard Nixon and Helen Gahagan Douglas (profiled below), the Nixon campaign arranged to have a half million anonymous phone calls made to California voters asking them, "Did you know that Helen Gahagan Douglas is a communist?"[211] The effects of these calls—made just as the red-baiting McCarthy era was getting underway—were devastating. The spread of TV beginning in the 1950s and the widespread use of PCs from the 1990s on have led to an exponential growth of dirty politics, not least the media manipulation discussed in the previous chapter.

Why Do Politicians Lie?

Some argue politics is inherently deceptive because it entails "saying only what needs to be said . . . to achieve a desired end."[212] Others have elaborated on politicians' motives for lying. Psychiatrist Charles V. Ford identifies four main reasons.[213] The first three are reasons you would expect: to get elected or reelected, to justify or implement political policies, and to defend national security. The fourth category is perhaps the most interesting: foolish lies. As an example, Ford cites the behavior of Joe Biden, who was forced to withdraw from the 1988 presidential race because of allegations he'd plagiarized from the speeches of Robert Kennedy, Hubert Humphrey, and British Labour Party leader Neil Kinnock. Biden also acknowledged that part of a term paper he'd submitted as a first-year law student at the Syracuse University College of Law in 1965 was plagiarized from a *Fordham Law Review* article.[214] His problems were compounded when a video surfaced showing him lashing out at a heckler at a campaign appearance by falsely claiming to have attended law school on a full scholarship, to have graduated in the upper half of his law-school class, and to have earned several undergraduate degrees. As David Greenberg puts it in a Slate.com article, "The sheer number and extent of Biden's fibs, distortions, and plagiarisms struck many observers at the time as worrisome, to say the least. . . . Quitting the [1988] race was the right thing to do."[215] Foolish lies like Biden's are extremely self-destructive because they're easily detected, yet they're surprisingly common among politicians. Ford attributes them to psychological rather than political imperatives, with a common motive being the desire to bolster self-esteem by increasing one's stature and power.[216] Ironically, they often have the opposite effect. One authority notes that "the stigma of plagiarism [like Biden's] seems never to fade completely, not because it is an especially heinous offense but because it is embarrassingly second rate; its practitioners are pathetic, almost ridiculous."[217]

Personality plays a major role in determining how people handle truth and deception. Those with obsessive-compulsive tendencies have control issues and may distort the truth to protect their autonomy and to reduce the intrusive or devouring behavior of others. People with antisocial tendencies often have little regard for the truth; they typically have poor impulse control and will lie and cheat to get what they want. Narcissism can lead to still other behavioral patterns. According to Ford, many politicians have narcissistic tendencies that manifest themselves in characteristic forms of deceit: "Descriptions of many politicians ... appear to be consistent with narcissistic issues. Obtaining power and prestige in the political arena may be a method of attempting to boost an underlying feeling of low self-esteem."[218] Narcissists tend to be easily recognizable by their grandiosity and manipulativeness. Ford distinguishes between several types of narcissists. As the term implies, *constructive* narcissists are relatively well-functioning. But *reactive* narcissists, who are the product of "rejecting and unresponsive parenting," can wield power ruthlessly: "They tolerate no disagreement and crush dissension. Their distorted reality (including their self-deceptions and overt lies) must be accepted by underlings if they wish to survive in the organization."[219] A third type, *self-deceptive* narcissists, had fawning parents and grew up seeing themselves as perfect. These individuals "frequently have interpersonal difficulties because of their emotional superficiality and lack of genuine empathy for others"; their leadership style tends to be manipulative.[220] In general, the self-esteem of narcissistic leaders is fragile, and in extreme cases when it is threatened, the outcome can be bloodbaths.

Test Your Skills

Give several examples of major lies by politicians that you or people you know have been taken in by. Were there warning signs of dishonesty that you or they overlooked? What could someone have done differently to avoid being duped? If you had to give advice to first-time voters on how to make sure they use their vote to elect candidates that best reflect their values, what would you tell them to watch for?

From the Pink Sheet to Hanging Chads: Dirty Politics in the Twentieth and Twenty-First Centuries

When it comes to chronicling deceptive or otherwise dirty politics, such a wealth of material is unfortunately available that it's necessary to be highly selective. I've had to pass over some well-known examples of dirty politics, including the 1828 election between Andrew Jackson and John Quincy Adams, often considered the dirtiest presidential election in U.S. history. That election featured class warfare, with Jackson attacked as an uncouth frontiersman and Adams (son of John Adams, the second U.S. president) as a pampered, Harvard-educated pedant. Adams supporters also produced the so-called Coffin Handbill, a leaflet accusing Jackson—who played a major political and military role in forcing Native Americans off their land—of having murdered six of his own soldiers in the 1813 Creek Indian war. The 1828 election showed, too, that there's nothing new about slurs against a candidate's family members. The attacks on Rachel Donelson Jackson—Jackson's wife—had tragic consequences, because she had a heart condition and suffered a setback. She survived long enough to see her husband win the election by a landslide but died on December 22, 1828. She was buried in Tennessee in the satin gown that was to have been her inaugural ballgown.

I'll also comment only in passing on another notoriously dirty election exactly a century later, the 1928 battle between Herbert Hoover (secretary of commerce and a millionaire Republican businessman) and Al Smith (a machine politician and four-term Democratic governor of New York). Smith was the first Catholic to be a serious contender for the presidency and anti-Catholicism was rampant. This problem was nothing new; Catholics had been blamed for everything from assassinating Abraham Lincoln to causing Woodrow Wilson's incapacitating stroke.[221] During the 1928 election the Ku Klux Klan, estimated to have between two and four million members, came out in full strength in the South and West, leading to cross burnings and other expressions of bigotry when Smith campaigned in those regions. In a foreshadowing of the prejudice greeting John F. Kennedy's campaign in 1960, it was widely proclaimed that Smith's primary allegiance was to the pope. Not surprisingly, Hoover won in a landslide. According to a popular joke in New York, Smith sent a telegram to the pope the day after the election with this succinct message: "Unpack!"[222] The public was blissfully unaware that the Great Depression would soon make a mockery of Hoover's campaign slogans like "A Chicken in Every Pot—Vote for Hoover" or "Hoover and Happiness."

In the remainder of this section I profile several examples of corrupt politics in more detail; I've chosen them for their historical importance and/or because they're representative of larger trends. I begin with the "carefully orchestrated whispering campaign of smear, fear, and innuendo that would go down in American history as the dirtiest ever—while also becoming the model for the next half century and beyond."[223] This is the notorious 1950 California senatorial contest, in which Richard Nixon used red-baiting tactics against Helen Gahagan Douglas—an election significant not only for its anticommunist smears but because it propelled Nixon along the path to higher office. It also foreshowed the use of misogynist attacks against more recent women candidates. My second example—Alabama's Democratic gubernatorial race between George Wallace and Albert Brewer in 1970—was one of the last old-style segregationist elections in the United States. Finally, I look at controversial aspects of the 2000 presidential election as well as subsequent elections.

Richard Nixon's Dirty 1950 Senate Campaign against the "Pink Lady," Helen Gahagan Douglas

Richard Nixon (1913–1994) first practiced law for five years in his hometown of Whittier, California, and served as a naval officer in the South Pacific in World War II, then was elected to Congress from California in 1946. He quickly rose to national prominence as a member of the House Un-American Activities Committee (HUAC). In a famous incident, Nixon doggedly pursued the allegations by *Time* magazine editor Whittaker Chambers that Alger Hiss—a former Justice Department and State Department official—had committed espionage on behalf of the Soviet Union. After an initial trial resulted in a hung jury, Hiss was retried on perjury charges; in January 1950, Nixon was vindicated when the jury came back with a guilty verdict.

The verdict gave Nixon's career a boost at an opportune moment, because he'd launched his campaign for a Senate seat two months earlier. It was a propitious time for an anticommunist crusader to be running for office, not least because Joseph McCarthy—the famous red-baiting senator from Wisconsin that you'll encounter in the next chapter— began his anticommunist witchhunts in the same period. Nixon's opponent in the 1950 Senate race was Helen Gahagan Douglas (1900–1980), the California congresswoman who had been a well-known actress and opera singer and was the wife of actor Melvyn Douglas. Both were left-leaning members of the Hollywood community and had long been active on behalf of progressive causes. Helen Douglas was a friend and protégée of Eleanor Roosevelt and Lyndon Johnson, and like them, she was a staunch advocate of civil rights. (Among other things, she was the first white member of Congress to employ a black secretary. She also forced the integration of the House cafeteria after discovering the secretary couldn't eat there and ensured that a staff member would always accompany her so she wouldn't have to eat alone.)[224] Douglas was not personally a communist, but her association with known communists in Hollywood and elsewhere—as well as her support for leftist causes more generally—left her open to Nixon's smear campaign.

Admittedly, Douglas was vulnerable to these charges, partly because of her less-than-cooperative attitude toward HUAC. Founded in 1938 on the eve of World War II, its purpose was to root out subversive organizations and activities wherever they might be found—including Hollywood. In the 1930s and 1940s, national and local government officials became increasingly concerned about the possibility that Communist Party members or sympathizers had infiltrated the Hollywood scene. In 1947, amid allegations that many actors, screenwriters, and other film-industry employees had communist ties or leanings, HUAC issued contempt citations to ten individuals who had incurred the committee's wrath because they declined to reveal any communist affiliations and had invoked their right to free speech under the First Amendment. The ten individuals became known as the "Hollywood Ten." (An eleventh witness, playwright Bertolt Brecht, did answer the committee's questions but fled to East Germany immediately afterward.) Douglas was one of only seventeen members of Congress to vote against the bill to cite the Hollywood Ten for contempt of Congress—a fact Nixon conveniently reminded voters of at every opportunity—though Douglas's vote was merely a protest vote against what she saw as HUAC's insidious tactics.[225]

Did You Know?

As a Congressman, Richard Nixon Supported Legislation That Would Have Prevented Presidents from Keeping Documents Secret!

In a section of her memoir covering the late 1940s, Helen Gahagan Douglas describes her conflict with Nixon over the legislation:

I tangled with Richard Nixon over a bill to allow the President the right to keep his documents secret. By one of the ironies of history, Nixon was *in favor* of forcing the President to surrender confidential files to Congress on demand. He wanted to see Truman's loyalty files. HUAC [the House Un-American Activities Committee] was hot on the campaign trail, getting a great amount of space in newspapers and on radio for charges that Truman's office and departments under his direction were riddled with communists.

I, on the other hand, supported Truman's position that such files were privileged....

The bill passed the House but was killed by the Senate.[1]

---

1   *Helen Gahagan Douglas, A Full Life (Garden City, NY: Doubleday, 1982), 271.*

Nixon had help in his campaign to smear Douglas. She'd already been dubbed the "Pink Lady" by the *Los Angeles Daily News*, a newspaper that, like the *Los Angeles Times, San Francisco Examiner*, and other influential California papers, was then strongly Republican and determined to paint Douglas as a left-wing pinko.[226] Nixon made much of the "pink" symbolism (suggesting communism or socialism) in his attacks on Douglas, partly by following the lead of another dirty campaign across the country.

In the Florida Democratic primary earlier in 1950, a leftist U.S. senator named Claude Pepper was defeated through a campaign of rumor and innuendo—a campaign that provided a blueprint for Nixon to follow against Douglas. Pepper's detractors called him "Red Pepper," analogous to the epithet "Pink Lady" used of Douglas. The Florida primary has gone down in history not only as an exceptionally dirty election but for amusing campaign rhetoric attributed to Pepper's opponent, Congressman George Smathers. While campaigning in rural areas, Smathers allegedly took advantage of voters' lack of sophistication with attacks like these on his opponent: "Are you aware that Claude Pepper is known all over Washington as a shameless *extrovert*? Not only that, but this man is reliably reported to practice *nepotism* with his sister-in-law, he has a brother who is a known *homo sapiens*, and he has a sister who was once a *thespian* in wicked New York. Worst of all, it is an established fact that Mr. Pepper, before his marriage he habitually practiced *celibacy*."[227] Though no recording survives of these statements and Smathers later denied making them, the use of the word *homo sapiens* (suggesting *homosexual* to the unsophisticated ear) and *thespian* (suggesting *lesbian*) represented the kind of innuendo and personal attack that permeated his campaign against Pepper.

Toward the end of the campaign, Pepper's enemies produced campaign literature using the tactic of guilt by association. In a booklet titled *The Red Record of Claude Pepper*, quotes from Pepper's speeches underscored his ties with the Soviet Union and its leaders (he had met with Joseph Stalin to discuss improving U.S.-Soviet relations), his opposition to President Truman's anticommunist policies, and other positions deemed subversive; photos showing Pepper together with prominent leftists also planted the idea in voters' minds that he couldn't be trusted.

Along the same lines, Nixon's staff distributed more than a half million copies of a "Pink Sheet" (a flyer printed on legal-sized pink paper) comparing Douglas's voting record to that of Vito Marcantonio, a well-known leftist congressman from New York.[228] The overlap between their voting records is discussed under alarmist, red-baiting headings like "Votes against Committee on Un-American Activities," "Communist Line Foreign Policy Votes," "Vote against National Defense," and "Votes against Congressional Investigation of Communist and Other Illegal Activities."

Nixon's dirty tricks didn't stop with the Pink Sheet. To court the anti-Semitic vote, he sometimes invoked the name Helen Hesselberg instead of Helen Douglas. (Helen Douglas says in her memoir that as an actor her husband was pressured to replace his original name of Hesselberg with something that would "fit on a theater marquee," so he "took his grandmother's maiden name, Douglas.")[229] And then there were the gender stereotypes. After Douglas dismissed Nixon as "peewee" in a speech, he angrily retorted that he would "castrate" her.[230] More often he used devious rhetorical strategies, taking his lead from Kyle Palmer, the influential *Los Angeles Times* political editor. Palmer had played on gender stereotypes by claiming Douglas was an "emotional artist . . . a veritable political butterfly, flitting from flower to flower," not to be confused with the heroic Nixon, who had courageously "pulled up the weeds, sprayed the plant lice, squashed the snails, killed the worms, and tilled the soil."[231] Nixon followed the strategy of announcing that "my opponent is a woman. And my advisers have warned me not to raise questions about her qualifications," assuring the public that "there will be no name calling, no smears, no misrepresentation. We do not indulge in such tactics."[232] By calling attention to Douglas's gender and insisting that he wouldn't question her right to run for office as a woman, Nixon—reportedly "personally affronted by the sheer brazenness of [Douglas's] ambition"[233]—was of course doing exactly what he denied he was doing. His insistence that there would be no dirty politics provided a cover for that very kind of politics. In view of these tactics, it's not surprising that the Douglas-Nixon battle is sometimes described as a clash of "the Beauty and the Beast."

Just as Smathers's red-baiting tactics had enabled him to defeat Pepper by a wide margin in Florida, Nixon's smear campaign paid off; he won by a 59-40 margin. His efforts destroyed Douglas's political career, making her "too radioactive" to be appointed to a position in the Truman administration or to run for office again. Despite what Nixon had done to her, Douglas refused to be vindictive, explaining that "when I woke up the next morning [after the election] I felt free, uninjured, whole. Nixon had his victory but I had mine."[234] She went on to lead an extraordinarily productive life working on behalf of causes she cared deeply about, from the plight of farmworkers to environmental issues, from civil rights to disarmament. When she campaigned with Jimmy Carter in the 1976 election and was honored with a standing ovation, Carter acknowledged: "It's you who should be running."[235] Douglas, who many believed would be the first woman president, has been lauded as "one of the grandest, most eloquent, deepest-thinking people we have had in American politics."[236]

As for Nixon, the rest is history. Dwight Eisenhower tapped Nixon as his running mate in 1952, only two years after the Nixon-Douglas battle. After eight years as vice president, Nixon was defeated by John Kennedy for the presidency in the hotly contested 1960 election. Aided by the disarray in the Democratic Party, which had splintered over the Vietnam War and other issues, Nixon captured the White House in 1968. In a repeat performance four years later, he defeated George McGovern in a landslide victory, taking every state except Massachusetts. In the end Nixon was derailed by his own dirty tricks—the burglary of the Democratic National Committee headquarters in the Watergate building in Washington in 1972 and the subsequent cover-up—and was forced to resign in 1974.

Douglas didn't die until 1980, so she lived to see Nixon's fall from grace. In her autobiography, *A Full Life* (published posthumously in 1982), she wrote that "there's not much to say about the 1950 campaign except that a man ran for the Senate who wanted to get there, and didn't care how."[237] "That same pattern emerged," she elaborated, "when Nixon was preparing for his second presidential campaign [in 1972]. It resulted in people close to him sending burglars into the Democratic party headquarters in the Watergate Hotel. . . . Under stress, Nixon reverted to what had served him in the past, which was to wage a dirty campaign."[238]

George Wallace's Segregationist Campaign against Albert
Brewer in the 1970 Alabama Gubernatorial Primary

On January 14, 1963, George Wallace (1919–1998)—who served as governor of Alabama for sixteen years and ran for president four times—stood on the spot where Jefferson Davis had taken the oath as president of the Confederacy a century earlier and delivered his first inaugural address. One line from that address has gone down in history: "In the name of the greatest people that have ever trod this earth, I draw the line in the dust and toss the gauntlet before the feet of tyranny . . . and I say . . . segregation now . . . segregation tomorrow . . . segregation forever."[239] Even by the Southern standards of that era, Wallace's demagoguery was startling, and it immediately earned him a reputation as one of the staunchest opponents of civil rights.

Wallace also became notorious for his efforts to block the integration of the University of Alabama by two African-American students, Vivian Malone and James Hood, on June 11, 1963. He planted himself in front of the university auditorium where registration was being held and refused to allow access to the building; it took Deputy U.S. Attorney General Nicholas Katzenbach, federal marshals, and the Alabama National Guard to force him aside. To Wallace's dismay, change was in the air in Alabama. While other Justice Department officials drove Hood to a men's dorm, Katzenbach walked Malone to her dorm, where she was welcomed by the house mother and—after she sat down by herself at a table in the cafeteria—was immediately joined by a half-dozen women students who brought their trays over and introduced themselves.[240] Change was also in the air on a national level. Ironically, the successful confrontation with Wallace at the University of Alabama led President Kennedy to give a hastily prepared televised address to the nation that evening to demand passage of a civil rights bill. That bill would become the Civil Rights Act of 1964, spearheaded by President Johnson after Kennedy's assassination in November 1963.

The surly, defiant Wallace blocking the University of Alabama entrance is the Wallace most people remember or have read about. He was more moderate on racial issues at the start of his political career—as a member of the Alabama House of Representatives and as a circuit judge in the 1940s and 1950s—but that didn't prove expedient for long. After he lost the Democratic primary for governor in 1958 to a candidate backed by the Ku Klux Klan, he adopted the racist tactics of his opponent. He told his finance director that he had been "out-[n-word]ed" and that he would "never be out-[n-word]ed" again.[241] Wallace's segregationist platform helped him win the 1962 gubernatorial race in a landslide. He explained his transformation this way: "You know, I tried to talk about good roads and good schools and all these things that have been part of my career, and nobody listened. And then I began talking about [n-word], and they stomped the floor."[242]

Wallace couldn't be reelected governor in 1966 because of term limits, so his wife, Lurleen Wallace, was elected in his place. But she died of cancer in May 1968 and was replaced by the lieutenant governor, Albert Brewer.

Meanwhile, George Wallace had presidential aspirations. He had made his first presidential foray by campaigning in several Democratic primaries in 1964, running on a platform supporting states' rights and opposing civil rights; he did surprisingly well, winning a third of the Democratic primary vote in states like Maryland and Wisconsin. In 1968 he ran on the American Independent Party ticket, hoping to siphon enough votes from the major-party candidates (Richard Nixon and Hubert Humphrey) to throw the election to the House of Representatives. He didn't succeed in doing that. But running on an anti-integration, law-and-order platform, Wallace prevailed in five Southern states and had substantial appeal to blue-collar workers in Northern states, garnering almost ten million votes.

If Wallace was going to make another run for the presidency, he needed to shore up the political base he'd lost in Alabama with his wife's death and Brewer's succession. So in 1970, Wallace challenged Brewer for the governorship, despite having promised him he wouldn't do so. That race was one of the dirtiest ever; it was also one of the last blatantly segregationist elections in U.S. history.

Brewer was a moderate respected by many people for his integrity—qualities mocked by Wallace when he labeled Brewer "sissy-britches."[243] Wallace, who was a charismatic campaigner, taunted his opponent at his rallies, charging that Brewer "used to stand on this platform behind me and my wife . . . who rode her skirttails to power [and now has] joined together with black militants to defeat me."[244] To win the support of rural and blue-collar white voters fearful about integration and resentful about class issues, Wallace hammered home the integration and "sissy-britches" themes, warning that a Brewer victory would lead to governance by a coalition of blacks and "sissy-britches from Harvard who spend most of their time in a country club drinking tea with their finger stuck up."[245] Brewer won most of his support from black voters as well as from urban and suburban white voters. As a Democrat, he also received support from an unlikely source: the Republican president of the United States, Richard Nixon! Nixon was concerned about Wallace's potential to draw off Republican votes when he (Nixon) ran for reelection in 1972, so he privately funneled money to the Brewer campaign—as much as $400,000, making up almost a third of Brewer's campaign funds, according to some sources.[246]

Brewer defeated Wallace in the primary, 422,000 to 414,000, with the remainder of the votes divided between five other candidates. Because Brewer had failed to win a majority of the votes, a runoff was held. Wallace and his supporters stepped up their dirty campaigning, and Wallace narrowly won, by a margin of only 32,000 votes out of more than a million cast. Overall, Wallace received 51.5 percent of the vote, but more than 90 percent of black voters turned out for Brewer, as did many urban and suburban whites. When it was all over, Brewer angrily complained about Wallace's racist smear tactics, telling a CBS interviewer that "if that's what it takes to win, the cost is too high."[247] Wallace may have outmaneuvered Brewer in the 1970 primary, but Brewer stood out as a symbol of integrity in the unusually dirty waters of segregationist politics.

Running for president a third time in 1972 (as a Democrat), Wallace survived an assassination attempt—on May 15 in Laurel, Maryland, where he was campaigning—and spent the rest of his life in a wheelchair.

He was reelected governor of Alabama in 1974 and made a fourth and final bid for the presidency in 1976, winning only three primaries and losing the Democratic nomination to another Southerner, Jimmy Carter. In the 1970s Wallace became a born-again Christian and publicly apologized for his segregationist past.[248] Many black voters obviously forgave him, because ironically, the candidate who had advocated "segregation now . . . segregation tomorrow . . . segregation forever" in 1963 gained considerable African-American support, enabling him to be reelected governor in his last election in 1982.

The 2000 Presidential Election and Beyond

The 2000 presidential election added a new term to the lexicon of most Americans: *hanging chad*, referring to the little fleck of paper that theoretically fell out when a stylus was pushed through the punch hole on a ballot but that sometimes remained attached, making it hard for the voting machine to read the ballot. Who could ever have imagined that an election would turn on something as trivial as pieces of confetti hanging from ballots?

It all came down to Florida. The evening of the 2000 election, George W. Bush and his family had left the Texas governor's mansion to have dinner at the Shoreline Grill in Austin. Keeping an eye on a TV set as he ate a crusted chicken dinner, Bush watched the networks declare Al Gore the winner in Florida. But Bush's younger brother, Florida Governor Jeb Bush, insisted his sources said the Republican ticket was winning, as did Karl Rove, the campaign's chief strategist. Indeed, two hours later the networks backtracked, and within a four- or five-minute period just after 1:00 a.m. Central Time, they declared Bush the forty-third president of the United States.

The mood at the Gore headquarters turned somber. Not long before, campaign workers had been drinking champagne; now their euphoria gave way to disbelief and sorrow. Anxious not to be seen as a sore loser, Vice President Gore lost no time conceding the election and calling Bush to congratulate him. It was a gesture many would later regret.

As the night wore on, Bush's lead dwindled from 50,000 votes to only 6,000. Like the general public, campaign operatives normally considered the projections of the TV networks infallible. What was going on? By this time Gore's entourage was on its way to the War Memorial in Nashville to publicly concede. A top strategist in Gore's campaign headquarters who was crunching the numbers tried desperately to get in touch with him to stop him from making the concession speech. Through the frenzied efforts of several staffers, Gore was reached minutes before he was to take the stage. Stunned, then elated at the news he was still in the race because a recount was mandated, Gore placed a second call to Bush to retract his earlier concession. In the ensuing chaos, the networks were forced to withdraw their predictions yet again—at NBC, an embarrassed Tom Brokaw said broadcasters didn't just "have egg" but "an omelette" on their faces—and the Castro administration in Cuba offered to send election monitors.[249]

Both camps turned to the courts, underscoring the accuracy of French visitor Alexis de Tocqueville's 1835 prophecy that "scarcely any political question arises in the United States which is not resolved, sooner or later, into a judicial question."[250] Court decisions seesawed back and forth, some benefiting Bush and others benefiting Gore; at issue was how to conduct a fair recount of thousands of questionable votes caused by poorly designed ballots (a confusing arrangement of candidates' names on the ballots), voting machines that couldn't read the ballots (the hanging-chad problem), or other irregularities. On December 12, 2000, the "nine scorpions in a bottle," as the members of the U.S. Supreme Court have been called, issued their sixty-five-page ruling on *Bush v. Gore*.[251] In a five-to-four decision favoring Bush, the court decided that the haphazard Florida recounts violated the equal protection clause of the Constitution and that time constraints and other practical problems made it impossible to remedy the situation. The next day, Gore took issue with the court's decision, conceded the election, and congratulated his opponent. Many critics, including some conservatives, were dismayed at the unprecedented role of the Supreme Court in determining the outcome of the election—a violation of the constitutional mandate that such disputes be resolved by the House of Representatives. Comedian Mark Russell spoke for many others when he quipped, "In this democracy of 200 million citizens, the people have spoken: all five of them."[252]

If the term *hanging chad* entered the political lexicon in 2000, *Swiftboating* made its appearance in 2004. The term *Swiftboating* acquired the connotation of blindsiding a candidate. The Democratic candidate, John Kerry, was a decorated Vietnam veteran and had been active in the antiwar movement after returning from Vietnam. A centerpiece of his campaign against George W. Bush in 2004 was that both his military experience and his antiwar credentials made him better qualified than Bush to handle the Iraq War. But Kerry's antiwar activism in the 1970s—especially his congressional testimony that U.S. servicemen had committed widespread atrocities in Vietnam—had rankled other vets, and they saw a chance to get even. Some founded a political group called Swift Boat Veterans for Truth, which produced ads alleging that Kerry had distorted his Vietnam record and had not legitimately earned the medals he was awarded. The ads proved effective, because for many voters they undermined Kerry's major claim to the presidency: his military background. The contentiousness of the 2004 election didn't stop with the Swiftboating campaign against Kerry.

"In November 2004," Steven F. Freeman and Joel Bleifuss write in their book *Was the 2004 Presidential Election Stolen?*, "concern about a possible fraudulent election based on an exit-poll discrepancy made headlines across America. However, it was not that month's U.S. presidential election that generated interest, but rather an election in a former Soviet republic halfway around the globe where the exit polls indicated election fraud was afoot."[253] They add that "the U.S. media never questioned why a comparable discrepancy here meant nothing, despite the fact that the U.S. exit poll suffered from none of the shortcomings observed in Ukraine."[254]

In the book's preface, Freeman (an expert on research methods and survey design, including polling) describes his surprise at the discrepancies between the exit polls the day of the 2004 election and the results as reported by the news media that evening. Listening to his car radio the afternoon of the election, he heard reports of exit polls that gave Kerry a substantial margin; that night and the next morning, the network news anchors gave the edge to Bush.[255] Freeman and Bleifuss (an investigative reporter) then spent considerable time analyzing the discrepancy between the exit polls, which favored Kerry by five million votes, and the actual vote tally, which gave Bush a margin of three million votes. From the beginning, allegations of fraud in battleground states like Ohio surfaced.

Freeman and Bleifuss's conclusion? Election fraud was highly likely, particularly in Florida and Ohio, with voting-machine irregularities playing a major role. They believe that Kerry actually won the popular vote in the 2004 election by a plurality of five to seven million votes nationwide—representing a 5 percent margin—and that if there had been a legitimate vote count, he would have garnered between 282 and 364 electoral votes (270 would have put him over the top).[256]

Especially troubling, Freeman and Bleifuss say, is the indifference of the media to these problems. They think this reveals a serious erosion of standards: "That a journalistic examination of the exit-poll discrepancy is deemed 'not fit to print' by both the corporate and the independent media indicates how far our standards have devolved. It seems undeniable to us that the very same set of facts applied to a foreign election anywhere in the world would have garnered front-page coverage in every American newspaper and would have been the lead story on every American news program. If election fraud in Ukraine or in Haiti is news, why isn't election fraud in the United States?"[257]

Allegations of election fraud also surfaced in the 2008 presidential election, especially in the lengthy Democratic primary. In Texas alone, thousands of complaints were filed alleging voter-registration fraud, voter intimidation, ballot-box stuffing, and other irregularities. Many allegations across the country involved the activities of the Association of Community Organizations for Reform Now (ACORN). In the aftermath of the election ACORN faced a host of problems, including investigations into its activities in many states, defunding by federal agencies, a drop-off in donations from the public, and undercover videos made public in 2009 that seemed to show misconduct by ACORN workers in several cities. As a result, ACORN announced it would shut down in 2010, though some of its components appear to have reorganized under other names.[258]

Conclusion

Politics provides some of the murkiest waters you'll ever have to dive through to find truth, but there are few areas of society where finding truth is more important. By giving you a glimpse of the history of deceptive politics in the United States, this chapter has tried to alert you to an array of political problems that need to be avoided or remedied. The next chapter, on bigots and demagogues, shows how things can go terribly wrong if these problems are not addressed.

What You Can Do

√*Be an informed voter.* The days are long gone when you can be a passive consumer of political news, relying on the mainstream media to give you anything approaching a balanced view of the issues. As the media become increasingly partisan, the only way to be a responsible, informed voter is to take the initiative in educating yourself on the issues. This means reading widely, consulting diverse sources, and using critical-thinking skills in evaluating those sources. Online news sites and blogs have become so important that it's now almost impossible to be well informed on political issues without doing at least some of your research online.

√*Speak out against corporate intrusion in the political system.* You don't have to be told that many politicians are beholden to corporate interests or to other groups that often fail to represent citizens' interests. Corporate involvement in politics is deeply entrenched and is likely to become worse in light of the 2010 *Citizens United* Supreme Court decision striking down limits on corporate spending in elections. These problems can only be addressed if enough members of the public are vigilant and speak out against them.

√*Get involved with organizations supporting open and transparent government, election reform, and similar goals.* Watchdog groups dedicated to responsibility and transparency in government include Citizens for Responsibility and Ethics in Washington (CREW) (www.citizensforethics.org) and OpenTheGovernment.org (www.openthegovernment.org). You can also join some of the many nonpartisan organizations working toward fair and accurate elections, like the Verified Voting Foundation (www.verifiedvotingfoundation.org) and its sister organization, VerifiedVoting.org (www.verifiedvoting.org).

√*More generally, work to strengthen democratic institutions.* Democratic institutions emphasize leadership that responds to the needs of the people rather than being autocratic; these institutions emphasize fairness, the equal participation of all citizens, and respect and tolerance even toward those we disagree with. Ensuring an equal voice for everyone rests on an egalitarian social structure. Poverty and despair can breed disenfranchisement and rebellion, so it's in all of our best interests to try to create a healthy middle class, not a social structure with a few haves at the top and many have-nots at the bottom.

√*Do your part to ensure that the media treat politicians fairly.* Try to hold journalists and bloggers accountable when they dehumanize politicians or their families based on gender, race, age, physical appearance, sexual orientation, or other factors, and demand equally fair and accurate coverage regardless of candidates' political affiliation. Also be vigilant about the tendency of the media to idealize certain politicians or officials; in the worst-case scenario, this tendency can devolve into the demagoguery profiled in the next chapter.

Further Reading

For a readable, informative book on dirty politics in the United States, see Kerwin C. Swint, *Mudslingers: The Top 25 Negative Political Campaigns of All Time* (Westport, CT: Praeger, 2006). Also see Joseph Cummins, *Anything for a Vote: Dirty Tricks, Cheap Shots, and October Surprises in U.S. Presidential Campaigns* (Philadelphia: Quirk Books, 2007). There are short write-ups (including useful references) on several of the elections touched on in this chapter in Paul F. Boller Jr., *Presidential Campaigns: From George Washington to George W. Bush*, 2nd ed. (New York: Oxford University Press, 2004). An older but still useful source on dirty politics in general is Kathleen Hall Jamieson, *Dirty Politics: Deception, Distraction, and Democracy* (New York: Oxford University Press, 1992).

On Richard Nixon's dirty campaign against Helen Gahagan Douglas, see Greg Mitchell, *Tricky Dick and the Pink Lady: Richard Nixon vs. Helen Gahagan Douglas—Sexual Politics and the Red Scare, 1950* (New York: Random House, 1998), and Sally Denton, *The Pink Lady: The Many Lives of Helen Gahagan Douglas* (New York: Bloomsbury Press, 2009), 139–174. For Helen Gahagan Douglas's own take on that campaign, see her memoir, *A Full Life* (Garden City, NY: Doubleday, 1982); she discusses the 1950 election on pp. 289–341.

For a comprehensive look at the 1970 Wallace-Brewer election as well as other aspects of George Wallace's controversial life and politics, see Dan T. Carter, *The Politics of Rage: George Wallace, the Origins of the New Conservatism, and the Transformation of American Politics* (New York: Simon & Schuster, 1995).

Many books cover alleged fraud in the last few presidential elections. For a collection of articles, see Mark Crispin Miller, ed., *Loser Take All: Election Fraud and the Subversion of Democracy, 2000–2008* (Brooklyn, NY: Ig Publishing, 2008). On the 2000 election see David A. Kaplan, *The Accidental President: How 413 Lawyers, 9 Supreme Court Justices, and 5,963,110 (Give or Take a Few) Floridians Landed George W. Bush in the White House* (New York: William Morrow, 2001), as well as Ellen Nakashima and the *Washington Post* Political Staff, *Deadlock:*

The Inside Story of America's Closest Election (New York: Public Affairs / Perseus Books Group, 2001). On the 2004 election, see Steven F. Freeman and Joel Bleifuss, *Was the 2004 Presidential Election Stolen? Exit Polls, Election Fraud, and the Official Count* (New York: Seven Stories Press, 2006); also see Freeman's website, www.electionintegrity.org. For general accounts of the 2008 election, see Dan Balz and Haynes Johnson, *The Battle for America 2008: The Story of an Extraordinary Election* (New York: Viking, 2009), and John Heilemann and Mark Halperin, *Game Change: Obama and the Clintons, McCain and Palin, and the Race of a Lifetime* (New York: Harper, 2010). Two books that attempt to bring to light problems in the 2008 Democratic primary are Anita Finlay, *Dirty Words on Clean Skin: Sexism and Sabotage, a Hillary Supporter's Rude Awakening* (Golden Middleway Books, 2012), and P. G. Abeles, *Admit the Horse: A Political Thriller* (Rockville, MD: Oak Leaf Press, 2012).

For more on issues related to voting technology and election administration, see Bev Harris, with David Allen, *Black Box Voting: Ballot Tampering in the 21st Century* (Renton, WA: Talion, 2004), as well as Harris's website, www.blackboxvoting.org. Also see Aviel D. Rubin's *Brave New Ballot: The Battle to Safeguard Democracy in the Age of Electronic Voting* (New York: Morgan Road Books, 2006).

For a short but insightful book that touches on plagiarism by politicians like Joe Biden, see Richard A. Posner, *The Little Book of Plagiarism* (New York: Pantheon Books, 2007).

7. BIGOTS AND DEMAGOGUES

This chapter focuses on two types of individuals who not only deceive others, but who do so in ways often profoundly hurtful and destructive—bigots and demagogues. After providing some basic definitions, I profile several notorious examples: Adolf Hitler, whose name is synonymous with demagoguery; Theodore Bilbo, one of the worst racists in U.S. history; and Joseph McCarthy, the Wisconsin senator who whipped up anticommunist hysteria in the early 1950s. While these cases are extreme, they're instructive; there is much we can learn about truth and deception from them.

Some Definitions

The words *bigot* and *demagogue* overlap but don't mean exactly the same thing. *Bigot* has been used in English at least since 1598 and originally meant a "religious person" or "superstitious person." In its earliest history in French, it was especially associated with women—for example, it was used as a derogatory term for the Beguines, members of a Roman Catholic women's community. Now, of course, a bigot is a prejudiced or intolerant person of either gender.

Demagogues are often bigoted, but demagoguery has other implications as well. *Merriam-Webster's Collegiate Dictionary* defines *demagogue* as "a leader who makes use of popular prejudices and false claims and promises in order to gain power"; he usually relies on emotional rhetoric and propaganda as well as on fear tactics to achieve his ends. Demagoguery also often has overtones of fascism; in his classic work, *The Nature of*

Prejudice, Gordon W. Allport elaborates: "Demagoguery invites the externalization of hatred and anxiety; it is an institutional aid to projection; it justifies and encourages tabloid thinking, stereotyping. . . . It bifurcates life into clear-cut choices: follow the simple fascist formula or disaster will occur. There is no middle ground, no national solution. While the ultimate objective is vague, still the need for definiteness is met by the rule, 'Follow the Leader.' . . . [The demagogue's] technique is one of arousing hope (e.g., 'share the wealth') and also of arousing fear."[259]

As these definitions suggest, it's impossible to talk about bigotry or demagoguery without talking about prejudice. In their book *Mistakes Were Made (but Not by Me)*, Carol Tavris and Elliot Aronson note that "a stereotype might bend or even shatter under the weight of disconfirming information, but the hallmark of prejudice is that it is impervious to reason, experience, and counterexample."[260] They add that prejudice helps reduce the cognitive dissonance people experience between their self-image as a good person and their bad behavior toward others, because the prejudice provides a rationale for that bad behavior. In short, prejudice can be a "self-justifying servant,"[261] whether it's rooted in conflicting customs or religious beliefs, the desire to preserve one's power or privilege, competition over jobs, or simply a fear of the Other.

From Nazism to McCarthyism: Three Examples of Bigotry and Demagoguery

History is full of examples of bigots and demagogues who have destroyed lives or even entire societies. Any list of international examples would include names like

- Joseph Stalin (1879–1953), remembered for political purges, gulags, and other repressive practices in the Soviet Union, especially in the 1930s
- Adolf Hitler (1889–1945), whose Nazi regime was responsible for the deaths of millions in war and in concentration camps in the 1930s and 1940s

- Pol Pot (1925–1998), the despot whose Khmer Rouge movement killed or tortured a third of the Cambodian population in the 1970s
- Idi Amin (1925–2003), the Ugandan dictator said to have been responsible for 200,000 deaths, also in the 1970s

Closer to home, well-known U.S. bigots and demagogues include

- Pitchfork Ben Tillman (1847–1918), a South Carolina governor and U.S. senator known for his populism but also for his racism (he earned his nickname when he threatened to stab President Grover Cleveland with a pitchfork)
- Huey Long (1893–1935), a Louisiana governor and U.S. senator whose political machine ran the state; he proposed a national "Share-the-Wealth" program (of the type mentioned in the quote on demagoguery from Allport above) in 1934 but was assassinated the following year
- Father Coughlin (1891–1979), a Canadian-born priest in the United States who became known for expressing anti-Semitic and pro-Nazi sympathies in radio addresses and magazine articles
- Theodore Bilbo (1877–1947), an influential Mississippi politician and white supremacist
- Joseph McCarthy (1908–1957), the Wisconsin senator whose anticommunist witchhunts in the early 1950s left a trail of damaged lives

In this section I trace the rise and fall of three representative bigots and demagogues (Hitler, Bilbo, and McCarthy), showing how they used manipulation and deception to wreak havoc on those around them.

Adolf Hitler, "One of the Greatest Demagogues of All Time"

Hitler's life story is well known. Born on April 20, 1889, in the town of Braunau on the Austrian-Bavarian border, he grew up in a middle-class family that was financially comfortable.[262] Yet all was not well. Hitler's father—a minor civil servant—was abusive toward Hitler and his siblings and probably also toward their mother, who was unable to protect the children. "Beneath the surface," in the words of a biographer,

> the later Hitler was unquestionably being formed. Speculation though it must remain, it takes little to imagine that his later patronizing contempt for the submissiveness of women, the thirst for dominance (and imagery of the Leader as a stern, authoritarian father-figure), the inability to form deep personal relationships, the corresponding cold brutality towards humankind, and—not least—the capacity for hatred so profound that it must have reflected an immeasurable undercurrent of self-hatred concealed in the extreme narcissism that was its counterpoint must surely have had roots in the subliminal influences of the young Adolf's family circumstances.[263]

Later remembered by his teachers as a capable student but also a troublemaker,[264] Hitler entered adulthood with little sense of direction. His two rejections by the Vienna Academy of Fine Arts in 1907–1908—where he'd hoped to get the training necessary to become a painter—blocked an obvious career path. Even in those years, his anti-Semitism and other extremist views alienated many of those around him. He moved to Munich in 1913, and with the outbreak of World War I the following year, he joined the Bavarian army. He served in France and Belgium; wounded in the leg and gassed in separate incidents, he was decorated twice for bravery.

Did You Know?

A Failed Art Exam Could Have Determined the Course of History

As a boy, Adolf Hitler showed a talent for drawing and dreamed of a career as an artist. In September 1907, at the age of eighteen, he went to Vienna to take the entrance exam at the Vienna Academy of Fine Arts. One of more than a hundred candidates, Hitler made the preliminary cut based on the "pile of drawings"[1] he brought from home. The real test came in October, when the applicants had to produce drawings on required subjects during two intensive, three-hour exams. Only twenty-eight applicants passed and Hitler wasn't one of them.

Hitler was stunned. He explains in *Mein Kampf* that he was "convinced that it would be child's play to pass the examination. . . . I was so convinced that I would be successful that when I received my rejection, it struck me as a bolt from the blue."[2] After asking for an interview with an academy official, Hitler learned that the professors judging the applicants' work "felt something was missing from [his] portfolio—a human touch—because the pictures over-emphasized landscapes and buildings. What seemingly struck the professors was that the pictures were not alive."[3] The academy administrator suggested that Hitler's gifts lay in architecture, not painting.

---

1   Adolf Hitler, *Mein Kampf*, trans. Ralph Manheim (Boston: Houghton Mifflin, [1925, 1927] 1943), 19.
2   Hitler, *Mein Kampf*, 19–20.
3   Fritz Redlich, *Hitler: Diagnosis of a Destructive Prophet* (New York: Oxford University Press, 1999), 22.

Did You Know?

Though Hitler later claimed that this advice resonated with him, he didn't pursue an architecture career and instead reapplied to the painting program the next year, suggesting that he held out hope for a career as an artist. The failure of the Vienna Academy of Fine Arts to recognize what Hitler considered his obvious artistic talent was a blow to his self-esteem and contributed to his festering resentment toward the world. In Chapter 1, we noted that self-deception sometimes has horrific consequences; Hitler's delusions of grandeur about his artistic gifts seem to be an obvious example. Many still wonder how a few obscure art professors may have influenced the course of history by rejecting Hitler's drawings as not being "alive" enough.

After the war Hitler returned to Munich. He became involved with politics, especially with the German Workers' Party (DAP), whose anti-Semitism, nationalism, and socialism appealed to him. In 1921 he was elected leader of the party and changed its name to the National Socialist German Workers' Party (NSDAP). Building support through his oratorical skills and with the aid of Nazi thugs, Hitler soon saw his opening. On November 8, 1923, he and his supporters staged what is called the Beer Hall Putsch—an attempt to overthrow the government. But the coup was unsuccessful and Hitler was arrested and tried for treason. Though he was sentenced to a five-year prison term, he was pardoned and released after serving just over a year. He took advantage of his time in prison, composing most of the first volume of *Mein Kampf* (My Struggle) and dictating it to two fellow prisoners.[265] This book was published in two volumes in the mid-1920s and became a bestseller, thanks partly to the fact that newlyweds and soldiers were later presented with free copies. Written in a turgid style, *Mein Kampf* contains autobiographical material, surveys party history, and presents Hitler's social Darwinist ideology (emphasizing the survival of the fittest and justifying conquest and genocide).

By tapping into the resentment stemming from Germany's humiliating defeat in World War I, Hitler won increasing support for himself and his cause. As Ian Kershaw writes in his *Hitler 1889–1936: Hubris*, "The First World War made Hitler possible. . . . Without the trauma of war, defeat and revolution, without the political radicalization of German society that this trauma brought about, the demagogue would have been without an audience for his raucous, hate-filled message. The legacy of the lost war provided the conditions in which the paths of Hitler and the German people began to cross. Without the war, a Hitler on the Chancellor's seat that had been occupied by Bismarck would have been unthinkable."[266] But it was thinkable, and on January 30, 1933, Hitler assumed the chancellorship of Germany. On learning that Hitler had become chancellor, Erich Ludendorff—a German general and former Nazi supporter—reportedly made this chilling prophecy to President Paul von Hindenburg: "By appointing Hitler Chancellor of the Reich, you have handed over our sacred German Fatherland to one of the greatest demagogues of all time. I prophesy to you this evil man will plunge our Reich into the abyss and will inflict immeasurable woe on our nation. Future generations will curse you in your grave for this action."[267]

The Nazis consolidated their power, manipulating the public through propaganda and strewing oppression and violence in their wake. As soon as they were able to, they implemented a deeply patriarchal ideology. Hitler's attitudes toward women have been the subject of much speculation. Those who knew him describe him as having been devoted to his mother; he carried a picture of her throughout his life and she "may well, in fact, have been the only person he genuinely loved in his entire life."[268] But this devotion did not preclude fear of and contempt for women in general:

He was an extreme male chauvinist. He had a low opinion of women's intellectual abilities, though he appreciated their intuition. He believed, as did his father, that the woman's task was to breed and devote herself to her husband and her children. Most of all, Hitler felt that women should not participate in politics. No woman must be a member of the Reichstag or play a significant role within the Party. In his view, the woman's role was to serve, a Wagnerian idea; yet Hitler contradicted himself in his extraordinary remark, "Once we have a men's society (*Männerstaat*), humanity will be on a downhill course." Intellectuals, and particularly intellectual women, were a horror for Hitler.[269]

Hitler did admire certain prominent women that he called *Paradefrauen* (parade women). Many were associated with the arts; the best known were the filmmaker Leni Riefenstahl and the ardent Hitler loyalist Winifred Wagner, the British-born daughter-in-law of the composer Richard Wagner. As for Hitler's personal relationships with women, this topic has given rise to endless discussions of possible "perversions," "asexuality," physical abnormalities, impotence—even, in the case of Geli Raubal, murder. Angela (Geli) Raubal was Hitler's niece and lived with him for a time; in 1931 she was shot and killed with his gun, possibly after they had a violent argument. Though the incident was labeled a suicide, many have suspected foul play on Hitler's part. While living with Raubal, Hitler was consorting with other women, including Eva Braun, whom he married the day before their deaths in 1945. As one author sums up, "Just what sexual or erotic experiences Hitler had with these [and other] women is a matter of conjecture. What is known is that one of them, Angela (Geli) Raubal, died a violent death and that at least four—Eva Braun, Valkyrie Mitford, Susi Liptauer, and Maria Reiter—made suicidal attempts, by any measure an extraordinary record."[270]

Hitler's sordid behavior was not confined to misogyny. As Nazism became more entrenched, Hitler and other Nazi leaders began to put their obsession with racial hygiene or racial purity into practice. In keeping with the Nazis' harsh social Darwinist ideology, those deemed "unfit to live" were exterminated. The outcome was the Holocaust, in which six million Jews and as many as eight million others lost their lives. The first group targeted by the Nazis for systematic killings were children with physical and mental disabilities, but the program was expanded to include Jews, non-Jewish Poles, communists, anti-Nazi clergy and other dissidents, homosexuals, Soviet prisoners of war, and others. Besides being gassed in concentration camps like Auschwitz, the victims were killed in mass executions, were worked to death, or starved or succumbed to disease in ghettos and other locations. Hitler apparently never visited any of the concentration camps and no documentation survives of a direct order from him authorizing the extermination of Jews. But abundant evidence—including the testimony of his personal secretary—shows he was well aware of what was going on in the camps.

Hitler's grandiose dreams of creating a thousand-year Reich (empire) that would stretch across vast territories were dashed in World War II. Despite early German victories, the Allies increasingly prevailed, leading to Germany's defeat in 1945. Hitler celebrated his fifty-sixth birthday in his Berlin headquarters on April 20, 1945. On April 30, with Soviet troops only a few blocks away, Hitler poisoned his dog, Blondi, with a cyanide capsule to test the effectiveness of the cyanide. Then he and Eva Braun—they'd been married the day before—committed suicide by biting into cyanide capsules. Hitler also shot himself, leaving a swath of death and destruction behind him.

Theodore Bilbo, American Racist

Theodore Gilmore Bilbo (1877–1947) was a Mississippi politician closely allied with the white supremacy movement. His nickname "The Man" belied his short stature (5 feet 2 inches or 157 centimeters)—a trait he shared with other well-known demagogues like Napoléon and Josef Goebbels. Bilbo's segregationist views together with his long political career meant he had a pernicious influence on race relations in Mississippi that continued to be felt long after his death. ("The Man" wasn't Bilbo's only nickname; his detractors also called him the "Bilbonic Plague.")[271]

Bilbo grew up in a poor farming family in rural Mississippi. Though he studied for the Baptist ministry at Peabody College in Nashville, Tennessee, and attended law school at Vanderbilt University in the same city, he never received a college degree.[272] Between the two years he spent at Peabody College (1897–1899) and two years at Vanderbilt (1905–1907), Bilbo was an itinerant teacher in rural southern Mississippi schools, where he married a fellow teacher. When they were teaching at a boarding school in Wiggins, Mississippi, and supervising a girls' dorm there, Bilbo caused a scandal by having an affair with an orphaned female student.[273] Neither his lack of a law degree nor the scandal prevented him from being admitted to the Tennessee bar or from setting up a law practice in Poplarville, Mississippi, in 1908. But he had higher ambitions. A Democrat, he served as a Mississippi state senator between 1908 and 1912 (the state senate tried unsuccessfully to oust him in 1910 after he became involved in a bribery scandal). He was lieutenant governor from 1912 to 1916, then was elected governor. As an indication of how some Mississippi residents viewed his election, the editor of the *Jackson Daily News* recommended that the eagle on the statehouse dome be replaced with a "puking buzzard."[274]

But Bilbo was elected on a populist platform, and in many respects he delivered. Earning the epithet "Bilbo the Builder," he backed many infrastructure projects, including a new highway system, a charity hospital and a tuberculosis hospital, and lime-crushing plants. He was also responsible for major tax reform and for the largest education appropriations ever. After Bilbo's first term (1916–1920), he was prevented by state law from succeeding himself. Eight years later he was reelected, despite having become embroiled in some memorable controversies. In the Democratic primary, he'd complained that his opponent (the incumbent governor) had called in the National Guard to thwart a lynching in Jackson—a misdirected effort, according to Bilbo, since the lives of African Americans weren't worth protecting. During the presidential election the same year (1928), Bilbo had campaigned for Al Smith, the Democratic candidate. Smith was Catholic and opposed Prohibition, but Bilbo helped him win in Mississippi despite the state's virulent anti-Catholic bias and support for Prohibition. Engaging in the kind of appeal to prejudice that demagogues often engage in, Bilbo trumped up a supposedly scandalous story about Herbert Hoover. He claimed that during a recent visit to the state to inspect flood damage, "Hoover insisted that his train be routed through Mount Bayou . . . in order that he might visit Mrs. Mary Booze, a negress, socially." (Booze was a member of the Republican National Committee.) The coup de grâce was that "Hoover danced with her."[275] The reference to dancing wasn't accidental, because Mississippi Baptists considered dancing sinful. Despite Bilbo's best efforts, Hoover was elected in a landslide.

The Hoover incident provided a hint of things to come. But before Bilbo's white supremacy campaign intensified, he became embroiled in a different controversy. Contemptuous of liberal intellectuals and of the university system in Mississippi, he decided to take action. In 1930, as part of a plan to consolidate the state's universities, he had dozens of faculty members fired and went after top administrators as well, gloating that "Boys, we've just hung up a new record. We've bounced three college presidents and made three new ones in the record time of two hours. And that's just the beginning of what's going to happen."[276] The students and remaining faculty at the University of Mississippi, Mississippi A&M (a precursor to Mississippi State University), and the Mississippi State College for Women suddenly discovered that their institutions were being led by a real estate agent, a press agent, and a recent college graduate, respectively. Another casualty was the dean of the University of Mississippi Medical School, replaced by someone the Bilbo administration considered qualified: a man who had once taken a course in dentistry. The result was a loss of accreditation for Mississippi's major colleges and universities for the next two years, until they could satisfy accrediting agencies that they met professional standards again. Although Bilbo was burned in effigy by students and brought scorn on himself and his state, he didn't seem to care.[277]

Bilbo's racist demagoguery burst into full bloom after his second term as governor ended in 1932. Two years later he was elected to the U.S. Senate. In what would today be considered a strange mixture of political views, he backed President Franklin D. Roosevelt's New Deal platform, while at the same time trying to advance his white supremacy agenda.[278] This agenda included membership in the Ku Klux Klan (which Bilbo admitted to in an interview on the *Meet the Press* radio show), relentless efforts to oppose the right of African Americans to vote, and several other actions for which he became notorious.

Bilbo was an outspoken critic of an antilynching bill debated in the Senate in 1938. His inflammatory rhetoric invoked racist stereotypes that persisted in milder forms into later eras: "If you succeed in the passage of this bill, you will open the floodgates of hell in the South. Raping, mobbing, lynching, race riots, and crime will be increased a thousandfold; and upon your garments and the garments of those who are responsible for the passage of the measure will be the blood of the raped and outraged daughters of Dixie, as well as the blood of the perpetrators of these crimes that the red-blooded Anglo-Saxon white Southern men will not tolerate."[279]

On April 24, 1939, Bilbo introduced the Greater Liberia Act in the Senate, calling for the voluntary repatriation of African Americans to West Africa at government expense. Ironically, though the bill was defeated, it had the support of some black nationalists, like Marcus Garvey, who saw repatriation as a solution to the racial oppression in the United States and other countries.

Bilbo was reelected to the Senate for a second term in 1940 and his racist rhetoric became increasingly vicious, in part as a response to the looming civil rights movement.

In 1945, he delivered a memorable attack on Richard Wright's autobiography, *Black Boy*: "Its purpose is to plant the seeds of devilment and troublebreeding in the days to come in the mind and heart of every American Negro. . . . It is the dirtiest, filthiest, lousiest, most obscene piece of writing that I have ever seen in print. I would hate to have a son or daughter of mine permitted to read it; it is so filthy and so dirty. But it comes from a Negro, and you cannot expect any better from a person of his type."[280]

Bilbo also expressed his bigotry in print. In 1947, he published a scurrilous book with the self-explanatory title *Take Your Choice: Separation or Mongrelization*.[281] Unless something was done, Bilbo warned in the preface, the "mongrelization" of the races was inevitable:

Surely every decent white man and woman in America should have cause to be alarmed over the mongrelization of their white race and the loss of their white civilization when Dr. Ralph S. Linton, a leading Professor of Anthropology of Columbia University, New York City, said just recently that at the present rate of intermarrying, interbreeding, and intermixing within nine generations, which is only 300 years, that there would be no white race nor black race in America—that all would be yellow. And in a recent article entitled "Who Is A Negro," Herbert Asbury makes the alarming and sickening statement that "more than two million United States Negroes have crossed the color line, contributing, among other things an ever-widening stream of black blood to the native white stock." . . .

Personally, the writer of this book would rather see his race and his civilization blotted out with the atomic bomb than to see it slowly but surely destroyed in the maelstrom of miscegenation, interbreeding, intermarriage and mongrelization. The destruction in either case would be inevitable—one in a flash and the other by the slow but certain process of sin, degradation, and mongrelization.[282]

The obvious answer, Bilbo argued, was separation—that is, the deportation of African Americans to Africa, as he had proposed in the Greater Liberia Act.

Bilbo was reelected to the Senate for a third term in 1946. Before he could be seated—the Republican-dominated Senate refused to seat him because of his bigotry and because of bribery allegations—he became seriously ill and returned to the South for medical treatment. Theodore "The Man" Bilbo died in New Orleans at age sixty-nine in 1947, leaving a poisonous legacy of racism behind.

<hr>

Test Your Skills

Identify a political figure in the world today that you regard as a bigot and another that you regard as a demagogue, or as showing tendencies toward demagoguery. Explain your choices.

<hr>

Joseph McCarthy, Anticommunist Witchhunter

Joseph Raymond McCarthy (1908–1957) was a very different kind of demagogue from Theodore Bilbo. But he, too, left considerable damage in his wake.

McCarthy grew up on a farm near Appleton, Wisconsin, and attended Marquette University, where he received his law degree in 1935. While practicing law, McCarthy ran for district attorney as a Democrat in 1936 and lost, but he won an election for circuit court judge in 1939. World War II interrupted what might have been a long judicial career. Though McCarthy didn't have to serve—he was exempt because of his judicial position—he joined the Marine Corps in 1942, supposedly because he thought experience in that branch of the service would advance his political career.[283]

McCarthy's military service was controversial. He seemed to share a need with other demagogues to appear more heroic than he actually was. Scholars have documented that he fabricated several aspects of his war record. Though his position as a judge earned him an automatic commission as an officer, he later insisted he'd joined the Marines as a "buck private." He also took credit for flying thirty-two combat missions in the South Pacific, making him eligible for the Distinguished Flying Cross he received in 1952. But the evidence shows he flew only twelve missions. Most embarrassingly, a wound he claimed to have received in combat was actually the result of a shipboard initiation ritual for sailors crossing the equator for the first time.[284]

While still in the Marines, McCarthy tried unsuccessfully to win the Republican Senate nomination in Wisconsin. After leaving the service in 1945, he was reelected to his position as a judge. In 1946 he battled again for the Republican Senate nomination, this time against Robert M. La Follette Jr. La Follette was a formidable opponent; he was part of a forty-year family political dynasty in Wisconsin. But McCarthy was up to the task. In a foreshadowing of the smear tactics he would later be famous for, McCarthy challenged La Follette's patriotism because he hadn't fought in the war (La Follette was in his mid-forties when the war began). McCarthy also accused his opponent of war profiteering, glossing over the fact that he too had profited from wartime investments. McCarthy's smear tactics dealt La Follette's campaign a major blow, and McCarthy won the election. Demoralized by the attacks, La Follette left politics. He committed suicide a few years later.

McCarthy's Senate term began in 1947, and he kept a low profile for the first two years. Though popular on the social circuit, his bad temper and irritability soon angered many of his Senate colleagues, especially in a case that took shape in 1949. Early that year, frustrated that his career had stalled and against the advice of friends, McCarthy decided to get involved with the Malmédy prisoner-of-war case. In the Battle of the Bulge in December 1944 and in the following weeks, German SS troops had massacred more than 500 U.S. prisoners and Belgian civilians in the vicinity of Malmédy, Belgium. After Germany surrendered in 1945, the U.S. military rounded up many of the perpetrators.

Seventy-four soldiers were charged with the atrocities and tried at Dachau. All but one—a French national—were found guilty. Forty-three were given death sentences; most of the sentences were later commuted to life imprisonment, with twelve death sentences remaining. A public outcry arose, because the German soldiers alleged that their confessions had been elicited under torture. McCarthy stepped into this volatile situation, siding with the Germans and arguing for the commutation of the remaining death sentences. His lobbying efforts outraged many senators and members of the public, and in a foreshadowing of his later censure by the Senate, the Senate press corps voted him the "worst" senator in office.[285] As one biographer writes, McCarthy's "brief but explosive encounter with the Malmédy case was a portent of his rendezvous with anti-Communism. He entered the picture perhaps thinking about his political future, quickly became swept away by a Cause, and was vicious and reckless toward all who challenged him."[286]

McCarthy's "rendezvous with anti-Communism" got underway in 1950. On February 9 of that year he gave a notorious speech in Wheeling, West Virginia. The details of his speech—delivered to the Republican Women's Club of Wheeling—are uncertain since no recording was preserved. But according to audience members, he waved a sheet of paper in the air and said something along these lines: "I have here in my hand a list of 205—a list of names that were made known to the Secretary of State as being members of the Communist Party and who nevertheless are still working and shaping policy in the State Department."[287]

In a different era, the speech might have gone unnoticed. But with the communist threat looming larger and larger in the collective psyche of Americans—China had fallen to the "Reds" in 1949 and the Soviets were solidifying their power in Eastern Europe—McCarthy's accusations took on added meaning.

The government responded swiftly. The Tydings Committee—a subcommittee of the Senate Foreign Relations Committee chaired by Maryland Democrat Millard E. Tydings—was convened to investigate the accuracy of McCarthy's charges. The highly partisan committee split along party lines, with Tydings concluding that McCarthy's accusations were "a fraud and a hoax" and the Republicans countering that the Democratic majority had whitewashed the problem. The full Senate voted three times on whether to accept the committee findings, each time splitting along party lines.

McCarthy got his revenge against Tydings; when Tydings ran for reelection to a fifth Senate term in 1950, McCarthy campaigned for his Republican opponent and helped him win. The conduct of McCarthy and his staff was so sleazy that a Senate subcommittee held an investigation, blaming them for "a despicable, back-street type of campaign."[288] Among other things, McCarthy's staff had helped produce campaign literature containing a doctored photo purportedly showing Tydings conversing with Earl Browder, a communist leader.

McCarthy stepped up his attacks on what he claimed was the subversive element in the U.S. government, which brought him a growing following but caused growing dismay among civil libertarians. One person who looked askance at McCarthy's witchhunting tactics was the cartoonist Herb Block, better known as Herblock, who is credited with coining the term *McCarthyism* as a synonym for demagoguery. He first used this term in a cartoon that appeared in the *Washington Post* on March 29, 1950.

McCarthy's relationship with the Democratic administration of Harry S. Truman was hostile. His 1950 West Virginia speech had targeted Truman's State Department for harboring communists. McCarthy reserved some of his most vicious attacks for George Marshall, Secretary of Defense under Truman. Using the inflammatory rhetoric typical of demagogues, McCarthy lambasted Marshall for being involved in "a conspiracy so immense and an infamy so black as to dwarf any previous venture in the history of man."[289] This accusation seemed especially inappropriate because Marshall was a distinguished public servant. Before serving as Truman's Defense Secretary, he had been Army Chief of Staff in World War II. As the architect of the Marshall Plan—charged with reconstructing postwar Europe—he received the 1953 Nobel Peace Prize.

McCarthy had exclaimed of Truman that "the son of a bitch should be impeached."[290] Truman's successor, Dwight D. Eisenhower, didn't fare much better at McCarthy's hands, despite the fact that McCarthy and Eisenhower were both Republicans. As he had with Truman, McCarthy alleged that Eisenhower was soft on communism. In late 1953, he stopped speaking of the "twenty years of treason" under Democratic administrations, changing the phrase to "*twenty-one* years of treason" to encompass Eisenhower's first year as president.[291] Eisenhower refused to counterattack, saying he wasn't willing to "get into the gutter" with McCarthy.[292]

McCarthy's anticommunist crusade received considerable support from the Catholic community, including the Kennedy family. A major backer was Joseph P. Kennedy Sr., who was staunchly anticommunist and may have subtly reinforced McCarthy's opposition to the "Reds." The Kennedys were fond of McCarthy and often invited him to Hyannisport, flying him there in their private plane. He dated both Eunice and Patricia Kennedy; when Eunice married R. Sargent Shriver in 1953, he gave them a silver cigarette box with this inscription: "To Eunice and Bob, from one who lost. Joe McCarthy."[293] McCarthy became the godfather of Robert F. and Ethel S. Kennedy's oldest child, Kathleen, born in 1951, gave Robert Kennedy a job in 1952, and served in the Senate together with John F. Kennedy beginning in 1953.

After his reelection to the Senate in 1952, McCarthy was named chairman of the Senate Committee on Government Operations. Subsumed under this committee was a subcommittee called the Senate Permanent Subcommittee on Investigations, which became the engine of McCarthy's anticommunist crusade. In January 1953 he chose Roy Cohn as his chief counsel and Robert Kennedy—only twenty-seven and a recent University of Virginia Law School graduate—as an assistant counsel.

McCarthy lost no time demonstrating his underhanded tactics. The committee first zeroed in on the Voice of America (VOA), then a unit of the United States Information Agency. VOA employees were dragged before television cameras, where McCarthy grilled them mercilessly about their alleged communist sympathies. Though none of these allegations were substantiated, the VOA was thrown into disarray, and one VOA engineer committed suicide.

One of McCarthy's subsequent targets put up greater resistance, and in fact led to his undoing. In the fall of 1953, he went after the U.S. Army. Various ill-advised and unsuccessful attempts to turn up evidence of subversion in the army so angered its supporters—including President Eisenhower—that they mounted a counterattack. This took the form of the Army-McCarthy hearings, which convened on April 22, 1954. Lasting thirty-six days and broadcast live to a television audience of about twenty million, the hearings badly damaged McCarthy's career.

Though McCarthy was not found to have exercised improper influence, the public got a prolonged look at his demagogic, bullying tactics and many didn't like what they saw. The most memorable attack on McCarthy's character during the hearings came in a confrontation between him and Joseph Welch, the army's chief legal representative. Offended by McCarthy's attempt to slander one of his (Welch's) legal associates, Welch asked, "Have you no sense of decency, sir? At long last, have you no sense of decency?"[294]

Some senators had spoken out against McCarthy from the beginning. On June 1, 1950, Senator Margaret Chase Smith (R-ME) had presented her "Declaration of Conscience," which urged an end to smear tactics but did not mention McCarthy by name. On June 1, 1954, Senator Ralph E. Flanders (R-VT) gave a speech comparing McCarthy to Hitler, and he subsequently introduced a resolution to censure McCarthy. After much deliberation and modification of the resolution, the Senate voted on December 2, 1954, to "condemn" him for various forms of misconduct. The vote was sixty-seven to twenty-two, with all the Democrats present favoring condemnation and the Republicans evenly divided. The only senator who didn't vote was John Kennedy, who was in the hospital for back surgery. Kennedy never said how he would have voted and was always reluctant to criticize McCarthy, because of their social ties and because McCarthy continued to have widespread support in Massachusetts.[295]

McCarthy remained in the Senate for another two and a half years after his censure but became a broken man. Though he continued to harangue against communism, he was ignored by his colleagues as well as by the press. On May 2, 1957, he died in Bethesda Naval Hospital of liver problems assumed by most of his biographers to be related to alcoholism.

Test Your Skills

In the March 9, 1954, episode of *See It Now*—the TV program he hosted—legendary newscaster Edward R. Murrow launched a devastating attack on Senator Joseph McCarthy for his witchhunting tactics. Murrow said of McCarthy: "His primary achievement has been in confusing the public mind, as between the internal and the external threats of Communism. We must not confuse dissent with disloyalty. We must remember always that accusation is not proof and that conviction depends upon evidence and due process of law. We will not walk in fear, one of another. We will not be driven by fear into an age of unreason, if we dig deep in our history and our doctrine, and remember that we are not descended from fearful men."[1] Based on your understanding of McCarthy's behavior and on the charges Murrow makes in this famous passage, describe as many of McCarthy's demagogic tactics as you can

---

1   "*Edward R. Murrow: A Report on Senator Joseph R. McCarthy,*" *See It Now,* CBS, March 9, 1954, transcript, *www.lib.berkeley.edu/MRC/murrowmccarthy. html.*

Conclusion

This chapter has provided a window into the lives of three bigots and demagogues: Adolf Hitler, Theodore Bilbo, and Joseph McCarthy. Though they represented different cultural backgrounds and time periods and the scale of their activities differed—only Hitler killed millions—the politics and behavior of all three reflected certain commonalities. Engaging in simplistic, stereotypical thinking, all three accepted the prejudices of their time unquestioningly and magnified them. And all three used hate-filled oratory and propaganda to demonize the "Other": Jewish people and other "non-Aryans" in the case of Hitler, African Americans in the case of Bilbo, communists in the case of McCarthy.

Certain types of social and economic conditions are more conducive than others to the kinds of problems just discussed. Allport writes in his influential book *The Nature of Prejudice* that prerequisites to antisocial behavior often include "a tottering social structure," while "prosperity and stability are poor soil" for troublemakers.[296] It behooves all of us to work toward social stability and justice, in order to create "poor soil" for bigotry and demagoguery.

In the next chapter, I explore a different, more specific arena of conflict between truth and falsehood: the legal system.

What You Can Do

√*Watch for telltale signs of bigotry and demagoguery.* Both these problems play on people's fears and insecurities by scapegoating certain groups and falsely holding them accountable for social or economic ills. These groups are often demonized by means of propaganda techniques, so you should be on the lookout for ethnic slurs, stereotyping, scare tactics, and the other propaganda techniques you learned about in Chapter 2.

√*Head off problems before they get out of control.* As you've seen in this chapter, bigots and demagogues are often exceptionally dangerous and must be thwarted before they gain power—otherwise it may be too late. Some of these individuals provide a blueprint of their antisocial program ahead of time; these warning signals should be taken very seriously. One of the great tragedies of history is that Hitler provided just such a blueprint in *Mein Kampf,* yet most readers dismissed this book as the work of a madman until it was too late. As one scholar explains,

> Intellectuals, as well as the masses for whom the writing was intended, found it difficult and obnoxious to follow Hitler's tortuous thinking, his redundancies, and his convoluted, crude language [in *Mein Kampf*]. Many politically neutral readers, and even sympathizers, were stunned by the unmitigated hatred. Outside the Third Reich, the book was widely depicted as a piece of propaganda produced by a sick mind, rather than as the work of a major statesman. Because readers were shocked by Hitler's style, some of his remarks on nationalism and socialism and his critical and constructive comments about the social and political evils of the period were minimized and overlooked. If the book had been carefully studied, the probability of underestimating Hitler during his ascent as a major political figure might have been smaller.[297]

√*Take collective action.* To be effective, resistance often requires collective as well as individual action. Defusing the threat posed by bigots and demagogues may necessitate complex, long-term strategies on the part of many individuals working together. As distasteful as it may seem, you and your fellow citizens may have to build bridges with the zealots or bigots so as to allow them to air their grievances. You will also need to find a way of broadening their horizons, especially by humanizing the groups targeted by their prejudice. Concrete social reforms that address the problems of these disaffected individuals—such as by creating more educational or economic opportunity—may also be essential. While these measures may seem daunting, the stakes are high.

√*Address the underlying causes of antisocial behavior.* Even a brief exploration of the lives of history's most notorious demagogues turns up a striking fact: almost all of these men seem to have been bullied or abused as children. And many were ridiculed for being too short, too "effeminate," or otherwise failing to measure up to norms of masculinity. Obviously, few men who are abused become demagogues; complex psychological, social, and historical factors had to come together to produce a Hitler or his counterparts in other cultures. But the message is obvious: one of the most important things you can do to eliminate the conditions that lead to demagoguery—as well as other antisocial behavior—is to combat child abuse, including all forms of bullying in and outside of school.

Bullying deserves special attention because of its pernicious effects. The Internet has offered new opportunities for bullying, and children are especially vulnerable: "About 30 to 40 percent of young Americans responding to recent surveys reported having been bullied online. Every moment of every day, in instant messages, e-mails, and postings, millions of children demean their peers, sully their reputations, threaten them with physical harm, and even call for their deaths. This online mean-spiritedness makes its toxic effects very much felt offline."[298] For more information on cyberbullying and on what you can do to combat it, go to sites like these:

- Stop Cyberbullying (www.stopcyberbullying.org), associated with WiredSafety.org (www.wiredsafety.org)
- Cyberbullying Research Center (www.cyberbullying.us), a clearinghouse of information on many facets of bullying

- Workplace Bullying Institute (WBI) (www.workplacebullying. org), a source of information on work-related bullying

√*Take advantage of the resources provided by human rights organizations and other groups combating antisocial behavior.* Well-known examples include the following:

- Simon Wiesenthal Center (www.wiesenthal.com), an influential Jewish human rights organization
- Museum of Tolerance (www.museumoftolerance.com), a unique Los Angeles museum that serves as the educational arm of the Simon Wiesenthal Center; each year, hundreds of thousands of visitors see or take part in its interactive exhibits on the Holocaust and other topics related to bigotry and hatred
- Southern Poverty Law Center (www.splcenter.org), an organization that began as a civil rights law firm in Alabama in 1971 and monitors hate groups, including the many groups now targeting women

Further Reading

For general works on bigotry and demagoguery, see R. S. Robins and J. M. Post, *Political Paranoia: The Psychopolitics of Hatred* (New Haven, CT: Yale University Press, 1997); Robert M. Baird and Stuart E. Rosenbaum, eds., *Hatred, Bigotry, and Prejudice: Definitions, Causes, and Solutions* (Amherst, NY: Prometheus Books, 1999); and Michael Signer, *Demagogue: The Fight to Save Democracy from Its Worst Enemies* (New York: Palgrave Macmillan, 2009). Gordon W. Allport's classic book on prejudice is still timely after more than a half century; see his *The Nature of Prejudice*, 25th anniv. ed. (Reading, MA: Addison-Wesley, [1954] 1979). For a readable case study, see Antero Pietila, *Not in My Neighborhood: How Bigotry Shaped a Great American City* (Lanham, MD: Ivan R. Dee / Rowman & Littlefield, 2010).

For an overview of Hitler's formative years and the years in which he came to power, see Ian Kershaw, *Hitler 1889–1936: Hubris* (New York: Norton, 1998). Kershaw discusses Hitler's misogyny and other aspects of his relationships with women on pp. 44–46, 351–355. Also see Anna Maria Sigmund, *Women of the Third Reich* (Richmond Hill, Ontario: NDE Publishing, [1998] 2000); Guido Knopp, *Hitler's Women*, trans. Angus McGeoch (New York: Routledge, [2001] 2003); and Alison Owings, *Frauen: German Women Recall the Third Reich* (New Brunswick, NJ: Rutgers University Press, 1993). In his *Hitler: Diagnosis of a Destructive Prophet* (New York: Oxford University Press, 1999), Fritz Redlich provides a detailed review of the pathologies underlying Hitler's behavior; see especially the chapter titled "A Psychopathological Profile" (pp. 255–339). Ron Rosenbaum's *Explaining Hitler: The Search for the Origins of His Evil* (New York: Random House, 1998) is a provocative look at the attempts to explain Hitler's behavior.

On Bilbo, see Chester M. Morgan, *Redneck Liberal: Theodore G. Bilbo and the New Deal* (Baton Rouge: Louisiana State University Press, 1985). Also see Robert L. Fleegler, "Theodore G. Bilbo and the Decline of Public Racism, 1938–1947," *Journal of Mississippi History*, spring 2006, http://www.mdah.state.ms.us/pubs/bilbo.pdf, as well as Thayer Watkins,

"Theodore G. Bilbo of Mississippi," Department of Economics, San José State University, http://www.applet-magic.com/bilbo.htm. For the larger context, see Keith M. Finley, *Delaying the Dream: Southern Senators and the Fight against Civil Rights, 1938–1965* (Baton Rouge: Louisiana State University Press, 2008).

For accounts of McCarthyism, see David M. Oshinsky, *A Conspiracy So Immense: The World of Joe McCarthy* (Oxford: Oxford University Press, 2005); Tom Wicker, *Shooting Star: The Brief Arc of Joe McCarthy* (Orlando, FL: Harcourt, 2006); and Arthur Herman, *Joseph McCarthy: Reexamining the Life and Legacy of America's Most Hated Senator* (New York: Free Press, 2000).

On other bigots and demagogues, see Alan Brinkley, *Voices of Protest: Huey Long, Father Coughlin, and the Great Depression* (New York: Knopf, 1982).

8. THE LEGAL WEB

Have you heard these lawyer jokes?
What do you know when you find a lawyer up to his neck in concrete?

Someone ran out of concrete.[299]

How do you know when a lawyer is lying?

His lips move.[300]

Why does New Jersey have so many toxic waste dumps and California have so many lawyers? Because New Jersey got first choice.[301]

Surveys rank lawyers among the least popular professionals. In their book *Devil's Advocates: The Unnatural History of Lawyers*—a collection of unflattering anecdotes about lawyers throughout history—Andrew Roth and Jonathan Roth cite a survey in which "only 19 percent [of respondents] credited lawyers with 'high or very high' ethical standards, ranking them below druggists, dentists and funeral directors. In yet another, only 12 percent expressed a 'great deal of confidence' in lawyers—last out of fifteen major institutions studied."[302] The perception of the legal profession as corrupt is nothing new; in the 1780s, both Prussia and France went as far as to abolish it, though they later restored it when it became apparent that lawyers were necessary to the smooth functioning of those countries' political and social institutions.[303]

Why this lack of popularity? Over the centuries in the United States and other countries, many people have found the justice system isn't always just. Instead it has often rested on a legal web of deceit and misconduct that can result in unfair verdicts, sometimes even involving the death penalty or life in prison for innocent people. As a Scythian sage named Anacharsis put it about 600 BCE, "Laws are just like spider's webs, they will hold the weak and delicate who might be caught in their meshes, but will be torn to pieces by the rich and powerful."[304]

In the following pages, I explore problems with the legal profession and recommend some things you can do to keep from becoming entangled in the legal web.

"Even the Rich Have Rights!"

One of the most persistent complaints is that money buys justice. The idea that money buys justice is reflected in the ironic title of one of the chapters of Irving Stone's bestselling biography of Clarence Darrow, *Clarence Darrow for the Defense*.[305] The chapter—titled "Even the Rich Have Rights!"—describes Darrow's handling of the famous Leopold and Loeb murder case. The brutality of this crime, the affluence of the defendants, and other aspects of the case led it to be billed as the "crime of the century."

Early in the morning of Sunday, June 1, 1924, Darrow and his wife Ruby were wakened in their Chicago home by the insistent ringing of the doorbell. Then sixty-seven, Darrow was America's most famous trial attorney; he was a brilliant orator and cross-examiner who often won victories against seemingly impossible odds. The four men who burst in implored him to represent two teenage boys who had just confessed to a horrific crime. The group included the uncle of one of the accused, who got down on his knees and begged Darrow to save his nephew from execution.

Ten days earlier (on May 22), a fourteen-year-old boy named Robert Franks had been found bludgeoned to death in a culvert along the Illinois-Indiana border. Several clues—mainly a pair of distinctive glasses carelessly dropped at the scene—cast suspicion on two young men from prominent families. Nathan F. Leopold Jr. (who was nineteen) and Richard A. Loeb (eighteen) confessed to the crime, admitting it was a thrill killing. The scions of millionaires, neither needed the $10,000 ransom they demanded. They led lives of extraordinary privilege:

Nathan F. Leopold, Jr., and Richard A. Loeb had been raised in the fashionable South Shore section of Chicago. Leopold's father was a retired millionaire box manufacturer, while Loeb's father was the multimillionaire vice-president of Sears, Roebuck and Company. The Loeb estate at Charlevoix, Michigan, was set in the midst of hundreds of acres of magnificently wooded country. The two boys were raised amidst great wealth from their early childhood, with governesses, chauffeurs and the soft, luxurious appurtenances that can be bought by millionaires. Loeb had an allowance of two hundred and fifty dollars a month, with three thousand dollars in the bank under his own name and a standing order from his father to the family secretary that "Dickie" was to be given a check for any sum of money at any time without question. Though Leopold was given only half as large a monthly allowance, he had the family chauffeur to drive him, his own car, charge accounts in the big stores and could have any amount of money for which he asked.[306]

The public was intrigued not only by their wealth but also by their prodigious intellects; in 1923 Leopold and Loeb had graduated from the University of Chicago and the University of Michigan, respectively, supposedly the youngest graduates ever of those institutions.[307] Leopold in particular was known for his brilliance. Widely read in philosophy, science, and other fields, he was an ornithology expert who published articles on the subject and had a highly regarded bird museum in his home. Chillingly, Leopold had discovered the German philosopher Friedrich Nietzsche in his early teens and had become fascinated with Nietzsche's concept of superman. This fascination played a key role in the murder.

The salacious details of the case aroused even more interest than the intellectual precocity of the young men. Reporters and court psychiatrists brought out the fact that at least one of the youths had been sexually abused by a governess, made much of the homosexual relationship between the two (who may have abused their victim, either before or after his death), and noted Leopold's gender ambiguity. Leopold had been partly raised as a girl; his mother—disappointed he was not the daughter she longed for—briefly sent him to a girl's school, where he was one of only two boys.[308]

Leopold's gender ambiguity, together with his conservative assumptions about gender roles, seemed to manifest themselves in his obsession with Nietzsche's idea of superman. For Nietzsche, a superman (or "overman," as the German *Übermensch* is sometimes translated) was a superior being destined to rule the world unencumbered by ordinary moral and legal constraints.[309] But Leopold "did not want to become a superman at all; he wanted to become a superwoman, a superwife, the female slave of the superman above him, a voluntary and joyous slave who served out of the overwhelming love which he bore for the superman."[310] Leopold (or "Babe," as his family and friends called him) ended up being superwoman to Richard Loeb's superman: "Babe, who never performed sexual acts with any other boy, implored Dickie Loeb to have relations with him. Loeb, who had been seeking eagerly for several years for a crony who would carry out his orders in committing crimes, decided that he had found the perfect mate in Leopold to help him plan and execute these crimes. He agreed to a homosexual relationship with Leopold, if Leopold would agree to a crime relationship with him. Leopold consented unquestioningly, and the complex was formed."[311] William Alanson White, an influential psychiatrist, testified at the trial that the "interdigitated" or interlocking personalities of the two young men made the Franks murder possible; Leopold alone wouldn't have been motivated to do it because he had no criminal tendencies and Loeb couldn't have pulled it off without an accomplice.[312]

Popular sentiment against the defendants ran high, and Darrow was pilloried for taking the case of such notorious (and notoriously rich) defendants. Justifying his actions by explaining that the case gave him a platform for his campaign against capital punishment, he managed to save Leopold and Loeb from execution. His case rested on the argument that they were mentally ill; why else, for example, would Loeb have claimed that "it is just as easy to justify such a death as it is to justify an entomologist in killing a beetle on a pin"?[313] Darrow prevailed and the two young men received a life sentence. Loeb was killed in prison in

1936 at the age of thirty; the inmate alleged to have slashed him more than fifty times with a straight razor in the shower was acquitted, apparently because of the jury's homophobia. (The jury foreman wrote years later that "nobody liked a queer, a homo, or a lesbian . . . so it was a good thing to get rid of such people.")[314] Leopold was paroled to Puerto Rico in 1958, when he was in his early fifties. After working as a hospital technician and medical researcher, earning a master's degree, writing a book on Puerto Rican birds, and getting married (to a florist and former social worker from Baltimore), the sixty-six-year-old Leopold died of a heart attack in Puerto Rico in 1971.

For years, large segments of the public remained outraged by the verdict in the Leopold and Loeb case and by Darrow's role in it, convinced that only the very rich could have escaped the gallows for so brutal and senseless a crime.

The Legal Profession: "Enveloping the Whole of Society"

Lawyers like Darrow have become so ubiquitous in recent centuries that you might think they've always been around, but they haven't. Legal history is closely intertwined with political history. Legal systems would have been superfluous in small, traditional societies where ethical behavior was enforced by social norms. But with the emergence of urban civilization in Mesopotamia, Egypt, China, and elsewhere, elaborate systems of rules defining people's rights and responsibilities were developed. One of the earliest examples is the Code of Hammurabi, a set of laws inscribed on an eight-foot-high stela (stone slab or pillar) about 1760 BCE in Babylon. Another example is the Hebrew Bible or Old Testament—composed between about the fifteenth and second centuries BCE—which contains moral injunctions or rules of conduct still influential in the United States and other countries. Roman law also connects the ancient world with contemporary Western society, because many of its principles found their way into European and English law.

In the United States, lawyers came into their own in the nineteenth century, as Alexis de Tocqueville observes in his classic work, *Democracy in America.*[315] Tocqueville and a friend were sent by the French government to study the U.S. penal system in 1831–1832. During their nine and a half months in the United States (and a few days in Canada), they covered more than 7,000 miles in an area bounded by New England in the East, Wisconsin in the West, Louisiana in the South, and Canada in the North. Published in two volumes in 1835 and 1840, *Democracy in America* offers wide-ranging insights into U.S. institutions, including the legal profession. Tocqueville doesn't mince words about the inordinate power wielded by this profession in the young country: "Lawyers in the United States constitute a power that arouses little fear, that is barely perceived, that flies no banner of its own, that supplely bends to the exigencies of the times and surrenders without resistance to every movement of the social body. Yet it envelops the whole of society, worms its way into each of the constituent classes, works on the society in secret, influences it constantly without its knowledge, and in the end shapes it to its own desires."[316]

In the decades after Tocqueville's visit, the United States was transformed by industrialization and urbanization. These trends led to the emergence of corporate law firms around the turn of the twentieth century. Corporate law firms proliferated and became influential out of any proportion to their numbers. Their priorities and the priorities of their clientele "shaped professional education, career patterns, ethics, mobility, and the availability and distribution of legal services—indeed, the very meaning of law and justice."[317] One result was a higher proportion of lawyers in the United States than in other countries and a very litigious society:

In 1989, the United States held over 750,000 practicing lawyers, about one for every 350 people. In New York, one out of every 230 inhabitants is a lawyer; in Washington DC, one out of every twenty-two.

Compare these figures with the more fortunate Europeans: in Great Britain, the ratio is one lawyer for every 1,500 citizens; in Italy, 1 in 1,500; and in France, 1 in 6,000. Japan comes out on top yet again: It has managed to keep its lawyer population down to a startling and admirable one for every 14,000 people.[318]

Today there are over a million lawyers in the United States, and U.S. lawyers are estimated to make up between a quarter and a third of the world's attorneys.[319]

That doesn't mean the legal profession in the United States has always flourished. Its nadir occurred in the aftermath of the Watergate burglary in 1972. Unfortunately for the profession's image, twelve of the fifteen major players were lawyers. This group included Attorney General John Mitchell, Vice President Spiro Agnew—not to mention President Richard Nixon, a 1937 graduate of the Duke University Law School. One outcome was the growth of the legal self-help movement, designed to enable ordinary people to cut lawyers out of the loop and to take care of their own legal problems.

No amount of legal help, whether self-help or otherwise, is enough to address problems when society doesn't want to take responsibility for them. The notorious Glen Ridge case provides a well-known example.

The Glen Ridge Case

When "Leslie Faber" (not her real name) rushed home from school, gulped down a glass of milk, grabbed her basketball and portable radio, and headed out the door to the park nearby to shoot some hoops, neither she nor her parents had any way of knowing that their lives would be forever changed after that day. The setting was the New Jersey suburb of Glen Ridge in March 1989, and Leslie was a seventeen-year-old with mental disabilities. As Bernard Lefkowitz shows in his excellent book *Our Guys: The Glen Ridge Rape and the Secret Life of the Perfect Suburb*, Glen Ridge appeared to be an idyllic, "picture-perfect" suburb, but like many other American suburbs, it hid an unsavory reality.[320]

When Leslie got to the basketball court, she found that the boys' baseball team was holding an informal practice on a nearby baseball diamond, and a bunch of football players and other star athletes were hanging out and watching the practice. A good athlete, Leslie had grown up with many of the boys and idolized them. But they were the cool jocks who belonged to the in crowd; she was the mentally disabled girl who usually played alone and was never invited to the other kids' parties. Leslie shot baskets alone for a half hour, then to her surprise five or six of the boys walked over to the basketball court.

The ringleader was a boy named Chris whose older brother Leslie adored. When Chris invited her to a party, Leslie demurred because something didn't seem right; after all, this had never happened before. But after Chris told her his brother would be there and would go out with her, she eagerly accompanied the boys to a house in the neighborhood. They took her into the basement, where they joined a group of boys already there. What happened next made the national news.

At first Leslie was thrilled to be in the basement, which seemed to her to be a sort of athletic clubhouse; sports trophies lined some of the shelves, and other shelves held basketballs, bats, gloves, and other equipment. The boys were initially friendly and joked around about sports and other topics. But their banter soon gave way to an uglier mood. Alarmed, some of the young men left, but seven remained. Over the next hour they forced Leslie to have oral sex and assaulted her repeatedly with a baseball bat, broomstick, and other objects.

The case caused a sensation in Glen Ridge and left the town bitterly divided. It exposed the ugly underbelly of many communities in America: the adulation of young male athletes, who are allowed to engage in destructive behavior with impunity: "The most heartless acts of the Jocks hadn't been publicized in Glen Ridge. They hadn't been arrested for wrecking houses and trashing the country club. They hadn't been thrown out of school for exposing themselves or for assaulting girls. The boys' behavior had always been the town's best-kept secret. None of the institutions in Glen Ridge had said anything to alert the parents of vulnerable children. Their transgressions remained hidden from folks like the Fabers."[321]

Leslie's ordeal wasn't over. In the courtroom proceedings, the boys' lawyers essentially put her on trial, dragging her through the mud as being promiscuous and as having provoked the attacks. One lawyer "shredded [her] reputation in an opening statement to the jury that had courtroom spectators gasping at its ferocity."[322] Leslie did receive justice to some extent: three of the four principal defendants (including the ringleader, Chris) were convicted of sexual assault, and a fourth was convicted of lesser charges. But reasoning that "you didn't want to lock up all-American boys and throw the key away,"[323] the judge reduced what could have been forty-year sentences for some of the defendants to a few months in prison. This case, and others like it, reveal some disturbing truths about U.S. society:

> In the Glen Ridge case, at the moment of decision, the judge decided that the damage done to this woman weighed less heavily than concern for the futures of the rapists and sympathy for their families. . . . These misguided and ultimately dehumanizing values were not exclusive to this one small town. As the continuing revelations of sexual harassment and abuse in the military, in colleges, in the workplace, and in many other spheres suggest, these values have deep roots in American life. . . . The law follows culture, and until we reexamine how we mold children and what we expect of our creations, we don't have a right to hold judges and lawyers to a higher standard than our own.[324]

As the Glen Ridge case indicates, rape and harassment cases consistently bring out some of the most unethical conduct on the part of lawyers and judges. One district attorney has admitted that more often than not, "'Trash the victim' is the only real form of defense . . . no matter what the law says."[325] A public defender's comments typify the attitude of many lawyers trying these cases: "The bottom line is getting my client off. [I am] more concerned with this one guy and his freedom than the ethical issue of sexism."[326] Another attorney, asked about the humiliating cross-examination he'd subjected a harassment victim to, was equally unconcerned with ethical issues: "It's certainly something I'd prefer not to do—but I don't allow myself the luxury of regret."[327] This unethical conduct by lawyers helps explain why more than 90 percent of sexual assault and harassment cases go unreported.[328]

A systemic problem contributing to these abuses has been the exclusion of women from the legal profession until relatively recently.

Though the first woman lawyer arrived in America from England in 1638, settling in Maryland, it would take two or three centuries for women to be admitted to the bar and to be accepted by law schools.[329] Women were admitted to practice law in most states between about 1870 and 1920. Law school admissions took longer; public institutions in the more egalitarian Western states led the way in the nineteenth century, but Harvard Law School didn't admit women until 1950. The most influential male lawyers fought vehemently against women's entry into the legal profession. These male lawyers included Clarence Darrow, who reportedly offered this advice to a group of women attorneys in Chicago: "You can't be shining lights at the bar because you are too kind. You can never be corporation lawyers because you are not cold-blooded. You have not a high grade of intellect. You can never expect to get the fees men get. I doubt if you [can] ever make a living. Of course you can be divorce lawyers. That is a useful field. And there is another field you can have solely for your own. You can't make a living at it, but it's worthwhile and you'll have no competition. That is the free defense of criminals."[330]

Ironically, the legal web has ensnared more than its share of victims in the criminal-defense cases Darrow recommended women lawyers handle without pay, as the problem of wrongful convictions shows.

Test Your Skills

The legal web can be especially pernicious in family law cases, such as divorce and child custody cases. Vengeance often prevails among warring spouses, and many lawyers are complicit. One attorney asks male clients, "Has it occurred to you that in divorce action, children can be a valuable commodity?"[1] From personal experience or from your knowledge of disputes involving public figures, discuss the way participants in these disputes are often drawn into a web of recriminations and distortions. Can you envision a better system, one that, for example, doesn't pit spouses against each other or force children to take sides? What would this system look like?

---

1   *Maurice Franks; quoted in Deborah L. Rhode, In the Interests of Justice: Reformsing the Legal Profession (New York: Oxford University Press, 2000), 85–86.*

Wrongful Convictions

In January 2000, Illinois Governor George Ryan's decision to declare a moratorium on the death penalty in his state attracted media attention around the country. Arguing that the system was badly flawed, Ryan noted that since Illinois reinstated capital punishment in 1977, more people had been freed because of wrongful convictions (thirteen) than had been executed (twelve).[331] One of the thirteen, Anthony Porter, was freed just two days before his scheduled execution. Journalism students at Northwestern University uncovered evidence that led to his release after he'd spent sixteen years on death row. Ryan called for an investigation into cases like Porter's to determine what had gone wrong. Despite being a death-penalty advocate, he said he did not feel the state should go forward with executions until the system could ensure that "everyone sentenced to death in Illinois is truly guilty."[332]

Two years later, the Illinois panel investigating the death penalty released a report recommending sweeping changes in the system. The panel's eighty-five recommendations included the following:

- Videotaping of all interrogations of capital suspects conducted in a police facility.
- Reducing the number of crimes eligible for a death sentence from 20 to five. . . .
- Forbidding capital punishment in cases where the conviction is based solely on the testimony of a single eyewitness.
- Barring capital punishment in cases where the defendant is mentally [disabled]. . . .
- Intensifying the scrutiny of testimony provided by in-custody informants during a pre-trial hearing to determine the reliability of the testimony before it is received in a capital trial.
- Requiring a trial judge to concur with a jury's determination that a death sentence is appropriate; or, if not, sentence the defendant to natural life.[333]

In 2011, the Illinois legislature approved a permanent ban on the death penalty, and one of Ryan's successors as governor, Pat Quinn, signed the bill.

The death-penalty debate in Illinois and other states was foreshadowed decades earlier by a book titled *Convicting the Innocent: Sixty-Five Actual Errors of Criminal Justice* (1932).[334] The book's author was a Yale law professor named Edwin Borchard, whose review uncovered irrefutable evidence that eight murder convictions were erroneous: the so-called victims subsequently turned up alive. Especially since 1989, when innocent prisoners began to be freed with the aid of DNA tests, many other investigations have uncovered abuses of the justice system. The evidence shows that a disproportionate number of these abuses have affected defendants who are African American and poor—for example,

African Americans make up 57 percent of exonerated defendants.[335] In a typical case, Alan Crotzer was exonerated in Florida in 2006 after spending more than twenty-four years in prison for crimes he didn't commit. He and two codefendants had been convicted of a 1981 rape, kidnapping, and robbery. But DNA tests proved Crotzer's innocence and his 130-year prison sentence was overturned. In 2008 the State of Florida awarded Crotzer $1.25 million in compensation for the time he'd spent in prison—more than half his life.[336]

Many organizations have been created to address injustices of this nature. One of the best known is the Innocence Project, consisting of many nonprofit legal clinics in the United States and Canada.[337] The project was founded in affiliation with Yeshiva University in New York in 1992, after investigations uncovered major problems in the justice system. These problems included a rate of wrongful convictions estimated at 5 percent, so that as many as 100,000 prisoners could be unjustly incarcerated in the U.S. system at any given time. (Other studies have estimated that the figure could be as high as 10 percent.)[338] The mission of the Innocence Project's nonprofit clinic at Yeshiva University, like that of its counterparts elsewhere, is to exonerate wrongfully convicted individuals through DNA analysis as well as to push for legal reform. The efforts of the Innocence Project and other organizations have led to the exoneration of several hundred prisoners by means of postconviction DNA testing. Unjust convictions are only part of the problem; putting the wrong person in prison often means the actual perpetrator is still at large. About 45 percent of the DNA exonerations to date have led to the identification of the real perpetrator.[339]

Did You Know?

The Judgment of Solomon Could Have Had a Disastrous Outcome If Lie Detectors Had Existed

In the famous biblical story of the "Judgment of Solomon" (1 Kings 3:16–28), King Solomon was confronted with two women who each claimed a baby as her own. To resolve the dispute, he said he'd split the baby in half with his sword so each woman could have half. One woman found this plan acceptable, but the other was horrified and agreed to give up her claim in order to save the baby's life. King Solomon gave the baby to the latter mother, believing the maternal instinct would compel the real mother to save the life of her child. In other words, he interpreted the woman's emotional plea as a sign of truthfulness. The outcome wouldn't necessarily be the same today, because to many law enforcement professionals and others who administer lie-detector (polygraph) tests, "emotional arousal is associated with deceit"![1]

---

1   Charles V. Ford, *Lies! Lies!! Lies!!!: The Psychology of Deceit* (Washington, DC: American Psychiatric Press, 1996), 222.

The high rate of wrongful convictions has been attributed to many factors, apart from the racial and economic biases just mentioned. The Innocence Project has identified seven common causes of wrongful convictions:

- Eyewitness misidentification
- Unreliable or limited science
- False confessions
- Forensic science fraud or misconduct
- Government misconduct
- Informants or snitches
- Bad lawyering[340]

The first cause is the most important; more than 75 percent of wrongful convictions reversed through DNA analysis have been attributed at least partly to eyewitness misidentification.[341] Eyewitnesses often make honest mistakes, because of faulty memories or other factors. But as the list suggests, other individuals may be more unethical. For example, a certain percentage of expert witnesses engage in deliberate misconduct (sometimes called "testilying") and wreak havoc with the justice system.

Juries tend to see forensic scientists and other expert witnesses as infallible, but many of these individuals have been known to inflate their credentials, to lie about the tests they've performed, to contaminate or otherwise mishandle evidence, or to fabricate results. All these problems came together in the notorious case of Fred Zain, a West Virginia police chemist who testified as a forensics expert in hundreds of cases. Increasingly viewed as a star witness who knew his subject and could be counted on to produce convictions, he received a more attractive job offer in Texas and "he did for Texas what he had done for West Virginia. He lied."[342]

Zain's stellar career began to unravel after his testimony helped convict a man named Glen Woodall of sexual assault and other crimes in 1987. Though Woodall was sentenced to a prison term of 203 to 335 years, subsequent DNA testing showed he was innocent, and he was freed in 1992. Woodall sued the State of West Virginia and won a $1 million judgment. The West Virginia Supreme Court ordered an investigation of all of Zain's work, and the investigation raised doubts about the guilt of 134 people because of Zain's role in their convictions. In the late 1990s, charges of misconduct were brought against Zain in both Texas and West Virginia, but the charges didn't stick. He died in 2002, leaving a trail of damage behind him.[343]

Because a wrongful conviction is "one of the worst professional errors you can make—like a physician amputating the wrong arm,"[344] professionals in the justice system have a powerful incentive to resolve the dissonance by denying or rationalizing their behavior. Many members of the public, too, have resisted the idea that the system is flawed. Yet through the collaborative efforts of many individuals and groups, the problem of wrongful convictions has finally begun to be addressed, offering hope that in time, other legal injustices can be addressed as well.

Test Your Skills

Consider the following examples, involving the ethical and legal duty of lawyers to keep information revealed to them by clients confidential:

- In 1915 a man confessed to his lawyer, Arthur Powell—a prominent Atlanta attorney—that he'd committed a murder for which someone named Leo Frank had been given a death sentence. Powell relayed the information that Frank was innocent to the governor, who then commuted the death sentence. But because Powell felt he would be breaking the law and violating his professional oath if he provided full details, Frank could not be given a new trial. Instead of having his name cleared, Frank was hanged by a lynch mob.

- In a recent version of the Frank case, an attorney said nothing while an innocent man spent twelve years on death row. The attorney not only failed to report that his own client was guilty of the crime, but advised his client not to confess to the crime. Again the attorney felt he had a professional duty to remain silent.

- In a survey of attitudes on the confidentiality issue, respondents were given a hypothetical case in which a company manufactured an airplane with a defective part that could weaken and lead to explosions at high altitudes. The part met government safety standards and the company's board of directors felt the evidence of a safety hazard was inconclusive, so they were not required to disclose the problem. Interestingly, more than 75 percent of lawyers surveyed said they would not reveal the risk (a position in keeping with the ethical code of the New York Bar), while 85 percent of nonlawyers thought they should do so.[1]

Discuss the pros and cons of confidentiality in the legal profession. Do you think the advantages of this system outweigh the disadvantages?

---

1   *The three examples in this list are from Deborah L. Rhode, In the Interests of Justice: Reforming the Legal Profession (New York: Oxford University Press, 2000); the first two are from p. 108 and the third, from pp. 112–113.*

Conclusion

This chapter has underscored the elusive role truth often plays in our society by looking at the legal web and the injustices it can cause. You've seen that because of racial prejudice, eyewitness errors, flawed science, and other factors, you can't always depend on the truth to come out—it's whether you're able to convince a judge or jury of the truth. Thus this book's metaphor of diving deep to find truth is especially apt with regard to the legal system, because ordinary citizens' lives often hang in the balance unless they're able to navigate the morass of half-truths or outright lies, character assassination, prejudice, and other problems that plague the system.

The next chapter looks at a different type of problem plaguing the system: financial scams.

What You Can Do

√*If you need legal help, inform yourself about your options and avoid lawyers if you can.* A good place to start is with the Nolo website (www.nolo.com). Nolo (formerly Nolo Press) was founded in 1971 to demystify the U.S. legal system and to give everyone equal access to it. They offer hundreds of easily understandable legal products—books, newsletters, legal forms, software, blogs, podcasts, and free articles—to help you avoid the legal web described in this chapter. Other organizations that make information on legal topics available include HALT (Help Abolish Legal Tyranny) (www.halt.org) and FindLaw (www.findlaw.com). With the help of these resources, you may be able to cut lawyers out of the loop and resolve your dispute through mediation rather than litigation, draw up a business contract, handle a Workers' Comp claim, protect your rights as a renter, or write your own will.

Another alternative is to handle your own case in small claims court. The jurisdictional limit varies from state to state; it currently ranges from a low of $2,500 in several states to a high of $25,000 in Tennessee.[345] If the limit in your state seems feasible, small claims court may be a cost-effective alternative to hiring a lawyer.

If you do have to hire a lawyer, use resources like those provided by Nolo to become as knowledgeable as you can about how the process works and about what to expect in terms of legal fees and other details. That way there will be fewer surprises.

√*For information on the problem of wrongful convictions, take advantage of the resources provided by organizations like the Innocence Project.* The Innocence Project is dedicated to overturning wrongful convictions through DNA testing and other techniques, and their website (www.innocenceproject.org) is a rich source of information on many facets of this problem. Similar organizations include the Center on Wrongful Convictions at the Northwestern University School of Law (http://www.law.northwestern.edu/wrongfulconvictions/) and Truth in Justice (www.truthinjustice.org).

√*Report misconduct by lawyers to the proper authorities.* The U.S. legal profession relies on self-regulation to address the problem of attorney misconduct—an inherently flawed system.[346] But you can report cases of misconduct to the appropriate office in the state or other jurisdiction where your attorney practices.[347]

√*Work for legal reform.* Injustices and inadequacies in the legal system—including unequal access to legal services, the insufficient commitment of the legal profession to social justice and diversity, the adversarial nature of the system, and inadequate disciplinary mechanisms for attorney misconduct—have spawned a cottage industry of organizations committed to legal reform. A web search under "legal reform" will produce the names of dozens of national and local organizations; one place to start is with the website of HALT (www.halt.org), the largest legal reform organization in the United States.

If you're interested in redressing the problem of wrongful convictions, the Innocence Project suggests many actions you can take, including joining their online community to receive news and other information, working with prisoners in your community, and taking political action (see http://www.innocenceproject.org/fix/What-can-I-do.php). For a useful list of reforms you can get involved with, also see "Appendix 1: A Short List of Reforms to Protect the Innocent" in Barry Scheck, Peter Neufeld, and Jim Dwyer, *Actual Innocence: Five Days to Execution and Other Dispatches from the Wrongly Convicted* (New York: Doubleday, 2000), 255–260. Brandon L. Garrett provides more detail on these and other reforms in his book *Convicting the Innocent: Where Criminal Prosecutions Go Wrong* (Cambridge, MA: Harvard University Press, 2011), 241–274.

Further Reading

For a collection of lawyer jokes and anecdotes, see Andrew Roth and Jonathan Roth, *Devil's Advocates: The Unnatural History of Lawyers,* ed. Barbara Repa (Berkeley, CA: Nolo Press, 1989). For cartoons, see *The New Yorker Book of Lawyer Cartoons* (New York: Knopf, 1994).

As a general indictment of the legal profession, Jerold S. Auerbach's *Unequal Justice: Lawyers and Social Change in Modern America* (New York: Oxford University Press, 1976) is somewhat dated but still suggestive. For a hard-hitting attack on corporate lawyers and law firms, see Ralph Nader and Wesley J. Smith, *No Contest: Corporate Lawyers and the Perversion of Justice in America* (New York: Random House, 1996).

Bestselling novelist Scott Turow is also a lawyer, and his *One L*—describing his first year as a Harvard Law School student—has become "a virtual bible for prospective law students," according to the jacket copy. This book offers interesting glimpses of the corporatization of legal education as well as some tentative suggestions for reform. See Scott Turow, *One L*, rev. ed. (New York: Farrar Straus Giroux, 1988).

Besides Irving Stone's well-known *Clarence Darrow for the Defense* (Garden City, NY: Doubleday, Doran & Company, 1941), intriguing accounts of the Leopold and Loeb case include Simon Baatz, *For the Thrill of It: Leopold, Loeb, and the Murder That Shocked Chicago* (New York: HarperCollins, 2008); Hal Higdon, *Leopold and Loeb: The Crime of the Century* (Urbana: University of Illinois Press, [1975] 1999); and John Theodore, *Evil Summer: Babe Leopold, Dickie Loeb, and the Kidnap-Murder of Bobby Franks* (Carbondale: Southern Illinois University Press, 2007). Also see Douglas Linder, "Famous American Trials: Illinois v. Nathan Leopold and Richard Loeb, 1924," University of Missouri at Kansas City Law School, 1997, http://www.law.umkc.edu/faculty/projects/ftrials/leoploeb/leopold.htm. There have been many fictional treatments of the Leopold and Loeb case; for a short survey, see the section "Leopold and Loeb in Fiction" in Baatz's book *For the Thrill of It* (pp. 449–451). For a well-known novel based on the Leopold and Loeb murder, see Meyer Levin, *Compulsion* (New York: Carroll & Graf, [1956]

1996). This novel was made into a 1959 film by the same name starring Orson Welles as the fictionalized character based on Clarence Darrow. For an engrossing biography of Darrow that includes a chapter on Leopold and Loeb (pp. 333–360), see John A. Farrell, *Clarence Darrow: Attorney for the Damned* (New York: Doubleday, 2011).

For a thought-provoking exploration of the Glen Ridge case, see Bernard Lefkowitz, *Our Guys: The Glen Ridge Rape and the Secret Life of the Perfect Suburb* (Berkeley: University of California Press, 1997).

Many books have appeared on wrongful convictions and related topics. For a readable and comprehensive survey, see Brandon L. Garrett, *Convicting the Innocent: Where Criminal Prosecutions Go Wrong* (Cambridge, MA: Harvard University Press, 2011). For another compelling treatment, see *Actual Innocence: Five Days to Execution and Other Dispatches from the Wrongly Convicted* (New York: Doubleday, 2000) by Barry Scheck, Peter Neufeld, and Jim Dwyer. (Scheck and Neufeld founded the Innocence Project; Dwyer is a Pulitzer Prize–winning columnist.) For a collection of cross-disciplinary articles on the causes of wrongful convictions and possible solutions, see Saundra D. Westervelt and John A. Humphrey, eds., *Wrongly Convicted: Perspectives on Failed Justice* (New Brunswick, NJ: Rutgers University Press, 2001). On problems with eyewitnesses, see James M. Doyle, *True Witness: Cops, Courts, Science, and the Battle against Misidentification* (New York: Palgrave Macmillan, 2005). Novelist John Grisham makes a foray into nonfiction with his book *The Innocent Man: Murder and Injustice in a Small Town* (New York: Doubleday, 2006). Grisham explores the wrongful conviction and subsequent exoneration of Ron Williamson, a local baseball hero from a small Oklahoma town.

Deborah L. Rhode discusses legal reform and related issues in her books *Access to Justice* (New York: Oxford University Press, 2004) and *In the Interests of Justice: Reforming the Legal Profession* (New York: Oxford University Press, 2000).

9. FIGHTING SCAMS

When Bernard Madoff confessed to the FBI in 2008 that his investment fund was a giant Ponzi scheme that had bilked 13,500 individuals and charities out of $50 billion, he not only sent shockwaves through the community of investors and philanthropists who'd lost everything. He also created intense speculation about the kind of person that could have blithely destroyed so many lives. Many of Madoff's victims described him in retrospect as a sociopath, but this wasn't the image he'd presented to most who knew him.

Madoff seemed to have everything. He'd grown up in a middle-class suburb of Queens, New York, and married his high school sweetheart, Ruth Alpern. In 1960 he founded Bernard L. Madoff Investment Securities (BLMIS) with $5,000 earned from high school and college jobs like installing sprinkler systems in tract housing. From the beginning he appeared to have a knack for inspiring confidence in tycoons looking for a place to invest their money, like the Boston philanthropist Carl J. Shapiro. The good returns Madoff earned for Shapiro beginning in the early 1960s attracted other wealthy investors and allowed Madoff's firm to take off. As it turned out, Shapiro—who considered Madoff a surrogate son—was one of many close friends Madoff duped; he lost more than $500 million.

Madoff's initial successes gave him an entrée into exclusive circles, producing an ever-expanding web of potential clients. When he was caught by the FBI, Madoff had spent years hobnobbing with the rich and famous; his lavish lifestyle included a $7.4 million penthouse in New York, a $9.4 million Palm Beach estate, getaways in the Hamptons and in the south of France, several yachts, a jet he co-owned, and many other assets. Tellingly, all of Madoff's boats were named *Bull*, and the federal marshals who inventoried and photographed the contents of the Madoffs' Palm Beach home discovered that it was decorated with a bull motif. They found bull statues, bookends, images on clothing, and other items, leading one marshal to quip: "There's a lot of bull in the house. I've never seen so much bull in my life."[348]

BLMIS was a legitimate brokerage firm located at the time of Madoff's arrest on the eighteenth and nineteenth floors of the upscale Lipstick Building in midtown Manhattan. On the seventeenth floor he ran a secretive investment advisory business—so secretive that many of the BLMIS brokers knew little about the business operating only a floor or two below them.[349] The advisory business was a phony hedge fund that had no name. It was fraudulent because the money from "investors" wasn't actually invested. Both components of Madoff's operation were initially profitable; he used the money from the "investors" in the advisory firm to pay himself as well as to trade in BLMIS and make large profits, out of which he would pay the "investors" the 20 percent returns he had offered them. Madoff managed to follow this strategy throughout the 1970s and 1980s and may not have seen it as unethical, because after all he was making good on his promise to pay his clients high returns.

At some point—possibly during the financial crash of 1987—BLMIS sustained significant losses that could only be covered by a large flow of money from the advisory business. Madoff also needed to keep up the generous payouts to the "investors" in that business. Many analysts think this may have been the point at which the Ponzi scheme began on a large scale, as Madoff scrambled for new "investments" with which to compensate older "investors" and with which to provide capital to BLMIS. By the crash of 2008 the scheme had spiraled out of control; anxious "investors" were demanding more than $7 billion back and Madoff didn't have the money. Out of options, he confessed and left his victims to fend for themselves. In the words of one observer, the result of Madoff's Ponzi scheme was a "financial holocaust."[350]

Investigators trying to unravel the mystery of the kind of person who could have become a "Svengali for rich people," as Donald Trump called Madoff, portray a private Madoff very different from the cordial Madoff known to friends and business associates.[351] The private Madoff is said to have been controlling and to have ruled his family by fear and intimidation. Many accounts describe his obsessive-compulsive behavior; even small objects out of place in a room or small scuffmarks on furniture would drive him to distraction.[352] One colleague would taunt him by putting a piece of thread on the floor and waiting for Madoff to go ballistic when he noticed it. The manager of Madoff's London office offered this picture: "We'd spend days before his arrival leveling blinds, making sure the computer screens were an identical height, lining every picture up straight. No paper was allowed on the desks. We'd use black marker pens to touch up the doors. Anything that looked as if it had a mark or a scratch on it, we'd have to retouch. Things like that would drive him nuts."[353] Madoff has also been described as arrogant and disdainful toward those he doesn't consider his equals. These and other traits hint at a picture of a rigid, insecure person deficient in empathy and with a need to advance himself at others' expense.

Longtime acquaintances trace these traits to Madoff's childhood. His father claimed to be a plumber, but his parents were apparently operating a dubious broker-dealer business called Gibraltar Securities in their home. It was listed in the name of Sylvia Madoff (Madoff's mother), possibly because his father had financial problems. In 1963 the SEC initiated proceedings against her for failing to file the proper financial reports, but the proceedings were dropped after she agreed to withdraw her registration and shut the business down.[354] Madoff is not only thought to have acquired questionable business ethics at home. Childhood friends attribute his compulsiveness and avarice to his mother's frugality; they say he was humiliated by her bargain-basement shopping habits, which deprived him of the fashionable clothes and shoes other kids had.[355] The Ponzi scheme that damaged thousands of lives, in short, may have been Madoff's effort to get even and to make sure he would always have the best of everything.

The thousands Madoff victimized ranged from his own family members and employees to millionaire financiers and socialites to ordinary, hard-working people—teachers, firefighters, secretaries, construction workers—whose hopes and dreams were destroyed when their savings or pension funds were invested with Madoff. The smaller-scale crimes described in the following pages have also damaged or destroyed lives, as well as eroding the fabric of society.

Scams: An Overview

There are as many types of scams as there are ingenious perpetrators. If we include related forms of deception, like hoaxes, the field is even broader. Hoaxes often emphasize trickery for purposes other than financial gain, but that doesn't mean they're victimless crimes. One of the best-known hoaxes was the *War of the Worlds* hoax in the 1930s. In a Halloween broadcast on October 30, 1938, Orson Welles did a radio adaptation of H. G. Wells's science fiction novel *The War of the Worlds* (1898), about a Martian invasion. For purposes of the broadcast, the scene was shifted from England to New Jersey; panic broke out not only in New Jersey but in many other parts of the country, and a few people are said to have had heart attacks. The station was besieged with threats—the male cast and other personnel reportedly hid in the ladies room until it was safe to leave—and CBS made a public apology.[356] Many commentators were appalled at the gullibility of the public. Dorothy Thompson, a noted columnist, said acerbically that "nothing about the broadcast was in the least credible. . . . Mr. Orson Welles and his theater have made a greater contribution to an understanding of Hitlerism, Mussoliniism, Stalinism, anti-Semitism and all other terrorisms of our times than all the words about them that have been written by reasonable men."[357] In fairness, many listeners tuned in to the broadcast belatedly and missed the introductory announcement that it was a dramatization of a novel. These were the 12 percent of the audience of a popular competing show—the *Edgar Bergen and Charlie McCarthy* ventriloquist show—who switched to Welles's broadcast when Bergen and his dummy took a break at 8:12

p.m. Nerves were also frayed because of the impending war in Europe and fears of an invasion—by Germans, not Martians.[358]

Other well-known hoaxes include the quiz-show scandals from the 1950s. The most notorious involved Charles Van Doren, a member of a prominent literary family (his father was the poet and critic Mark Van Doren and his uncle was the Pulitzer Prize–winning author and Columbia University Professor Carl Van Doren). Charles Van Doren had his moment of fame for fourteen weeks in 1956–1957, when he appeared on an NBC quiz show called *Twenty-One*. A few weeks earlier a producer had approached Van Doren and enticed him to take part in the rigged show with the promise of earnings that would dwarf his Columbia University instructor's salary (he eventually took home about $128,000 from the show). Contestants were told what to wear and how to behave down to the smallest details—one contestant was usually cast as sympathetic and the other as unappealing, like Van Doren's first opponent, who'd been instructed to get an unflattering haircut as well as to wear an ill-fitting suit and a cheap watch—and were secretly shown the script ahead of time. The show was so carefully orchestrated that each time the contestants entered the studio, they knew exactly how many points they were supposed to win or lose, what answers they were expected to give, and how to deliver them (hesitating at certain points, adding brief comments, and so on). After Van Doren's run of luck came to an end on March 11, 1957—he was required to lose to a lawyer named Vivienne Nearing that evening—he was hired by NBC as a high-paid educational consultant. Eventually the scandal was exposed and the show went off the air. Together with other contestants, Van Doren pleaded guilty to perjury and got a suspended sentence. He also lost both his NBC job and his teaching position at Columbia and had to live down the scandal for the rest of his life.[359]

For reasons of space, I limit myself in this chapter to more traditional scams, which usually have a major financial component. I profile the main types of scams in the following pages and suggest ways you can dive through the layers of deception to protect yourself against them.

Test Your Skills

Have you or someone you know been victimized by a scam?
Why did you or they fall for the scam? If you had to tell
someone what to watch out for so they won't be victimized
the way you were, what warning signals would you describe?

Sweetheart Scams

I'll start with a simple but pernicious type of scam that's the stuff of novels and films: sweetheart scams. You may know someone who's been victimized in one of these scams. This is where a person worms their way into someone's life, and the next thing you know, the perpetrator has access to the victim's bank account, owns the deed to their house, or has been written into their will. In the stereotypical case, a sensitive, attentive man turns up in the life of a widowed woman and sweeps her off her feet—but anyone can perpetrate or be the target of this type of fraud.

The core element is the use of friendship or love to win the liking and trust of the victim. The con artist uses many tactics to win that liking and trust. They'll show an interest in the victim's life, asking questions about family and friends; they'll flatter the victim; they'll appear to have similar values and interests; they'll do favors (or appear to do favors) for the victim; and they'll do other things that in real life would be a sign of empathy and caring—except that in the context of a sweetheart scam these emotions are contrived. The con artist is often so successful at creating a bond with the victim that many victims are depressed after the scam has been exposed, not only because of their financial loss but because they feel they've genuinely lost a friend or loved one.

A commonality between sweetheart scams and other types of scams is the use of friendship and trust as a basis for defrauding the victim. We saw this practice with Madoff, who defrauded many of his closest friends and associates, and it's a common practice in many other scams.

Sweetheart scams have traditionally been carried out by solo operators, but the Internet has made it possible for unscrupulous online dating services, foreign-bride schemes, and the like to proliferate. Victims may not only be risking a broken heart. Sweetheart scams are sometimes intertwined with other illegal activity, like prostitution or the Nigerian schemes discussed later. Victims lured into traveling to foreign countries, or even into face-to-face encounters in their own country, can face physical danger.

Investment Scams

There are dozens of types of investment scams; here is a sampling:

- *Ponzi schemes*, like the one masterminded by Madoff, are among the most common. These schemes utilize the money coming in from new investors to pay previous investors. As happened with Madoff, the system eventually collapses and only the scammers and possibly the earliest investors are likely to come out ahead. Some particularly exploitative Ponzi schemes are of a religious nature; they pressure people to invest by taking advantage of their religious faith and their trust in their church. Scammers infiltrate the church, distributing propaganda literature and videos on how successful the investment scheme is and using religious language to persuade parishioners to take part.[360]
- Other investment scams involve *business opportunities*. Ads, flyers, spam emails, seminars, and other efforts to promote business and franchise opportunities are everywhere. While many of these ventures are legitimate, others are not. Fraudulent deals often involve high-pressure tactics. Scammers may be trying to lock you into a disastrous investment scheme that could deprive you of many thousands of dollars, or they may just be trying to rip you off to the tune of a few hundred dollars

for worthless investment seminars and other materials. Either way, buyer beware.

- Still other common scams involve *oil and gas investments.* These investments can seem appealing because of rising energy costs, but since they usually require the investment of large sums, fraudulent oil and gas deals can be especially costly.
- *Rare-coin scams* are also common. Here the victim usually receives the gold coins or other types of coins they've been promised, but the coins turn out not to be authentic or to be worth less than advertised. Hefty shipping and handling fees can also be tacked on.
- These and other investment scams can involve *affinity fraud,* where scammers target members of the same ethnic, religious, or political group they belong to, making the pitch that they're trustworthy because they share the same background as their potential victims. Affinity fraud played a big role in the Madoff scandal, since he disproportionately targeted wealthy Jewish investors who moved in the same business and social circles he moved in.

Did You Know?

Ponzi Schemes Are Named for Charles Ponzi, an Early Twentieth-Century Swindler

Bernard Madoff and others like him have followed in the footsteps of Charles Ponzi (1882–1949), an Italian immigrant who scraped by as a fruit peddler, waiter, dishwasher, factory worker, sign painter, and petty criminal before he discovered his true calling: swindling. Late in 1919 Ponzi hit on the idea of soliciting capital from people and offering a high rate of return (50 percent within three months, later shortened to forty-five days), then repaying earlier investors with funds acquired from later investors. This was the ancient "robbing Peter to pay Paul" scheme. When Ponzi made good on his promise to the initial investors, word spread and he was deluged with more money, especially at the peak of his scam in the spring and summer of 1920: "There were days when Ponzi's office looked like a hurricane had hit. Incoming money littered the place, stuffed in closets, desk drawers and overflowing in wastebaskets."[1] Ponzi made more than $2 million a week at the height of his scam.[2] He became a hero in Boston and adopted a lavish lifestyle, appearing in public in elegant suits (he owned 200) and with gold-handled canes (he had dozens).

It was not to last. After a Boston newspaper revealed in August 1920 that Ponzi had been imprisoned for forgery in Canada and had been involved in other nefarious activities, his flow of investors dropped off. The result was predictable: his scheme crashed because he no longer had the money coming in to pay previous investors. After serving four years of a five-year federal prison sentence and seven years of a seven- to nine-year

1   Entry titled "Ponzi, Charles, Swindler" in Carl Sifakis, *Hoaxes and Scams: A Compendium of Deceptions, Ruses, and Swindles*, 208–210 (New York: Facts On File, 1993) (quote on 209).
2   Mitchell Zuckoff, *Ponzi's Scheme: The True Story of a Financial Legend* (New York: Random House, 2005), dust jacket; also see pp. 172, 187.

Did You Know?

state prison sentence, Ponzi was extradited to Italy in 1934. He ended up a few years later in Brazil, lured by the promise of employment with an Italian airline (the position had been arranged by a cousin friendly with the son of dictator Benito Mussolini). When that position fell through, Ponzi was forced to make ends meet with low-paying jobs and a small Brazilian pension. Impoverished and disabled, he died in the charity ward of a hospital in Rio de Janeiro in 1949.

These and other types of investment scams have in common that they promise a spectacular rate of return on investments, unusually lucrative oil and gas leases, "one-of-a-kind" gold coins, or other benefits that sound too good to be true. If investment opportunities sound too good to be true, they probably are.

Identity Theft

Whether done the old-fashioned way by retrieving your bills or bank statements from an unlocked mailbox or a dumpster, through lost or stolen credit cards, by using a device to skim your credit card number while processing the card, by peering over your shoulder at an ATM, or through Internet fraud, this category of scams is a fast-growing problem. One identity thief said in an interview that "in terms of how drug addicts get their money, ID theft has completely replaced armed robberies, house burglaries, ATM holdups . . . nobody wastes their time with that anymore."[361] The common denominator is that scammers are after your information so they can help themselves to your financial resources, but their methods are infinitely variable.

The losses from Internet fraud alone are in the billions of dollars, with no letup in sight. Contributing factors include the erosion of privacy standards and the increased access to personal data like home addresses, employment history, Social Security numbers, and credit card numbers. Criminals obtain this information in myriad ways—sometimes just by buying it. They may also get you to turn over the information under false pretenses. You've almost certainly run into con artists posing as legitimate companies or institutions. They'll email you that "there's a problem" with your account and ask you to verify or update your personal information. In the past the letter would have a makeshift logo and would be full of grammatical and spelling errors. Scammers have become more sophisticated, and their websites and correspondence now look like the real thing. Another problem is the emergence of malware like fraudulent antivirus software. This software often has believable names and looks legitimate. But if installed on your computer, it can tamper with security settings and otherwise leave it open to predatory practices.

Full-fledged cases of identity theft can damage or destroy lives by costing victims their jobs, homes, and peace of mind. One case involved a California man who was a department store salesman. Seven months after his wallet was stolen containing his driver's license, Social Security card, and other items,

> he was called into the [department store's] main security office and told he had been caught shoplifting at one of the chain's other stores. He had done no such thing. In fact, he had been working in his usual store at the time. He even produced a letter from his boss confirming that. Still, he was fired. The man who had stolen his wallet had assumed his identity and done the shoplifting.

He got other jobs, but was dogged by the crimes of the thief. He'd apply for a job, a check would be done on him, and he'd be told, sorry, his services weren't needed. He later found out from the police that the rap sheet in his name included arrests for shoplifting, burglary, and arson. He went bankrupt. He lost his home. Finally, he legally changed his name to distance himself from the identity theft, but his life is only a shadow of what it once was.[362]

Nigerian Scams

Nigerian scams—sometimes called *Nigerian advance-fee scams* or *419 fraud* after the applicable section of the Nigerian criminal code—have been the butt of jokes because some have been outlandish, but they're no joke to those conned by them. These are foreign money-offer scams, in which individuals or organizations receive a letter, fax, or email asking for their assistance in return for a generous fee, often in the millions. The letter conveys a sense of urgency; the writer claims to be in trouble and identifies himself or herself as a member of the royalty, a high-level civil servant, a political insider, a lawyer or other professional person, or the family member of a persecuted leader. Typically, the writer asks for help transferring money out of the country on some pretext; the list of pretexts grows all the time but includes:

- The letter writer's need to escape persecution (the scammer may pose as a deposed leader or as a relative of such a leader; they have access to millions of dollars in political or other funds but are in hiding and need help escaping from Nigeria with the money)
- Overpayment of invoices (for example, the scammer says the Nigerian government has overpaid on a contract and they need assistance getting the money out of the country before government officials realize their error)
- The need to transfer other ill-gotten gains out of the country (the letter writer has accumulated money from questionable business deals or government corruption and wants to transfer it to a foreign bank account)
- Disbursement of an inheritance (the scammer claims to have received a multimillion-dollar inheritance and needs help transferring it abroad; in other versions, they claim a wealthy Nigerian has bequeathed a fortune to a U.S. charity, which must submit the proper paperwork in order to claim the inheritance)

The recipient of the letter is often flattered to be singled out (in reality, they're probably the target of a mass mailing) and may be tempted by the offer of a 10 to 30 percent share of millions of dollars. If the victim innocently contacts the scammer for more information, the scammer begins to reel them in. Victims foolish enough to provide accurate contact information will soon find themselves deluged with official-looking documents on the letterhead of the Nigerian government, law firms, or petroleum companies. If the victims are even more foolish and provide the banking information they're asked for, they may find their account has suddenly been cleaned out. More typically, they'll be told that bureaucratic problems have arisen and that they'll have to pay government fees, bank fees, or lawyers' fees before the millions can be transferred into their account. This is where the term *advance fee* comes in; as soon as they pay an advance fee of, say, 2 percent of the money or $215,000, the transaction can be completed. The victims may be able to talk the fee down to $50,000 or $75,000, but as soon as they make the payment, other fees and taxes are unexpectedly required, like insurance fees, transfer taxes, or bribes. The more money the victims pay, the more desperate they become to keep on paying in order to reap the profits they've been promised, if only to recoup their investment. These advance fees are usually the criminal's real goal in a Nigerian scam.

Not only is it illegal for you to assist in plots of this nature by bringing foreign money into the United States, but it could be dangerous. Many scam victims are asked to come to Nigeria or adjoining countries to carry out business transactions, and there have been reports of scam victims being murdered or disappearing.

Charity Scams

In an era of frequent natural disasters and human-made tragedies, charity scams have to be taken seriously. The most common variants of charity scams include:

- *Exploitation of legitimate charities.* In small-scale but ubiquitous charity scams, scammers submit fraudulent claims to the Red Cross or other relief organizations for a few hundred dollars' or a few thousand dollars' worth of free food or housing—aid that should have gone to needy citizens. Sometimes crooks bilk legitimate charities out of large sums if they're able to gain access to the charities' banking information. We've just glimpsed a typical example: a Nigerian scam in which a charity is urged to provide financial information in order to claim a donation from a Nigerian benefactor.

- *Fake charities.* In the aftermath of a disaster, many scammers prey on well-intentioned donors by setting up fake charities. The names of these charities tend to sound legitimate and may resemble the names of well-known organizations like the Red Cross or Catholic Charities.

- *Other fraudulent solicitations for help.* A natural disaster or other tragedy can become a pretext for fraudulent solicitations through a wide range of channels, not just from fake charities. For example, a telemarketer claiming to be from Publishers Clearinghouse could promise that a donation will be made to the Red Cross for every magazine subscription ordered or sweepstakes entered. Or the scammer can solicit funds on eBay with the promise that the money will go to the relief effort.

The obvious implication is that donors should do their homework, especially in dealing with smaller, more obscure charities. Misspellings and grammatical errors that indicate a lack of professionalism are not the only red flags on websites. Watch especially for a "donation" button linked to a private account rather than to that of a legitimate charity.

Online Auction Scams, Including eBay Scams

Millions of customers have had good experiences with eBay and other auction sites, but many have not been so lucky. Surveys suggest that as many as 40 percent of buyers have run into problems.[363] The item they've purchased may have arrived damaged, or some other item has been substituted, or nothing arrives at all. Sellers are also scammed; they're not always paid, or are paid with bogus checks or credit cards.

Scammers take advantage of several weak points in the auction process:

- *The seller's rating is easy to manipulate.* These ratings are not as infallible as they seem—for example, con artists sometimes buy and sell large quantities of cheap items like CDs to establish a good rating before they transition into criminal activity.

- *Some escrow services are fraudulent.* With a reputable escrow service, the buyer sends the payment to the service; after the buyer has received the goods and made sure they're acceptable, the escrow service forwards the payment to the seller. That's how it's supposed to work, but criminals sometimes set up fake escrow services. The buyer successfully bids on an expensive item; after being notified by an escrow service that it's holding the payment, the seller ships the item. The seller is never paid by the escrow service, and on further investigation, discovers the service has shut down.

- *The use of money-transfer services like Western Union makes it hard to recover stolen funds.* Scammers prefer wire services like Western Union because these services allow money to be transferred anywhere in the world and to be picked up with ease, often by someone showing minimal or no ID. By using Western Union, the criminals are also bypassing the U.S. Postal Service and the stringent federal laws governing postal crime. If you make a payment via a wire service like Western Union you're essentially paying cash, which can be impossible to retrieve if it falls into the wrong hands. Recognizing this problem, Western Union includes warnings about fraud on its website and advises against paying for Internet auction purchases by means of money-transfer services. For more tips from Western Union, see the "What You Can Do" section below.

- *Law enforcement agencies like the FBI and Secret Service don't have the resources to handle most low-level auction fraud.* A $5,000 or

$10,000 loss may be a lot to you, but major government agencies often won't get involved until it reaches the $100,000 mark. This works to the criminals' advantage, because many reap large profits from small-scale swindles with items like jewelry, consumer electronics, or cars.

Counterfeiting Scams

A type of scam that may overlap with others like auction scams involves counterfeit goods. Everyone has heard of merchants selling counterfeit items like Rolex watches or designer handbags on the streets of New York, but counterfeiting has become more sophisticated and dangerous. It's also extremely widespread, with factories springing up especially in China and other Asian countries to produce everything from fake food to fake car parts. The entry of counterfeit foods into the food supply is especially worrisome, as is the spread of fake pharmaceuticals and medical supplies, ranging from adulterated aspirin to phony birth control pills and condoms to reused syringes and syringe bottles. There have apparently been thousands of deaths from counterfeit drugs alone, including 3,000 deaths blamed on fraudulent meningitis vaccines in Africa. Another widespread problem involves fake machine parts. Counterfeit car and aircraft parts have been implicated in many fatal or near-fatal accidents, like a 1989 plane crash that cost fifty-five lives and was attributed to fake bolts in the tail section.[364]

Sweepstakes, Free-Prize, and Lottery Scams

In sweepstakes and related scams, the victims receive a phone call, letter, or email informing them that they've won a valuable prize. The prize can range from money, a car, or a trip to jewelry, electronic goods, or other items. To claim the prize, the victim typically has to pay a fee or tax or make a purchase. Prizes received, if any, are usually inferior to what the victims had been led to expect—sometimes ludicrously so, like a box of rocks instead of an electronic device. There's nothing new about this type of deception, but it's been aided and abetted by technological developments. Many scammers make use of the latest technology to replace their phone numbers on your caller ID with the names of legitimate-sounding government or consumer-protection agencies. They may also direct you to a bogus "government" website—even that of the FTC—that lulls you into trusting them.

These types of scams are hard to avoid; surveys show that almost all adults have encountered them.[365] You've probably received letters from companies informing you in big print that "You're a Winner!" or inviting you to "Fly to Florida to Claim Your Million-Dollar Prize!" Hopefully you didn't take the bait, but many others unfortunately have:

- A New York man has pleaded guilty to his role in a bogus sweepstakes scheme that bilked an elderly Iowa woman out of hundreds of thousands of dollars. . . . She paid about $200,000 in "taxes" and "advance fees" in installments of between $3,500 and $8,000 by using MoneyGram and Western Union.
- One California man, unable to convince his elderly father he was not a winner, flew with him to Florida to "claim" his prize only to find out it was all in vain.
- A 78-year-old woman, so convinced she had won the big prize after being asked for a map to her home, "so the Prize Patrol could find her," put a welcome sign for it in her front yard, ordered a cake and was ready to celebrate her great fortune with friends. Like the California man, she didn't win either.[366]

As one website devoted to exposing consumer fraud points out, "Even 'legitimate' sweepstakes companies have become masters at creating a web of deception. The headlines, the words, everything about their mailers are calculated to get people to buy products they wouldn't otherwise buy."[367] Using hyperbole and other deceptive practices, these companies prey on their targets. Once they've fallen for a sweepstakes come-on, victims are likely to become prime targets for other fraudulent schemes—including those that offer assistance in getting their money back.

Recovery or Reload Scams

These are operations that purport to help people recover money they've lost in scams. At a minimum, you'll have to pay a fee to a crook who won't get your money back. A more serious consequence is that you're almost certainly being set up to be victimized again—especially if you've been foolish enough to give out credit card or other personal information to the con artist. The con artist will either revictimize you himself through a scam or sell your information to someone else who will. The moral? Don't provide your information to anyone who says they can recover your money.

Scammers' Tactics

This section looks at who scammers target and how they do it.

Choosing Targets

One misconception we can lay to rest is that scam victims are necessarily poorly educated and frail older people. After all, many of Madoff's targets were affluent, highly educated movers and shakers, not uneducated, marginalized individuals. In the words of the Financial Industry Regulatory Authority (FINRA),

> Recent research has shattered the stereotype of investment fraud victims as isolated, frail and gullible. Do you know anyone who meets the following description?
>
> - Self-reliant when it comes to making decisions
> - Optimistic
> - Above-average financial knowledge
> - Above-average income
> - College-educated
> - Experienced a recent health or financial setback
> - Open to listening to new ideas or sales pitches

If so, you know someone who fits the profile of an investment fraudster's prime target.[368]

While anyone can be targeted, older people are especially attractive to scammers because criminals go where the money is and older people tend to have more money than other groups. Older people may also be more trusting because of having grown up in an era when ethical standards were higher. In the words of an experienced scammer,

> I would say that 80 percent of the [people I targeted] were senior citizens—if not senior citizens, then someone over the age of 45. Anybody younger than that, it was usually just a waste of our time. It's horrible but it's really true—they are the easiest victims out there. They have better credit, they have longer history at a job, they are on a pension plan, they have had the same bank forever, they are just plain and simple the best profile that's out there. Plus, they are the most trusting. They are the least likely to sit at home and think, "Who could steal from me today?"[369]

Young people are not immune; a few authors suggest that while older citizens are more likely to report having been victimized by financial scams, well-educated young people may be more likely to actually be scammed.[370] The vulnerability of young people has been attributed to a variety of factors, including a lack of maturity, insufficient life experience to realize they're being conned, and a higher level of materialism than earlier generations.[371]

Some demographic characteristics vary with the type of scam. According to surveys by the AARP and other organizations, investment victims are more likely to be well-educated, middle-aged men with high incomes, while lottery victims are more likely to be low-income women well into old age who are not financially literate.[372]

Psychological and behavioral factors also help to define who is likely or unlikely to be scammed. Risk takers, people with an attitude of invulnerability ("It can't happen to me!"), people who are easily persuadable, and those coping with an emotional loss may be more likely to be victimized.

Test Your Skills

It's sometimes said that "only the greedy are victimized by fraud." Do you agree with this statement? Why or why not?

The preceding paragraphs indicate that almost anyone can become a victim. How do scammers choose from among the pool of potential victims? In fraud that targets businesspeople, companies, or charities—as in many investment scams and Nigerian scams—criminals often mine business periodicals, trade journals, professional directories, or similar resources for prospects. Other sources of leads include investment workshops or tradeshows, because by participating, attendees have signaled that they're open to making future investments.

The perpetrators of investment scams don't always target wealthy individuals. Some con artists seek out people with financial problems, believing they'll be unusually receptive to get-rich-quick schemes. Another group whose vulnerability can make them a target are bereaved people, as in the sweetheart scams mentioned earlier that prey on widows.

Other methods of identifying victims are used in sweepstakes scams. A good guess is that people who have already entered sweepstakes, lotteries, or other contests will be unusually receptive to scams, so scammers buy lists of contest entrants and their contact information. One fraud investigator has explained the process as follows: "I really believe that telemarketing fraud problems all begin with the mail solicitations, the junk mail . . . the prize mail stuff that comes to a senior. If they participate in that, if they play those shady solicitations, sweepstakes solicitations that they get in the mail, if they get on those lists, fraudulent telemarketers will buy those lists. . . . I've seen seniors where, you know, they've told me over and over—once I started playing those solicitations, not only did my mail increase exponentially, but I also started getting calls."[373] Another way to get on fraudulent telemarketers' lists is to fill out entry forms for prize drawings in locations like shopping malls. When you fill out that slip of paper and drop it in the glass bowl, your information may end up in unexpected places, because not all those drawings are as innocent as they seem. Many are legitimate, but some are intended to generate telemarketing lists, including lists used by con artists.

Profiling

After identifying potential victims, con artists profile them to learn as much about them as possible. Profiling techniques depend on the type of scam. Complex financial scams may require extensive research in business publications so that the pitch can be perfectly tailored to the company or charity being targeted. More typically, profiling focuses on individuals—especially the emotional vulnerabilities that will motivate them to fall for the scam. This is because to be successful, scams not only have to be tailored to victims' circumstances, but have to tap into their deepest desires.

For most people this involves easy money, but it could involve an array of other goals, like gaining access to medical treatment, providing for children or grandchildren, buying land, or traveling to an exotic location. A scammer specializing in financial fraud explains how he elicits this information: "In the first conversation, I am asking a lot of questions about the person's personal life. I want to know where they used to work, are they married, how long have they been married, what they have invested in before. I am looking for things they care about. What motivates them? Is it their grand kids? Is it improving their relationship with their wife? It's kind of like a jewelry thief casing the local jewelry store."[374]

Making the Pitch

In making the pitch, con artists rely on a variety of persuasion tactics. Common to almost all of them is the manipulation of the victim's emotions. The goal is to get the victims so excited about their future windfalls that it will short circuit the rational part of their brains and cause them to make decisions based on emotion alone. The tactics used are typically variants on several basic approaches: establishing the scammer's credibility and authority; creating friendship and trust; emphasizing scarcity ("If you don't seize the chance to win the jackpot now, I'll be forced to give someone else the opportunity!"; "There are only seven rare coins left and they're going fast!"); and resorting to coercion and intimidation.

Gifted con artists know exactly how to use these tactics. In establishing credibility, for example, they provide just the right balance of information via phone calls, impressive brochures, and phony references from experts or satisfied customers to create a sense of authority and allay doubts. This requires knowing where to draw the line between providing enough information about a fraudulent business deal and too much information. Too few technical details and the potential victim will balk; too many technical details and they'll insist on consulting an expert, who will probably detect the fraud.

Closing the Deal

In closing the deal, timing is everything. Scammers realize a prospect is almost certainly not ready to buy if they're still scrutinizing brochures and manuals and asking technical questions. Anticipating and deflecting any objections the victims may have before these objections gain traction is a key part of the closing process. If the scammers have done their job properly, victims will eventually signal that they're ready to make a deal—for example, by suddenly using phrases indicating ownership of the goods or property ("my gold coins"; "my land"). The final step in the closing process is to create a sense of urgency to prevent prospects from backing out ("This is a limited-time offer"; "The cost of this deal could double tomorrow").

Revictimizing the Victim

Scammers have surprisingly good luck in revictimizing prospects shortly after the original scam. Victims don't expect to be contacted only a few days after they entered into the deal, and they haven't had enough time to discover the fraud. As with the Nigerian scams discussed earlier, the targets are sometimes told there's a problem with their original investment and additional investments or fees are required. In other cases they're informed of a fabulous new development—the sudden availability of new products or properties—but they have only a limited time to take advantage of the offer. Individuals who might otherwise be resistant often take the bait, sometimes because they fear a refusal could jeopardize their original deal or just because they're again caught up in a powerful emotional state.

Fighting Scams

The most basic step in fighting scams is obviously to be aware of them when you encounter them. Many scams have characteristic features—for example, Nigerian-type advance-fee letters usually originate in West African countries and purport to be from a prince, government official, or other high-ranking individual; they're typically addressed to a "CEO" or "president" or some other generic official rather than a specific person because they're being mass-mailed; and they're often marked "urgent" and typed in capital letters like an old-fashioned telegram.

The AARP offers a list of warning signals to watch for in detecting these and other types of scams:

1. You are asked to send money to claim a lottery or prize or to obtain credit or a loan.
2. You are sending money to someone whom you do not know personally or whose identity you can't verify.

3. Someone you don't know is requesting money sent via a wire service (the number one way money is transferred to fraud criminals).
4. An unknown caller claiming to be a lawyer or in law enforcement will help you get your money back (for a fee).
5. The deal is only good for today or a short period of time.
6. The seller offers "free gifts" in return for a minimum effort or a fee.
7. A "repair person" suddenly finds a dangerous defect in your car or home.
8. You are given little or no time to read a contract.
9. A sale item is suddenly unavailable but a "much better item" is available for slightly more money.
10. Someone is trying to scare you into purchasing a credit card or other protection plan.[375]

You should also be alert to any signs that relatives or friends are being taken in by scams, especially if it's an older family member whose well-being you're responsible for. Warning signs include excessive junk mail or phone calls about sweepstakes offers or other prizes or trips. Large or frequent payments made (especially via wire services or other unusual payment methods) to individuals or businesses located in other states or abroad should also be a major red flag, as are sudden, unexpected financial problems. Other warning signals include changes in the person's demeanor. Con artists often try to find out whether a victim lives with or is in close contact with family members who could interfere with the scam; they may try to get the victim to cut themselves off from others or at least to become more secretive about finances. The demeanor of a scam victim can change in other ways as well. Like the seventy-eight-year-old woman mentioned earlier who was so sure she'd won the sweepstakes that she put a sign in her yard welcoming the "Prize Patrol," some individuals experience euphoria, only to come crashing down when they realize they've been had and have lost part or all of their life savings.

As the Madoff scandal showed, scams can destroy lives. Many victims lose their homes, businesses, children's educational accounts, retirement savings, inheritance, or professional reputation. A few individuals commit suicide. Younger people may have time to recoup their financial losses, but older victims can face poverty or even the loss of their independence, if the scam causes family members to have them declared legally incompetent. An AARP official underscores just how much older victims can lose:

> While we might be tempted to say, "It's only money," for older people with little chance of recovering what they've lost, it's a lot more than money. It may mean the victim cannot afford to remain at home. It may mean not being able to enjoy hobbies or travel to visit the grandchildren. In the worst cases, the victim may no longer be able to afford necessities for daily living, keep a pet, or pay for healthcare needs and medications. The best thing to do is to first say, "I am sorry this happened to you," and then offer to help.[376]

Scams also take a psychological toll; many victims describe a sense of betrayal and violation and say they fear for their financial or even physical safety.

Protecting yourself and others from scams is only the first step in addressing these problems. Fighting scams on a societal level requires the concerted efforts of many individuals and organizations. These range from antifraud activists and government watchdog agencies to the media to the parents and teachers who instill ethical values in the next generation. This is a long-term process, because it involves changing the underlying value system in our society to make it more truthful and less exploitative.

Conclusion

This chapter of *Diving Deep* has only skimmed the surface of the multitude of scams perpetrated on a daily basis in our society. While some kinds of deception don't have a direct, concrete impact on our lives, the kinds of financial scams discussed above can be ruinous; the Madoff scandal is only one of many examples. Even when scams are not financially catastrophic, they rip at the fabric of trust and goodwill that holds any society together. Thus, fighting scams should be a high priority for all of us, both as individuals and as a society.

In the next chapter I explore issues of truth and deception in a different context, but one that can have equally pernicious consequences: scientific and medical misconduct.

What You Can Do

√*Educate yourself and others about scams.* A wealth of information is available online. The StopFraud.gov website is a clearinghouse for information from many government agencies; it includes instructions on how to report various types of fraud and links to the appropriate agencies (www.stopfraud.gov). The Federal Trade Commission (FTC) site provides dozens of articles on scams; see especially their resources on ID theft as well as Internet fraud and safety (www.ftc.gov). The Securities and Exchange Commission (SEC) (www.sec.gov) offers online resources on avoiding financial fraud. For more on scams and fraud, go to the AARP webpage on that topic (http://www.aarp.org/money/scams-fraud/). If you enter "scams" in the search box on the AARP site (www.aarp.org), you'll get additional links to articles and other resources. Because so many scammers use Western Union's money-transfer service, the Western Union website has a fraud section alerting viewers to types of scams and warning signs (www.westernunion.com). The Better Business Bureau provides resources for checking out charities (www.bbb.org/us/charity in the United States or www.bbb.org/canada/charity in Canada). The Canadian Anti-Fraud Centre (CAFC; formerly PhoneBusters) maintains an informative site; visit http://www.antifraudcentre-centreantifraude.ca for useful articles on various types of fraud as well as information on how Canadians can report and prevent it. (The CAFC is jointly run by the Royal Canadian Mounted Police, the Ontario Provincial Police, and the Competition Bureau Canada.)

√*Reduce your chances of being taken in by scammers by becoming hard to reach.* List your phone number with the National Do Not Call registry (www.donotcall.gov or 1-888-382-1222). You can also cut down on preapproved credit card offers (www.optoutprescreen.com or 1-888-567-8688).

√*Have an exit strategy for dealing with unsolicited calls from potential scammers.*

A defensive measure that most experts recommend is surprisingly simple: be prepared with a plan for getting off the phone when a potential scammer calls. Many scammers are masterful at using influence tactics, and some people—especially those who are unusually polite or shy—have a hard time saying no. The longer you stay on the phone, the greater your chances of being taken in by the scam. Have an exit strategy in mind: a phrase like "Sorry, thanks for your offer but I never take part in lotteries or sweepstakes," or "I never make a financial decision without discussing it with _____. I'll get back to you if we need more information."

√*Never furnish your bank account number, credit card number, Social Security number, password, or other personal information to a business or government agency unless you have initiated the transaction.* Even if unsolicited requests for information appear legitimate, you should obtain the web address or phone number of the company or agency on your own and initiate contact with them.

√*Monitor bank statements, credit card statements, and credit reports for suspicious activity.* Other warning signs include unexpected denials of credit, or conversely, receiving credit cards or correspondence about accounts you never applied for. Don't just throw your financial statements in a drawer without looking at them; the sooner you detect illegal activity, the greater your chances of resolving it.

√*Take commonsense steps to avoid being taken in by financial scams.* Thoroughly research potential investment or business deals. Personally choose your financial advisers—find them, don't let them find you—and monitor their handling of your accounts. Steer clear of affinity fraud, where members of groups you belong to take advantage of your relationship in order to con you. Above all, don't forget the rule that if something seems too good to be true, it almost certainly is.

√*Follow tips from companies like Western Union on how to protect yourself against auction fraud and other types of online scams.* Western Union—the payment method of choice for many online scammers— urges that you *always*

- Know the person you're sending money to.
- Buy goods and services from known and trusted sources.
- Be alert to internet advertisements for goods or services wherein the provider suggests you send funds via a wire transfer service.
- Avoid paying for online auction purchases through money transfer.
- Use extra caution if buying or selling items to someone outside of your country, especially when buying popular, high-dollar, items.
- Discontinue any transaction if someone coaches you on how to respond to questions asked by Western Union. This is a sure sign of fraud.
- Check with the Better Business Bureau if you are suspicious of a business.
- Contact your State Attorney General Office of Consumer Affairs if you think someone is trying to defraud you.[377]

√*Take precautions to avoid being victimized by sweepstakes and free-prize scams.* The FTC offers these suggestions:

Don't pay to collect sweepstakes winnings. If you have to pay to collect your winnings, you haven't won anything. Legitimate sweepstakes don't require you to pay "insurance," "taxes" or "shipping and handling charges" to collect your prize.

Hold on to your money. Scammers pressure people to wire money through commercial money transfer companies like

Western Union because wiring money is the same as sending cash. If you discover you've been scammed, the money's gone, and there's very little chance of recovery. Likewise, resist any push to send a check or money order by overnight delivery or courier. Con artists recommend these services so they can get to your money before you realize you've been cheated.

Look-alikes aren't the real thing. It's illegal for any promoter to lie about an affiliation with—or an endorsement by—a government agency or any other well-known organization. Disreputable companies sometimes use a variation of an official or nationally recognized name to try to confuse you and give you confidence in their offers. Insurance companies, including Lloyd's, do not insure delivery of sweepstakes winnings.

Phone numbers can deceive. Some con artists use Internet technology to call you. It allows them to disguise their area code: although it may look like they're calling from Washington, DC or your local area, they could be calling from anywhere in the world.[378]

√*Guard against identity theft.* The burgeoning problem of identity theft calls for extreme vigilance. At a minimum you should

- Give out your personal information as sparingly as possible, especially your Social Security number.
- Avoid leaving personal papers lying around in easily accessible places at home and in the workplace, and try not to carry crucial items like your Social Security card in your wallet unless you have to.
- Get a locked mailbox, retrieve your mail as soon as possible (even from locked boxes because thieves sometimes have master keys to mailboxes in apartment buildings), and avoid leaving outgoing mail in an open box.

- Investigate the privacy policy of any company you're considering doing business with (ask how long they retain sensitive information and how they dispose of it, whether they sell customers' information, whether they conduct criminal background checks on employees, and whether temps for whom no background checks have been done have access to confidential documents—an important issue because thieves often send temps into department stores or doctors' offices to steal information).

- Use secure passwords and avoid obvious choices like your Social Security number (even the last four digits), your birthdate, your mother's maiden name, your dog or cat's name, or a series of consecutive numerals.

- Conduct financial transactions only on secure sites you've accessed by typing in a legitimate URL yourself, as opposed to clicking on questionable links in emails.

- Reduce the number of credit cards you use.

- Consider reducing your use of checks, which can put you at risk for identity theft because of all the personal information they contain (your name, address, and signature; bank account information; and possibly other details like your driver's license number).

- Avoid ATMs that show signs of having been tampered with, and shield the keyboard when you use an ATM.

- Reconcile your bank statements and check your credit report often for signs of unauthorized activity.

- Use a shredder to shred financial documents and other personal papers.

√*To reduce cyberproblems, keep your computer and software updated and take appropriate security steps.* Use the most secure operating system, browsers, and antivirus and other antimalware software you can. Be sure to activate the firewall, spam filter, and other security features included in your operating system, ISP service, email program, or other software. Arrange for automatic or manual updates of security software to catch the latest viruses and other problems. Try to download software only from sites you know are reliable, and avoid conducting financial transactions on public computers like library computers.

√*Report actual or suspected scams to the proper authorities.* In fighting scams, this is one of the most important actions you can take. You don't need indisputable evidence that a scam has taken place; even suspected scams should be reported. Many government agencies handle fraud cases—including some agencies you may not think of. Many Americans don't know, for example, that the Secret Service investigates a wide range of financial crimes, encompassing everything from bank and credit card fraud to counterfeiting and ID theft to computer crime (for more, go to www.secretservice.gov).

If you've been victimized by a scam, you may have to file a police report, because creditors may ask for proof of the crime. Another appropriate starting place is to report the scam to your state attorney general's office, which probably has a fraud hotline. (The Justice Department provides a list of state attorneys general and contact information at http://www.justice.gov/usao/about/offices.html.) If you suspect you're a victim of identity theft, you should file a special identity theft report with the police, preferably in person rather than by phone or online (an identity theft report differs from an ordinary police report and may be required by the businesses you deal with in addressing your ID theft problem).[379] You can also file a complaint with the Federal Trade Commission; information and instructions are available on the FTC's ID theft site (http://www.ftc.gov/bcp/edu/microsites/idtheft/).

Agencies that handle fraud cases include:

- Better Business Bureau (www.bbb.org)
- Federal Bureau of Investigation (FBI) (www.fbi.gov)
- Federal Trade Commission (FTC) (www.ftc.gov)
- Internet Crime Complaint Center (IC3) (www.ic3.gov)
- Secret Service (www.secretservice.gov/criminal.shtml)

- Securities and Exchange Commission (SEC) (www.sec.gov or www.sec.gov/complaint.shtml)
- StopFraud.gov (www.stopfraud.gov)
- U.S. Postal Service (https://postalinspectors.uspis.gov/)

As noted earlier, the Canadian Anti-Fraud Centre (CAFC) website offers information on how Canadians can report fraud (http://www.antifraud-centre-centreantifraude.ca).

√*Get involved.* Join the fight against scams by getting involved with a fraud-fighting organization. An important step you can take is to help pressure the government to better regulate the way Social Security numbers and other data are utilized. In his book *The Art of the Steal*, Frank W. Abagnale urges that "if we're serious about combating identity theft, it's going to take a federal solution, beginning with changes in the way the Social Security number is used and the free and easy access businesses have to people's credit reports. . . . We need to restrict the selling of personal information by credit bureaus, state and federal agencies, and marketing firms. The federal government has to take this issue up—and soon."[380]

Further Reading

The Madoff scandal has generated a small industry of books and articles. For a compelling account, see Diana B. Henriques, *The Wizard of Lies: Bernie Madoff and the Death of Trust* (New York: Times Books / Henry Holt, 2011). Also see Brian Ross, *The Madoff Chronicles: Inside the Secret World of Bernie and Ruth* (New York: Hyperion, 2009); Andrew Kirtzman, *Betrayal: The Life and Lies of Bernie Madoff* (New York: Harper, 2009); Jerry Oppenheimer, *Madoff with the Money* (New York: Wiley, 2009); and Erin Arvedlund, *Too Good to Be True: The Rise and Fall of Bernie Madoff* (New York: Portfolio, 2009). Pulitzer Prize–winning author James B. Stewart considers the Madoff scam in the context of other scandals like those involving Martha Stewart and Lewis "Scooter" Libby; see Stewart's *Tangled Webs: How False Statements Are Undermining America—From Martha Stewart to Bernie Madoff* (New York: Penguin Press, 2011), 361–432.

For more on Charles Ponzi, see Mitchell Zuckoff, *Ponzi's Scheme: The True Story of a Financial Legend* (New York: Random House, 2005).

On scams in general, see Carl Sifakis, *Hoaxes and Scams: A Compendium of Deceptions, Ruses, and Swindles* (New York: Facts On File, 1993). Set up like an encyclopedia, this book contains hundreds of short write-ups on scams ranging from the promises of medieval alchemists to confer immortality to quack devices like the "pandiculator," a height-stretching contraption marketed in the early twentieth century.

For a good book on fighting scams, including excerpts from interview transcripts revealing the strategies used by criminals, tips for resisting the scams, and an appendix titled "Fraud-Prevention Resource List," see Doug Shadel, *Outsmarting the Scam Artists: How to Protect Yourself from the Most Clever Cons* (Hoboken, NJ: AARP/Wiley, 2012). For another AARP book, see Sid Kirchheimer, *Scam-Proof Your Life: 377 Smart Ways to Protect You & Your Family from Ripoffs, Bogus Deals & Other Consumer Headaches* (New York: Sterling, 2007). Also see Les Henderson, *Crimes of Persuasion: Schemes, Scams, Frauds*, 2nd ed. (Azilda, ON: Coyote Ridge Publishing, 2003); Silver Lake Editors, *Scams & Swindles: Phishing, Spoofing, ID Theft,*

Nigerian Advance Schemes, Investment Frauds, False Sweethearts: How to Recognize and Avoid Financial Rip-Offs in the Internet Age (Aberdeen, WA: Silver Lake Publishing, 2006); and Elisabeth Leamy, *The Savvy Consumer: How to Avoid Scams and Ripoffs That Cost You Time and Money* (Herndon, VA: Capital Books, 2004).

On how to avoid being victimized by identity theft—and on how to handle it if you or your family members have been victimized—see Denis G. Kelly, *The Official Identity Theft Prevention Handbook: Everyone's Identity Has Already Been Stolen—Learn What You Can Do about It* (New York: Sterling & Ross, 2011); Jim Stickley, *The Truth about Identity Theft* (Upper Saddle River, NJ: FT Press / Pearson Education, 2008); and Frank W. Abagnale, *Stealing Your Life: The Ultimate Identity Theft Prevention Plan* (New York: Broadway Books, 2007). Also see Abagnale's more general book on fraud, *The Art of the Steal: How to Protect Yourself and Your Business from Fraud—America's #1 Crime* (New York: Broadway Books, 2001).

10. SCIENCE: NOT ALWAYS "SCIENTIFIC"

This chapter looks at the role of bias and deception in science, and the way these problems have affected ordinary people's lives.

Fraudulent Science: From the Piltdown Hoax to Today's Ticking Time Bombs

In the following paragraphs you'll glimpse a few well-known cases of scientific fraud. I've selected these cases to illustrate a range of deceptive behaviors in science and medicine; my discussion is not meant to be exhaustive.

The Piltdown Hoax

Scientific fraud has a long history. In the late seventeenth and early eighteenth centuries, the physicist Isaac Newton apparently manipulated data to provide support for his theories. Nineteenth-century luminaries alleged to have engaged in wrongdoing include the geneticist Gregor Mendel, accused like Newton of manipulating data; Charles Darwin, criticized for borrowing from predecessors without proper acknowledgment; and the chemist and microbiologist Louis Pasteur, who apparently took credit for a vaccine actually produced by someone else.[381]

You've probably heard of one of the most famous cases of scientific fraud in the twentieth century: the Piltdown hoax. At a meeting of the Geological Society of London on December 18, 1912, a lawyer and amateur

archeologist named Charles Dawson announced the discovery of fragments of a skull and jawbone in the Piltdown gravel quarry in East Sussex,
England. Dawson explained that quarry workers had found the skull and
broken it into pieces, giving him a fragment in 1908. Dawson unearthed
other fragments on return trips and showed them to Arthur Smith Woodward, head of the British Museum's geology department. In the summer
of 1912, Woodward joined Dawson in searching the site, and they located
other skull fragments as well as a portion of the jawbone.

At the Geological Society meeting just mentioned, Woodward
informed the audience that the British Museum had pieced together the
skull and jawbone and that Piltdown man appeared to be the long-sought
"missing link"—a hominid spanning the evolutionary gap between apes
and humans. The discovery of a second Piltdown skull in 1915 lent credence to Dawson and Woodward's findings, causing a sensation in some
circles. Still, from the beginning there were skeptics. The circumstances
under which both skulls were found were vague; it wasn't clear exactly
how or when the quarry workers had found the first skull, and Dawson
provided few details on how he and an anonymous friend had unearthed
the second skull. The accuracy of Woodward's reconstruction of the skull
and jawbone was called into question. Most damning were allegations
that the skull and jawbone came from two different sources, with the jaw
being that of an ape.

Over the years Piltdown man was increasingly seen as an anom-
aly that didn't match other fossil discoveries. But several factors made
further investigation difficult, including the inaccessibility of the fragments. According to one account, they were on public view in the British Museum until an incident in 1914 in which a suffragist—angry that
the Piltdown hominid had been arbitrarily labeled male despite a lack
of evidence—vandalized the display case. After that the fragments were
locked in a safe, and most researchers had to work with plaster casts
of the fossils.[382] The hoax didn't begin to unravel until the late 1940s,
when sophisticated dating techniques became available. In 1953, Piltdown man was fully exposed as a fraud by three investigators, Joseph
S. Weiner, Wilfred Le Gros Clark, and Kenneth Page Oakley. They con-

cluded that the so-called missing link was an amalgam of three species: a human skull dating from the Middle Ages, a 500-year-old lower jaw from an orangutan, and chimpanzee teeth. The bones had been stained with a chemical solution to age them, and the chimpanzee teeth had been filed down to look more authentic. To this day the identity of the perpetrator is unknown, though Dawson—working alone or with any of several collaborators—is the leading suspect.

This scientific disaster wasted the lives of countless individuals. Woodward and others sacrificed years investigating archeological remains that turned out to be fraudulent, more than 500 articles and books were needlessly written about the fossils before the fraud was revealed, and the fake artifacts reinforced erroneous hypotheses about human origins. It also doesn't speak well for the scientific community that exposure of the Piltdown hoax took forty years. The hoax illustrates how uncritical and faddish science can be; once findings have won wide acceptance, they can be hard to dislodge. This is a problem we'll meet again in the following sections, though in the case of the thalidomide tragedy, an alert scientist prevented what could have been an unspeakable disaster in the United States.

The Thalidomide Tragedy

The scientist who averted the disaster was Frances Oldham Kelsey. Born in British Columbia in 1914, Kelsey received a master's degree in pharmacology at McGill University, then applied to the doctoral program in pharmacology at the University of Chicago. Confusion over her name may have led to the opportunity that set her career in motion: admission to the Chicago program. Her acceptance letter was addressed to "Mr. Oldham" (her maiden name), and she quickly realized that her first name had probably been mistaken for the man's name *Francis*. After wrestling with her conscience she accepted the research assistantship and financial aid she'd been offered and moved to Chicago. She later said, "To this day, I do not know if my name had been Elizabeth or Mary Jane, whether I would have had that first big step up." She added that "to his dying day," the professor who'd written the letter "would never admit one way or the other."[383]

After receiving her PhD in pharmacology as well as a medical degree from the University of Chicago, Kelsey taught and practiced medicine, then was hired by the Food and Drug Administration in Washington, D.C., in 1960. Only a month after she arrived, Kelsey was assigned the task that would thrust her into the headlines two years later: review of a drug application for thalidomide.

Thalidomide was being manufactured in Germany as a sedative and as an antidote to morning sickness. By the time it came to Kelsey's attention it had been sold over the counter in Germany for several years and was also widely available in other European countries as well as in Canada, South America, and other areas. In September 1960, the Richardson-Merrell pharmaceutical company applied to the FDA for authorization to begin selling thalidomide in the United States under the brand name Kevadon. Kelsey had misgivings from the start. She found the data provided by Richardson-Merrell on the drug's safety inadequate. Key questions were unanswered—for example, whether toxicity would appear if illness or other drugs were present. Kelsey was also wary of the animal research that had been used to justify the drug's safety, because she knew the results of animal experiments often couldn't be extrapolated to humans.

Kelsey's concerns proved well founded. Though the pharmaceutical company pressured her for quick approval, she refused to give in. Then in December 1960, alarm bells sounded when a physician named Leslie Florence sent a letter to the *British Medical Journal* saying some of his patients who'd taken thalidomide had developed peripheral neuritis, a condition involving nerve damage that caused painful tingling in the arms and legs. Knowing thalidomide was being prescribed to pregnant women, Kelsey began to worry about its effects on fetal development. She reasoned that a drug that could cause nerve damage in adults might be toxic to a fetus.

Tragically, she soon had her answer, as families and physicians in Europe and Canada began to report birth defects in babies born to mothers who'd taken thalidomide. Before it was over, there would be more than 10,000 cases of birth defects and thousands of fetal deaths in 46 countries. Many of the birth defects involved a condition called phocomelia, in which the limbs and other organs did not develop properly. Children with this condition were often ridiculed with the cruel epithet "flipper babies."

Kelsey received a firsthand report on these problems from Helen Taussig, a pioneering U.S. physician at Johns Hopkins University (she founded the field of pediatric cardiology). After hearing about a suspected link between thalidomide and increased birth defects in Germany and the United Kingdom, Taussig traveled to Europe to see for herself. She notified Kelsey that the problem was very real, and lent support to Kelsey's efforts by testifying before the Food and Drug Administration.

In the face of mounting evidence of thalidomide's toxicity, the German government removed it from the market, as did other countries. In March 1962, Richardson-Merrell withdrew its application for approval. Since the company had been allowed to make thalidomide tablets available to more than a thousand U.S. physicians on a trial basis and the tablets were given to patients, thousands of pregnant American women did receive thalidomide. Some also obtained the drug abroad. Not all the women could be tracked down, but at least seventeen children with thalidomide-related birth defects are known to have been born in the United States. Still, it would have been much worse if Kelsey (and Taussig) had not prevented the full-scale epidemic from spreading to the United States.

Kelsey's contribution made the headlines; she was written up in the *New York Times, Washington Post, Life, Saturday Review,* and other publications.[384] On August 7, 1962, President John F. Kennedy awarded her the medal for Distinguished Federal Civilian Service, the highest honor a civilian can receive in the United States. Two months later President Kennedy signed a new drug law designed to avert disasters like the thalidomide tragedy by strengthening the FDA's oversight of the review process and raising the standards drug manufacturers had to meet.

The thalidomide tragedy provides a painful lesson in how "unscientific" science can be; I'll return later to the misleading role of animal research in causing this tragedy. But many would agree that Kelsey's efforts show science at its best. In contrast, almost nothing positive can be said about the performance of the scientific and medical profession in the Tuskegee experiment.

The Tuskegee Syphilis Study

The Tuskegee Syphilis Study was one of the most horrifying cases of scientific misconduct in U.S. history. As James H. Jones reports in his book *Bad Blood: The Tuskegee Syphilis Experiment*, this unethical study was allowed to continue for four decades.[385] In 1932, the U.S. Public Health Service decided to study untreated syphilis in African-American men in Macon County, Alabama. These men—399 of them by the time the study ended—became unwitting participants because they were never told they had syphilis and never offered proper treatment, especially penicillin after it began to be the drug of choice in the 1940s.[386] Instead the investigators let the disease go unchecked so they could observe its progression in their subjects. As a newspaper later editorialized, "The fact is that in an effort to determine from autopsies what effects syphilis has on the body, the government from the moment the experiment began withheld the best available treatment for a particularly cruel disease. The immorality of the experiment was inherent in its premise."[387]

The study didn't end until an Associated Press reporter named Jean Heller blew the whistle and published an account in the *Washington Star* on July 25, 1972. Others had spoken out earlier but their voices hadn't been heard. A Public Health Service official had written a memo in 1970 criticizing the experiment as inconsistent with PHS goals. He had also denounced it as "bad science," arguing that its results were contaminated because no record had been kept of the penicillin and other drugs the men may have received for purposes unrelated to the syphilis study. The official concluded that "nothing learned will prevent, find, or cure a single case of infectious syphilis or bring us closer to our basic mission of controlling venereal disease in the United States."[388]

Many critics link the Tuskegee study with the atrocities committed by Nazi scientists and physicians, many of whom were executed or imprisoned after World War II for experimentation on human subjects. Some authors have also drawn parallels with the massive experimentation on animals that continues to this day in laboratories around the world. Deborah Rudacille writes, for example, that

> like the animals that were by then an integral part of a growing research industry, the men of the Tuskegee Syphilis Study were viewed primarily as a means to a scientific end. Racism certainly played a part in the tragedy, as did bureaucratic inertia, but the context in which the drama was enacted was the continued lack of oversight or accountability by biomedical researchers to anyone outside the closed community of science. . . .
>
> The German experience has been commonly viewed as an aberration, a bizarre chapter of history in which an entire nation went mad. Few were willing to see (and even fewer to say) that the seeds of that madness lay dormant in every nation.[389]

Test Your Skills

Gather more information on the Tuskegee Syphilis Study by doing a web search or by reading a book like James H. Jones's critically acclaimed *Bad Blood: The Tuskegee Syphilis Experiment*. The government officials and medical personnel who conducted the study believed the goal of finding a cure for syphilis took precedence over the men's right to informed consent and their right to treatment. Do you think this logic on the part of scientists and doctors is ever justifiable? Why or why not?

The Tuskegee study was only one of many developments that have undermined the public's faith in science and contributed to the view that it is not always "scientific." It has left a bitter harvest in other respects as well, as a public health specialist found to her surprise when she overheard a conversation between two HIV/AIDS clients. After learning that the first client had just been given prescriptions for vitamins and the drug AZT as well as an appointment for a breathing treatment that would help prevent AIDS-related pneumonia, the second client offered this advice: "'OK, here's what you do. Go down the street and fill the vitamins and AZT prescriptions, because they'll know if you don't—the doctors can look on their computer and see if you went to a pharmacy and filled your prescriptions or not—but don't take the AZT. Take the vitamins, and you definitely want to do the breathing treatment because you don't want to get the pneumonia, but don't take the AZT. None of us are taking it. . . . It's just like Tuskegee all over again. They are just using it to experiment on black people.'"[390] The public health worker said she sat there "stunned, enlightened, and amazed by what [she] had heard."[391] She also said she now understood the "worrisome clinic reports" suggesting African-American patients weren't responding to AZT as well as others did: "*Well, of course not. . . . Of course they wouldn't respond as well if they aren't taking the drug.*"[392]

The Love Canal disaster provides another example of deceptive, "unscientific" science that has left a lasting legacy.

Love Canal

A few years after Jean Heller blew the whistle on the Tuskegee experiment, another woman did the same at Love Canal, a neighborhood in Niagara Falls, New York. Love Canal was named after William T. Love, a businessman who built the mile-long canal in the 1890s as part of a grand scheme to construct a model city and shipping lane in the region. His money ran out before he could construct more than a few houses or extend the canal, and the short section of the canal that had been completed left a legacy far more negative than anything he could have envisioned.

In the 1920s, the city began to use the canal as a municipal dump-site. In the 1940s it was acquired by the Hooker Chemicals and Plastics Corporation for use as a waste dump; they lined the canal with clay, then began depositing barrels of toxic chemicals. Others utilized the canal, too: "The City of Niagara Falls and the United States Army used the site as well, with the city dumping garbage and the army dumping possible chemical warfare material and parts of the Manhattan project."[393] Incredibly, in 1953 the city of Niagara Falls pressured Hooker Chemical into selling it the land on which the dumpsite was located because it needed room for a new school. Hooker Chemical not only warned the city of the hazardous nature of the site, but insisted that a seventeen-line caveat be included in the sales agreement that reiterated the same warning. Not only did the city proceed with plans to build the school on landfill it had been warned was toxic, but construction crews damaged the clay barrier Hooker Chemical had put in place to prevent leakage. Construction on a sewer system for a housing development being built next to the waste site in 1957 led to further damage and leakage, and after the wet winter and spring of 1977, the toxic substances in the canal began to overflow.

In 1978, a Love Canal resident named Lois Gibbs began to suspect that her children's asthma, epilepsy, and other chronic health problems could be related to the toxic sewage that people could see and smell in the neighborhood. Gibbs discovered that their housing subdivision and school had been built on or near 21,800 tons of toxic waste. The hundreds of toxic substances identified included at least twelve carcinogens and other lethal chemicals, among them dioxin.[394] In August 1978 Gibbs founded the Love Canal Homeowners Association, which conducted surveys and determined, for example, that just over half the children born between 1974 and 1978 had birth defects, like deafness, a cleft palate, an extra row of teeth, or extra toes. The group spurred efforts to investigate the situation and to get the government to do something about it. Not only did Hooker Chemical (which had become a subsidiary of Occidental Petroleum) try to downplay the seriousness of the problem, but so did many government officials and scientists, some of whom claimed the health effects were unrelated to the chemical waste.

Some officials did express concern, however, such as an EPA administrator who came to Love Canal in the late 1970s. He reported seeing disturbing signs of pollution: "Corroding waste-disposal drums could be seen breaking up through the grounds of backyards. Trees and gardens were turning black and dying. One entire swimming pool had been popped up from its foundation, afloat now on a small sea of chemicals. Puddles of noxious substances were pointed out to me by the residents. Some of these puddles were in their yards, some were in their basements, others yet were on the school grounds. Everywhere the air had a faint, choking smell. Children returned from play with burns on their hands and faces."[395]

The efforts of Gibbs and others to get help finally paid off. On May 21, 1980, President Jimmy Carter declared a federal state of emergency at Love Canal. The government ultimately evacuated more than 900 families, reimbursing them for their homes. Congress also passed the Superfund Act, holding polluters accountable for their actions.

The Love Canal battle didn't end when the families were evacuated. In September 1988, the decision was made to allow resettlement of 200 homes in the area, despite inadequate cleanup measures and despite the fact that "the only separation between the homes declared habitable and those declared not habitable is a suburban street."[396] Describing the decision to allow the resettlement of Love Canal as "appalling," Gibbs speculates that this decision was part of a "political agenda, to convince the American people that such public health and environmental crises can somehow be corrected."[397] She elaborates:

I believe that it's a cover-up, a well-thought-out plan to protect corporate interests—not just Occidental Petroleum, but the entire industry. If Love Canal is resettled, corporate America can claim that chemical contamination in the environment isn't a threat forever, and that technology can be used to clean it up. Or maybe the Love Canal area is intended to set another precedent:

the setting of standards for residential exposures to low-level chemical contamination. If a person were to ask what the residential standard might be for a particular chemical like benzene, scientists would honestly tell you they don't know. However, scientists, government agencies, and corporate polluters can now say that they don't know, but at Love Canal the level was "x," and that level passed the test for habitability.[398]

Ticking Time Bombs

You might think we would have learned something from disasters like thalidomide and Love Canal, but in the early twenty-first century we're awash in current or potential problems caused by runaway science and technology. Many of these problems are ticking time bombs. Here are a few examples:

- *Genetically modified foods ("Frankenfoods").* A growing chorus of voices have been warning for years about the dangers of genetically modified (GM) foods. Good examples of these warnings include Jeffrey M. Smith's exposés, *Seeds of Deception* and *Genetic Roulette*.[399] Noting that "mice avoid eating GM foods when they have the chance, as do rats, cows, pigs, geese, elk, squirrels, and others," Smith asks, "What do these animals know that we don't?"[400] His books provide a wealth of detail on GM food debacles ranging from nutritional deficiencies to life-threatening allergic reactions. They also offer chilling insight into the collusion of scientists and industry in marketing these products as "safe."
- *Cell phones and laptops.* The health impact of the electromagnetic fields associated with wireless communication devices is a matter of growing concern. While some studies purport to find no ill effects, their validity has been questioned because many of these studies have been funded by the communications industry or the military, both of which have a vested interest in downplaying safety concerns.[401] Opposition to cell towers is growing in the United States and is even more intense

in the United Kingdom and Europe: "In recent years, protesters in England and Northern Ireland have brought down cell towers by sawing, removing bolts, and pulling with tow trucks and ropes. In one such case, locals bought the structure and sold off pieces of it as souvenirs to help with funding of future protests. In attempts to fend off objections to towers in Germany, some churches have taken to disguising them as giant crucifixes."[402]

- *Plastics.* Adverse health effects from components of plastics have long been known or suspected. The hazards of polychlorinated biphenyls (PCBs)—common in electrical transformers and many other products—came to light in the 1960s and 1970s, leading to the banning of these substances. Concerns have also been raised for years about perfluorooctanoic acid (PFOA) and other members of the perfluorochemical (PFC) family. PFOA is used in the manufacture of Teflon and is thought to be emitted by Teflon cookware when heated to unusually high temperatures. Though both DuPont (the manufacturer of Teflon) and the government have downplayed safety concerns, there have been disturbing reports of pet birds dying after exposure to fumes from Teflon pans, as well as reports of PFOA contamination in DuPont workers and in the environment surrounding DuPont facilities.[403] Another chemical in plastics that has given rise to widespread concern is bisphenol A (BPA), which mimics the hormone estrogen and is thought to cause neural, reproductive, and other problems. Studies have shown that BPA is leached from polycarbonate baby bottles and water bottles, cans lined with plastic, and other items. As a result, the Canadian government began to ban some of these items in 2008, and similar bans have been introduced or are expected in various U.S. jurisdictions.[404]

This list is unfortunately growing all the time.

Hubris

There's a deeper problem beneath the long history of the "unscientific," fallible, deceitful science touched on in this chapter: the urge to tamper with life. Some call this hubris, usually defined as exaggerated pride.[405]

Frankenstein

Few books encapsulate the problem of scientific and technological hubris better than Mary Shelley's *Frankenstein* (1818), which she began writing when she was only eighteen. The daughter of two radical thinkers, Shelley was well suited to the task of producing such an imaginative novel. Her mother, who died ten days after giving birth to her in 1797, was Mary Wollstonecraft. Wollstonecraft was a writer and social critic famous for her treatise *Vindication of the Rights of Women* (1792), usually taken as the starting point of the feminist movement. Shelley's father was William Godwin, a writer and political philosopher. Through her father she met the poet Percy Bysshe Shelley, with whom she eloped in 1814.

In the introduction to the third edition of *Frankenstein*, published in 1831, Mary Shelley explains how she came to write the novel. She and Percy spent the summer of 1816 in Geneva, near a villa rented by another prominent poet, George Gordon, Lord Byron. It was a wet summer, and they often spent rainy days telling ghost stories. One evening when Byron was entertaining the Shelleys as well as John Polidori, his physician, he proposed that they each write a horror story. The others accepted the challenge, then gave up; only Mary persevered. She explains what happened next: "Many and long were the conversations between Lord Byron and Shelley, to which I was a devout but nearly silent listener. During one of these, various philosophical doctrines were discussed, and among others the nature of the principle of life, and whether there was any probability of its ever being discovered and communicated."[406] Among other things, they discussed the idea (associated with "galvanism," named for the Italian physician and physicist Luigi

Galvani) that electricity could be the spark of life, the animating force of living beings. If true, "Perhaps a corpse would be re-animated; galvanism had given token of such things: perhaps the component parts of a creature might be manufactured, brought together, and endued with vital warmth."[407]

The subtitle of *Frankenstein* is *The Modern Prometheus*, and the novel also drew from conversations between the Shelleys, Byron, and their guests on the Prometheus story. In Greek myth, Prometheus defies the gods and brings fire to humankind; Zeus punishes him for this act of hubris by chaining him to the Caucasus, where an eagle feeds on his liver. In an alternative version, more common among the Romans, Prometheus is guilty of hubris because he gives life to a clay figure, thus creating or recreating humankind. In still other accounts in later centuries, Prometheus symbolizes the creative artist. Mary Shelley combined these themes in her depiction of Victor Frankenstein as a scientist who fashions a monstrous creature from bones he has obtained at a charnel house and who imbues the creature with the spark of life.

Test Your Skills

"Frankenfoods" (genetically modified foods) take their name from Mary Shelley's novel *Frankenstein,* to suggest they're the work of mad scientists. What other examples of human hubris in tampering with nature can you think of? From your experience or that of your family and friends, give a few examples where there have been negative consequences— injuries or illnesses resulting from defective products, harmful medical treatments, pollution-related problems, and so on. Tampering with nature is often attributed to corporate greed; do you think there are other motives as well?

The hubris symbolized by Frankenstein is perhaps at its worst in terms of the human destruction of nature, including the mistreatment of animals. Since animal cruelty is a thread running throughout many cases of deception and fraud in science and medicine, it's worth saying a few words on this topic.

Scientific Fraud and Animal Cruelty

Vivisection (experiments on live animals) came into prominence in Europe in the latter half of the nineteenth century. Claude Bernard, an influential professor of physiology at the Collège de France in Paris, wrote one of the first books justifying this practice. His *Introduction to the Study of Experimental Medicine*, published in 1865, presaged an era—still with us—in which the most excruciating torture of animals would be seen as justifiable in the name of scientific and medical "progress."[408]

If France became the world capital of vivisection in the late nineteenth century, England became the center of the antivivisection movement. An early animal rights leader was Anna Kingsford (1846–1888), who went to Paris to study medicine in the 1870s so she would be better equipped to fight the battle against the vivisectionists.[409] In France, she was tormented by the sights and sounds of animal torture. She wrote on August 20, 1879, that "I have found my Hell here in the *Faculté de Médecine* of Paris, a Hell more real and awful than any I have yet met with elsewhere, and one that fulfills all the dreams of the mediaeval monks."[410] She described her agonizing reactions in more detail:

> The idea that it was so came strongly upon me one day when I was sitting in the Musée of the school, with my head in my hands, trying vainly to shut out of my ears the piteous shrieks and cries which floated incessantly towards me up the private staircase where Beclard, Vulpian and other devils were tormenting their innocent victims. Every now and then, as a scream more heart-rending than the rest reached me, the moisture burst out on my forehead and on the palms of my hands, and I prayed, "Oh God, take me out of this Hell; do not suffer me to remain in this awful place."[411]

Kingsford got some measure of revenge. In 1877, she became embroiled in a ferocious argument with a professor. According to her friend and biographer, Edward Maitland, the argument was about vivisection and was set off by shockingly cruel animal experiments Bernard had just done. Kingsford continued to be distraught after she got home. Viewing Bernard as the primary symbol of the evil of vivisection, she "invoked the wrath of God upon him, at the same moment hurling her whole spiritual being at him with all her might, as if with intent then and there to smite him with destruction."[412] Two months later, she and Maitland discovered a notice posted at the medical school announcing Bernard's death. She continued to spiritually target vivisectionists for assassination. In 1888, Paul Bert—who had been Bernard's student and who was one of her targets—died, and Kingsford again took satisfaction in having enacted a death sentence.

With the growth of bacteriology, immunology, pharmacology, and other experimental sciences in the United States beginning about 1870, animal experimentation became increasingly normative. By the turn of the twentieth century, the United States had become a leader in animal experimentation, like France several decades earlier. Many antivivisection organizations arose to meet this challenge, with the U.S. groups, like their counterparts in England, usually spearheaded by women.[413] These groups, and their successors, proved mostly powerless to stop a growing litany of horrific acts of cruelty to animals at the hands of scientists.

Noting that "scientists do things to animals that, from the animals' point of view, are torture and would be regarded as such by almost everyone if done by nonscientists," famed primatologist Jane Goodall elaborates: "To test the safety of various products, animals are injected with or forced to swallow different amounts to see how sick they get, or if they survive. The effectiveness of medical procedures and drugs are tried out on animals. Surgical skills are practiced on animals. Theories of all sorts, ranging from the effects of various substances to psychological trauma, are tested on animals. What is so shocking is the lack of respect for the victims, the almost total disregard for their living, feeling, sometimes agonizing bodies. And often the tortures are inflicted for nothing."[414]

This history of cruelty is all the more disturbing because animal research is often irrelevant and in many cases spectacularly misleading with respect to human disease. Goodall has said of Robert Gallo, an influential AIDS researcher, that "only a few months after declaring that progress in understanding AIDS would come to a halt because of wicked legislation that prohibited the import of more chimps from Africa, he presented a paper at an international AIDS conference in Arusha, Tanzania, which announced that progress in AIDS research was now 'boxed in by inappropriate results from chimpanzees and gibbons.'"[415] Even the writings of early vivisectionists like Claude Bernard suggest that animal experiments exist not because they have any intrinsic usefulness or accuracy but because they lend medicine a more "scientific" aura, leading to greater career advancement and sources of funding for researchers.[416]

AIDS research is only one of many areas of research jeopardized by unreliable animal studies. Problems with drugs provide another notable example. Thousands of human fatalities are attributed each year to drugs that have been tested on animals, and many more people suffer other serious ill effects. An expert on animal testing has compiled the following list of major disasters:

- The arthritis drug Vioxx, withdrawn from the global market in September 2004, appeared to be safe and even beneficial to the heart in animals, but caused as many as 140,000 heart attacks and strokes in the US alone. The associate safety director of the US Food and Drug Administration (FDA) described it as the "single greatest drug-safety catastrophe in the history of the world." . . .
- Hormone-replacement therapy (HRT), prescribed to many millions of women because it lowered monkeys' risk of heart disease and stroke, increases women's risks of these conditions significantly. The chairman of the German Commission on the Safety of Medicines described HRT as "the new thalidomide." In August 2003 *The Lancet* estimated that HRT had caused 20,000 cases of breast cancer over the past decade in Britain, in addition to many thousands of heart attacks and strokes.

- Dr. Richard Klausner, former director of the US National Cancer Institute (NCI), lamented: "The history of cancer research has been a history of curing cancer in the mouse. We have cured mice of cancer for decades, and it simply didn't work in humans." The NCI also believes we have lost cures for cancer because they were ineffective in mice.
- Cigarette smoke, asbestos, arsenic, benzene, alcohol and glass fibres are all safe to ingest, according to animal studies. . . .
- Dr. Albert Sabin, the inventor of the polio vaccine, swore under oath that the vaccine "was long delayed by the erroneous conception of the nature of the human disease based on misleading experimental models of [it] in monkeys."
- Penicillin, the world's first antibiotic, was delayed for more than 10 years by misleading results from experiments in rabbits, and would have been shelved forever had it been tested on guinea pigs, which it kills. [The discoverer of penicillin] Sir Alexander Fleming himself said: "How fortunate we didn't have these animal tests in the 1940s, for penicillin would probably never have been granted a licence, and possibly the whole field of antibiotics might never have been realized."[417]

Did You Know?

Millions of Animals Are Used for Research Purposes in the United States Every Year

The extraordinary number of animals used in scientific and medical research in the United States is alarming, not only because of the cruelty involved but because of the unreliability of many animal studies. Here's a breakdown of the animal species used in U.S. research in 2010; the figures are listed in order of decreasing frequency:[1]

Guinea pigs	213,029
Rabbits	210,172
Hamsters	145,895
Nonhuman primates	73,317
Dogs	64,930
Pigs	53,260
Cats	21,578
Sheep	13,271
Other farm animals	38,008
All other covered species	303,107
Total	1,136,567

Note: Mice, rats, birds, and fish aren't included in this list because they aren't covered by the Animal Welfare Act. About twenty-five million of these animals are estimated to be used annually for research purposes, making up more than 95 percent of the animals utilized in U.S. research.[2]

1   *These figures are from U.S. Department of Agriculture, Animal and Plant Health Inspection Service, Annual Report Animal Usage by Fiscal Year, Fiscal Year: 2010, July 27, 2011, http://www.aphis.usda.gov/animal_welfare/efoia/downloads/2010_Animals_Used_In_Research.pdf.*
2   *Speaking of Research, "Statistics," 2012, http://speakingofresearch.com/facts/statistics/.*

One of the most notorious examples of the failure of animal studies to turn up potential drug hazards involved thalidomide. Thalidomide was deemed safe for human consumption after extensive animal testing was done. The problem is that thalidomide is not a teratogen (a substance that causes birth defects) in most animals, so birth defects were unlikely to occur. James Schardein, an expert on birth defects, has said: "In approximately 10 strains of rats, 15 strains of mice, 11 breeds of rabbits, two breeds of dogs, three strains of hamsters, eight species of primates, and in other such varied species as cats, armadillos, guinea pigs, swine and ferrets in which thalidomide has been tested, teratogenic effects have been induced only occasionally."[418] In short, based on the animal studies alone, there was no way of foreseeing the disaster that would occur after the drug was put on the market.

Ironically, the drug bill signed by President Kennedy in 1962—the Kefauver-Harris Act—mandated the animal testing still required in the drug-approval process due to the misconception that thalidomide had not been tested on animals. So if thalidomide were evaluated today based exclusively on that mandate, it would still be approved.

Animal rights advocates are increasingly pressuring scientists to use computer models and other alternatives to animal experiments. Promising alternatives include microchip technologies, in which microchips are built that contain miniature replicas of animal organs and systems. Drugs can then be tested on these so-called animals-on-a-chip. Chips replicating human physiology are also being developed for the same purpose.[419] If these and other technologies live up to their expectations, the accuracy of drug tests is likely to improve and the suffering inflicted on animals through the hubris of the scientific and medical community will be, if not halted, at least alleviated.

Conclusion

This chapter has focused on the disturbing history of deceptive, "unscientific" science surrounding us, and on the need to cut through it in order to avert tragedies like thalidomide, Tuskegee, and Love Canal—as well as the ticking time bombs awaiting us in the twenty-first century. After a few concluding remarks, the appendix to the book unifies many of the themes of this and the previous chapters by looking at the importance of critical thinking in our search for truth.

What You Can Do

√*Use critical-thinking skills in evaluating scientific and medical information.* In their book on self-deception, Carol Tavris and Elliot Aronson note that "at least public-interest groups, watchdog agencies, and independent scientists can eventually blow the whistle on bad or deceptive research. The greater danger to the public comes from the self-justifications of well-intentioned scientists and physicians who, because of their need to reduce dissonance, truly believe themselves to be above the influence of their corporate funders. Yet, like a plant turning toward the sun, they turn toward the interests of their sponsors without even being aware that they are doing so."[420] This tendency for a "plant to turn toward the sun" can be detected in the thalidomide tragedy, the problem of genetically modified foods, and a wide range of other disasters or potential disasters, so it's important to evaluate scientific and medical information critically and watch for harmful biases.

√*Take advantage of online resources.* To protect yourself and your family from food- and drug-related problems, toxic plastics, electromagnetic radiation, and other hazards, you'll find a wealth of information online. For example, before you purchase a cell phone, you can check the radiation levels of the most popular models using resources like the CNET staff's "Cell Phone Radiation Levels" (http://reviews.cnet.com/cell-phone-radiation-levels/). (Read the numbers carefully if you compare the ratings on several sites, because the ratings can vary.) The Seeds of Deception website (www.seedsofdeception.com) offers resources on genetically modified foods. The Environmental Working Group's website (www.ewg.org) is a rich source of information on environmental hazards and provides downloadable guides on everything from safe personal-care products for kids to healthy-home tips to how to reduce cell phone radiation.

√*Take commonsense precautions.* To guard against food-related problems, it's usually safer to buy local, organically grown food—for example, from farmers' markets and health food stores—and to reduce the use of packaged foods. Because tests by Consumers Union (the publisher of *Consumer Reports*) turned up evidence of bisphenol A (BPA) even in cans advertised as "BPA-free," they recommend these simple steps:

- Choose fresh food whenever possible.
- Consider alternatives to canned food, beverages, juices, and infant formula.
- Use glass containers when heating food in microwave ovens.[421]

These steps are only the bare minimum. You'll find more information on toxic chemicals in everyday products—including tips for avoiding these chemicals—on the Environmental Working Group website (www.ewg.org).

√*Get involved.* Love Canal showed that anyone can make a difference. When Lois Gibbs left home for Washington, D.C., in 1981 to try to start a movement to combat environmental problems, her mother cautioned her that "you're forgetting you're just a housewife with a high school education." Today the organization Gibbs founded that year— the Center for Health, Environment, and Justice (CHEJ; previously the Citizens Clearinghouse for Hazardous Waste)—has a large membership, and Gibbs has become an internationally known spokesperson and organizer in the environmental justice movement. These achievements led to a Nobel Peace Prize nomination for Gibbs in 2003. For more on CHEJ and how to get involved, go to www.chej.org.

On how you can help create a more life-sustaining food system, see the resources in the book edited by Karl Weber, *Food, Inc.* (a companion guide to the acclaimed film by the same name).[422] If you're specifically concerned about "Frankenfoods" and related problems, you can get involved in the anti-GMO movement. You'll find resources on local actions you can take and on other aspects of this movement in Smith's book *Seeds of Deception* and on the Seeds of Deception website (www. seedsofdeception.com).

√*Both to alleviate the suffering of animals and to reduce the risk of unreliable animal studies, work to end animal tests and other forms of animal cruelty.* Don't buy cosmetics, detergents, or other products unless they're labeled as not having been tested on animals. Some of the worst offenses occur in university labs, so if you study or teach at a university, investigate the role of animal research on your campus and work to end it. Do whatever else is in your power to stop this cruelty—for example, by contributing to the Humane Society (www.humanesociety.org) or other animal-welfare groups of your choice.

The Humane Society's website provides detailed information on the problem of animal cruelty and on ways you can fight it. See especially the page titled "Animals in Laboratories" (http://www.humanesociety.org/about/departments/animals_research.html), containing information, blog posts, videos, and suggestions for actions you can take to combat a wide range of animal abuses. For more on animal experimentation, see the website of People for the Ethical Treatment of Animals (PETA) (http://www.peta.org/issues/animals-used-for-experimentation/default.aspx). You'll find the names of other animal-protection organizations and their contact information in the "Resources" section of Deborah Rudacille's *The Scalpel and the Butterfly: The War between Animal Research and Animal Protection* (New York: Farrar, Straus and Giroux, 2000), 365–375.

Further Reading

General works on scientific fraud include William Broad and Nicholas Wade, *Betrayers of the Truth* (New York: Simon & Schuster, 1982), and David J. Miller and Michel Hersen, eds., *Research Fraud in the Behavioral and Biomedical Sciences* (New York: Wiley, 1992). For a selection of books on corporate science and medicine, see Sheldon Krimsky, *Science in the Private Interest: Has the Lure of Profits Corrupted Biomedical Research?* (Lanham, MD: Rowman & Littlefield, 2003); Jerome P. Kassirer, *On the Take: How Medicine's Complicity with Big Business Can Endanger Your Health* (New York: Oxford University Press, 2005); Stan Cox, *Sick Planet: Corporate Food and Medicine* (London Pluto Press, 2008); Marcia Angell, *The Truth about the Drug Companies: How They Deceive Us and What to Do about It* (New York: Random House, 2005); and Dan Fagin, Marianne Lavelle, and the Center for Public Integrity, *Toxic Deception: How the Chemical Industry Manipulates Science, Bends the Law, and Endangers Your Health* (Monroe, ME: Common Courage Press, 1999).

For a comprehensive website on the Piltdown hoax, including links and references, see Richard Harter, "Piltdown Man," December 4, 2011, http://www.tiac.net/~cri_a/piltdown/piltdown.html. Also see J. S. Weiner, *The Piltdown Forgery*, 50th anniv. ed., ed. Chris Stringer (Oxford: Oxford University Press, 2003), as well as Roger Lewin, *Bones of Contention: Controversies in the Search for Human Origins* (New York: Simon & Schuster, 1987), 60–75, 134–136. The following volume includes original correspondence otherwise hard to obtain: Frank Spencer, *The Piltdown Papers 1908–1955: The Correspondence and Other Documents Relating to the Piltdown Forgery* (London: Oxford University Press, 1990).

On thalidomide, see Rock Brynner and Trent Stephens, *Dark Remedy: The Impact of Thalidomide and Its Revival as a Vital Medicine* (New York: Perseus, 2001). For biographical sketches of Frances Kelsey, see "Frances Oldham Kelsey," National Women's Hall of Fame, 2000, http://www.greatwomen.org/women-of-the-hall/search-the-hall/details/2/92-Kelsey, and "Changing the Face of Medicine: Dr. Frances

Kathleen Oldham Kelsey," National Library of Medicine, 2003, http://www.nlm.nih.gov/changingthefaceofmedicine/physicians/biography_182.html.

For more on the Tuskegee experiment, see James H. Jones, *Bad Blood: The Tuskegee Syphilis Experiment*, rev. ed. (New York: Free Press, 1993), and Susan M. Reverby, *Examining Tuskegee: The Infamous Syphilis Study and Its Legacy* (Chapel Hill: University of North Carolina Press, 2009). Reverby's edited collection, *Tuskegee's Truths: Rethinking the Tuskegee Syphilis Study* (Chapel Hill: University of North Carolina Press, 2000), contains a selection of letters, interviews with survivors, and other documents and analysis. On the exploitation of African Americans by the medical profession, also see Harriet A. Washington's award-winning book, *Medical Apartheid: The Dark History of Medical Experimentation on Black Americans from Colonial Times to the Present* (New York: Doubleday, 2006). A provocative book on related themes is Stefan Kühl, *The Nazi Connection: Eugenics, American Racism, and German National Socialism* (New York: Oxford University Press, 1994).

On the Love Canal disaster, see Erika Engelhaupt, "Happy Birthday, Love Canal," *Chemical & Engineering News: Government & Policy* 86, no. 46 (November 17, 2008): 46–53, http://pubs.acs.org/cen/government/86/8646gov2.html. For Lois Gibbs's story, see Lois Marie Gibbs, *Love Canal: The Story Continues . . .* (Gabriola Island, BC: New Society Publishers, 1998). Benjamin Ross and Steven Amter discuss the larger context of the Love Canal fiasco in their book *The Polluters: The Making of Our Chemically Altered Environment* (Oxford: Oxford University Press, 2010).

On genetically modified foods, see Jeffrey M. Smith's *Seeds of Deception: Exposing Industry and Government Lies about the Safety of the Genetically Engineered Foods You're Eating* (Fairfield, IA: Yes! Books, 2003), as well as Smith's *Genetic Roulette: The Documented Health Risks of Genetically Engineered Foods* (Fairfield, IA: Yes! Books, 2007). Also see Peter Pringle, *Food, Inc.: Mendel to Monsanto—The Promises and Perils of the Biotech Harvest*, rev. ed. (New York: Simon & Schuster, 2005); Marie-Monique Robin, *The World According to Monsanto* (New York: New Press,

2010); and F. William Engdahl, *Seeds of Destruction: The Hidden Agenda of Genetic Manipulation* (Montreal: Global Research, 2007). Other popular books on food-related issues include Eric Schlosser, *Fast Food Nation: The Dark Side of the All-American Meal*, rev. ed. (New York: Mariner Books, 2012); Michael Pollan, *The Omnivore's Dilemma: A Natural History of Four Meals* (New York: Penguin Press, 2006); Barbara Kingsolver, with Steven L. Hopp and Camille Kingsolver, *Animal, Vegetable, Miracle: A Year of Food Life* (New York: HarperCollins, 2007); and Karl Weber, ed., *Food, Inc.: How Industrial Food Is Making Us Sicker, Fatter, and Poorer—and What You Can Do about It* (New York: PublicAffairs / Perseus Books Group, 2009).

For more on the writing of *Frankenstein*, see Dorothy Hoobler and Thomas Hoobler, *The Monsters: Mary Shelley and the Curse of Frankenstein* (New York: Little, Brown, 2006). Susan Tyler Hitchcock's *Frankenstein: A Cultural History* (New York: Norton, 2007) provides a lively history of the Frankenstein theme.

For two books by a husband-and-wife team (he is a physician and she is a veterinarian) exploring the destructive impact of animal-based research, see C. Ray Greek and Jean Swingle Greek, *Sacred Cows and Golden Geese: The Human Cost of Experiments on Animals* (New York: Continuum, 2000), and their *Specious Science: How Genetics and Evolution Reveal Why Medical Research on Animals Harms Humans* (New York: Continuum, 2002). Many of Jane Goodall's publications deal with the exploitation of animals in research labs; see for example Dale Peterson and Jane Goodall, *Visions of Caliban: On Chimpanzees and People*, rev. ed. (Athens: University of Georgia Press, 2000). For surveys of the treatment of animals in scientific and medical research, see Deborah Rudacille, *The Scalpel and the Butterfly: The War between Animal Research and Animal Protection* (New York: Farrar, Straus and Giroux, 2000), and Anita Guerrini, *Experimenting with Humans and Animals: From Galen to Animal Rights* (Baltimore: Johns Hopkins University Press, 2003).

CONCLUSION

The ten chapters that make up *Diving Deep* have explored major forms of deception—from dirty politics to financial scams, from advertising hype to scientific fraud—engulfing us in contemporary society. If this book helps you reduce the impact of these problems so you can make better political, medical, financial, and other decisions, it will have achieved one of its main purposes. A deeper purpose has been to suggest that we're drowning in a sea of deception because deception has become an ideology governing our way of life. We're at a crossroads. We can either opt for a society based on truth, whether in politics, business, advertising, science, or other areas of life, or we can continue along the path we're on.

I began this book with the example of Helen Gahagan Douglas, eulogized as someone who succeeded in "being true to oneself in one's own place and in one's own time."[423] We can't all be glamorous actors or spend our lives on the national stage. But we can all try to show the integrity and resilience Douglas showed in the face of the lies and distortions hurled at her in the 1950 California senatorial race and subsequently. Whether we dive deeply for our own truth, as Douglas did, or let ourselves be tossed around in the waters of deceit and fabrication is up to us, both as individuals and as a society. I hope you'll join me in choosing a society based on truth.

APPENDIX
DIVING DEEP AND THINKING
CRITICALLY

A theme reiterated throughout *Diving Deep* is that to make sound decisions, you should think critically about the information that comes your way. Many cultural and technological influences—a declining educational system, the anti-intellectualism of popular culture, sound-bite journalism, and other forces—have contributed to a dumbing down of our society. Some authors identify an *ignorance spiral*: "a cynical populace bombarded with more and more thoughtless propaganda that they have less and less skill and inclination to process and ability to understand."[424] By providing an overview of critical thinking, this appendix is meant to give you some tools to resist these forces.

Whole books have been written on critical thinking; no two authors understand this term exactly the same way.[425] But any definition would have to emphasize concepts like intellectual rigor, accuracy, clarity, reflection, insight, and ethics. As a starting point, I'll define critical thinking as *a cognitive process by which we gather information and evaluate it, arriving at insightful conclusions through the use of intellectual rigor, open-mindedness, and an awareness of our own biases and those of others.*

Critical thinking can also be defined in terms of what it is *not*. Critical thinking is the opposite of rigid, egocentric thinking that is self-serving and that disregards the perspectives and needs of others. Critical thinkers are curious, flexible, and try to be fair-minded in the way they interpret facts and ideas; they're tolerant of others' viewpoints and often seek common ground. Rigid thinkers tend to be dogmatic, rely on sweeping generalizations rather than nuanced thinking, are interested in winning arguments no matter how much they have to distort the facts, and often lash out with personal attacks if they're losing.

Table A.1 Critical thinking: A five-step approach

Step 1: Define the problem or issue as clearly as possible.
State the problem precisely.
Break the problem down into its component parts.
Look at the problem from different perspectives.
Identify the results you're trying to achieve by solving the problem.

Step 2: Gather as much information and supporting evidence as you can.
Investigate a wide array of sources and viewpoints.
Be alert to your biases and those of others.

Step 3: Evaluate the information by assessing the supporting evidence and arguments.
Assess the evidence.
Assess the arguments.

Step 4: Draw the conclusion that makes the most sense to you.
Draw a well-supported conclusion.
Make the conclusion consistent with your values and goals.

Step 5: Remain open to new perspectives.

In the following pages I outline a commonsense, five-step approach, summarized in Table A.1. Most critical thinkers follow this approach, or something similar, in making important decisions. As the table shows, the five main steps are:

Step 1: Define the problem or issue as clearly as possible.
Step 2: Gather as much information and supporting evidence as you can.
Step 3: Evaluate the information by assessing the supporting evidence and arguments.
Step 4: Draw the conclusion that makes the most sense to you.
Step 5: Remain open to new perspectives.

A few more details and concrete examples will help you see how a mastery of critical thinking can benefit almost every area of your life. Note that the critical-thinking steps outlined in this chapter apply equally to speech and writing; they'll make you a better judge of other people's arguments in a speech or article, or help you do a great job in a debate or on a written assignment for work or school. The accompanying box looks specifically at critical thinking in relation to the writing process.

Tips on Critical Thinking for Good Writing

Here are a few pointers on using critical-thinking skills to produce good writing.

1. *Be succinct and to the point.* Don't ramble. State your main point in the first or second paragraph, then develop it using the critical-thinking steps outlined in this appendix.

2. *Organize your piece of writing in the most logical way you can.* In a short article or essay you'll often have an introductory paragraph, followed by a separate paragraph for each of your main points, then a conclusion. In an even shorter piece like a blog post you could have an opening paragraph, a second paragraph that combines your main points and supporting evidence, then a concluding paragraph. In a nonfiction book, on the other hand, you would have the space to devote one or

more chapters to each of your main points. Regardless of what you're writing, well-organized material signals to readers that you're a critical thinker and increases their comprehension of the material.

3. *Strive for clarity.* Use good grammar and comprehensible vocabulary. Avoid jargon and technical terms or define these terms clearly. Also try to avoid ambiguity—for example, terms like *socialist, radical,* and *extremist* have very different (sometimes opposite) meanings depending on who is using them and on the context, so either steer clear of these words or define them. Keep in mind that your audience may include people from a wide range of educational, ethnic, cultural, and political backgrounds.

4. *Argue in a level-headed, respectful way.* In keeping with the points made in this appendix and elsewhere in this book, you should avoid ridicule and personal attacks, including slurs and stereotypes based on gender, ethnicity, age, appearance, or other factors. These attacks are not only disrespectful but can backfire by suggesting you have to resort to insults because you aren't competent or knowledgeable.

5. *If time permits, revise your work extensively.* Most writers—including highly experienced professional writers—revise their work multiple times before turning it in. It helps to put your draft aside, then come back to it. Also get as much feedback as possible from family, friends, and colleagues. Their responses should alert you to whether you've successfully used the critical-thinking principles discussed in this appendix.

Step 1: Define the Problem or Issue as Clearly as Possible

As you've seen throughout this book, problems or issues are often more complicated than they seem at first glance. You can't make an important decision without identifying exactly what you're trying to assess or solve. Luckily there are several ways you can tease a problem apart to make the decision-making process easier. You can state the problem precisely, break it down into its component parts, look at it from different perspectives, and identify the results you're trying to achieve by solving the problem.

State the Problem Precisely

An obvious place to begin is by stating the problem as clearly and succinctly as you can. I'll begin with a simple example. Let's say you consider the U.S. political system unjust or corrupt and want to help reform the system. You might begin with a general statement of the problem like "I want to help create a better political system in the United States." But what does this mean? You might refine your statement by saying that "I believe every American should have a voice in politics, and I want to help bring that about." Further refinements could lead to a statement like "I think voting rights are all-important, so want to start by helping people register to vote."

With even more specificity, you could end up with the statement that you plan to create an organization to mobilize voters in your community. Or you could commit yourself to working on a voter-education project. Alternatively, you could say you plan to obtain a political science or law degree and enter government service to work for electoral reform. Do you see how much more precise and useful these statements are than the one you began with—that you merely want to work toward a better political system? The process of defining your goal has put you in touch with what's really important to you and how best to achieve it.

Break the Problem Down into Its Component Parts

A second strategy that can help you define a problem is to break the problem down into its component parts. Dividing the election-reform issue into smaller units might lead you to look at factors like the history of dirty politics in the United States, previous attempts at reform, the role of the two main political parties as well as of the corporations and media in blocking reform, the precise nature of the desired reforms, and the political, legal, and financial hurdles that have to be overcome in order to improve the system.

Look at the Problem from Different Perspectives

A third strategy for defining a problem is to look at it from different perspectives. Sticking with the our previous example, if you're interested in working for political reform and want a better understanding of the relevant issues, a useful approach would be to look at the issues from a variety of viewpoints—say, those of voters of various political parties and outlooks, campaign organizers and activists, government officials, and scholars and journalists who've written on election-reform issues. You could also do an online search to see what people in different countries have to say about their political systems.

Identify the Results You're Trying to Achieve by Solving the Problem

A good way to pinpoint the problem you're trying to solve is to ask yourself what you're trying to accomplish by solving the problem. Returning to the political example, ask yourself what your specific priorities are in bringing about reform. Are you primarily concerned about the mechanics of voting, so that each eligible voter has an opportunity to cast a vote and can expect that their vote will be recorded? Or are you concerned about creating balanced media coverage of the candidates and issues? Or are you primarily focused on giving ordinary citizens more of a role and the corporations and political-party hierarchies less of a role in determining the outcome of elections? In short, once the problem or problems have been solved and you've helped implement the new system, what features would it have? Clarifying your goals will make it easier to research the subject and arrive at choices that are important to you.

Step 2: Gather as Much Information and Supporting Evidence as You Can

At this stage you'll want to assemble as much information on your topic as possible. You should be careful to investigate a wide array of sources and viewpoints and should be alert to your biases and those of others.

Investigate a Wide Array of Sources and Viewpoints

When possible, try to get a broad view of the problem or issue by looking at relevant materials from several sources. If you're researching a controversial political issue, for example, you might want to look at authoritative books for an in-depth treatment, newspaper or magazine articles to get a sense of what's appearing in the mainstream media, and blogs for the latest opinion and commentary.

Don't fall into the trap of including information that reflects only a single viewpoint; as a critical thinker, you should utilize sources reflecting a range of viewpoints. Doing web searches under terms like "Mexican perspectives," "Native American values," "liberal principles," or "conservative ideologies" (or other viewpoints that may be unfamiliar, depending on your background) may add depth to your research. Exploring various viewpoints doesn't obligate you to accept any of them, but it will almost always give you a better, more complex understanding of the problem you're trying to define and solve. In some cases, this approach will alert you to points of view you may not have thought of; it may also save you from embarrassing errors.

Be Alert to Your Biases and Those of Others

An essential part of the information-gathering step is to be aware of your biases and those of others. The more aware you are of the filters through which you see the world, the more you can correct for any distortions or omissions. If you're a college student and it's not "cool" to be a Republican on your campus, your anti-Republican bias may tempt you to filter out the GOP position on an issue without giving it a fair hearing.

The biases of others require the same vigilance. The researchers at the website FactCheck.org recommend subjecting a source of information to extra scrutiny if it's an advocate for a particular cause: "Claims made by political parties, candidates, lobbying groups, salesmen, and other advocates may be true but are usually self-serving and as a result may be misleading; they require special scrutiny. Always compare their information with other sources."[426]

Step 3: Evaluate the Information by Assessing the Supporting Evidence and Arguments

At this crucial stage, you'll need to evaluate the information you've gathered, discarding information that seems unreliable or irrelevant. As the above heading implies, this stage can be broken down into two separate tasks: assessing the evidence and assessing the arguments. Note that evaluating the evidence alone is not enough, because people can draw unsound conclusions from sound evidence.

Assess the Evidence

There are many ways of assessing evidence. I'll touch on five factors to look at: the source, adequacy, relevance, recency, and consistency of the evidence.

Source. In evaluating evidence, a place to begin is to ask yourself what the source of the evidence is. If it's provided by an "expert," what are the person's credentials and track record? If someone is genuinely knowledgeable, there's a good chance that that will be reflected in credentials, past accomplishments, or accolades from colleagues. Of course, you'll need to exercise caution in this area, because credentials are no guarantee of expertise or ethical conduct. As we saw in Chapter 8, so-called expert witnesses are capable of manipulating evidence in court; we noted in Chapter 10 that scientists sometimes distort their findings so as not to jeopardize their funding from industry or government. Conversely, a lack of credentials may be misleading. A woman with extensive foster-care experience may have more insight into parenting issues than a psychologist with a PhD; a mechanic with a lifetime of experience may be more knowledgeable about car engines than someone with an engineering degree.

Adequacy. It's important to look not only at who provided the evidence, but at how they obtained it. If the evidence was obtained through studies or surveys, how trustworthy was the method? Let's take an example involving political polls that gets at the adequacy of the evidence. Suppose you want to vote for the candidate in your party who has the best chance of winning the election. A major poll shows Candidate A is way ahead of Candidate B, and Candidate A's campaign staff and supporters tout those results as evidence that their candidate is the most electable. Should you take their word for it and vote for Candidate A?

Not necessarily. Especially if a single poll is all you have to go on, you should make sure it's reliable. How big was the sample of people polled? Did they survey hundreds of people from around the state or just a handful? And how representative was the sample? Did it include a cross-section of people drawn from different categories based on gender, race and ethnicity, age, religion, economic background, geographic region, and so on, or was it skewed in one direction or another? If you investigate the poll's reliability, you may find that Candidate A is not a sure-fire winner at all—just a candidate with strong support from the particular slice of the electorate that happened to be surveyed.

Relevance. Besides looking at the source and adequacy of the evidence, you can also assess the evidence in terms of its relevance. In Chapter 10, we saw that even the staunchest advocates of animal experimentation sometimes admit that conclusions derived from animal research can't be extrapolated to humans.

Recency. As a fourth criterion for judging the reliability of the evidence, you can look at its recency. In some cases the date of the evidence is unimportant; in other cases it's crucial. Earlier evidence is occasionally preferable to more recent evidence. Someone doing a study of a Native culture might prefer source material from the nineteenth or early twentieth century, because it could include firsthand accounts rather than material filtered through later generations of scholarship. For the same reason, documents from the first half of the twentieth century could have the advantage of including unusually detailed eyewitness accounts, say, of the sinking of the *Titanic*, the battles of World War I, or the Great Depression of the 1930s.

More typically, recent evidence is more useful. Examples abound from the medical and scientific fields. To take a simple example, if you were considering accepting a job that exposed you to a high level of radiation, you wouldn't read literature on radiation safety from the 1940s or 1950s, when radiation was thought safe enough that scientists, military personnel, and miners were routinely exposed to large doses. For that matter, radiation was considered so safe that between the 1930s and 1950s, many shoe stores used shoe-fitting x-ray machines or fluoroscopes to ensure that shoes were a good fit. Typically, the machine was a vertical wooden cabinet with an opening near the bottom for the customer's feet. At the top there were several viewing ports through which the customer, salesperson, and a third person (such as a parent if the customer was a child) could see the x-ray showing the outlines of the shoes in relation to the bones of the feet. Shielding against radiation was nonexistent; the customer's feet were essentially resting on the x-ray tube, with only a one-millimeter-thick layer of aluminum in between.[427] The text of a newspaper and magazine ad for the Adrian X-Ray Machine from the 1940s hints at how blasé scientists, manufacturers, and the public were about radiation hazards in those days:

> They'll Need Their Feet All Through Life. . . .
>
> The new Adrian "Special" shown here is the latest development in fluoroscopic X-Ray shoe fitting equipment. Built in full compliance with American Standards Association requirements as well as all other applicable government specifications, the new Adrian has met rigid requirements and has been awarded the Parent's Magazine Seal of Commendation. The new ADRIAN can be found in better retail shoe and department stores everywhere. Ask for fitting by ADRIAN . . . it will assure you of foot health and comfort. And remember, SHOES THAT FIT WELL - LAST LONGER![428]

Fortunately no adverse effects experienced by customers using these machines have come to light. Salespeople and other personnel utilizing them on a regular basis weren't so lucky. One of the worst cases was that of a shoe model who had to have her leg amputated because of severe radiation burns.[429]

The moral? With medical and scientific topics you'll almost always want to consult the latest studies, especially when the stakes are high, as with the radiation-safety example. Knowledge in these fields may increase exponentially and you don't want to be left behind at the shoe-fitting fluoroscope stage of awareness.

Consistency. A fifth way you can assess the evidence is in terms of its consistency, both internal and external. *Internal consistency* refers to the internal logic of the evidence. Here's an example of a piece of evidence that lacks internal consistency: "Because of the tremendous potential benefits of genetic engineering I have outlined, we need to proceed immediately with experimentation on recombinant DNA research using human genetic materials. Because of the dangers associated with human genetic research, current legislation allows for experimentation on animal and plant genetic structures only. It is my view that the current laws should remain in place until adequate safeguards are established for human genetic research, and such safeguards may take years to develop."[430] In this passage, the first and last sentences seem to contradict each other.

To meet the criterion of *external consistency*, evidence should be consistent with most other available evidence considered authoritative. An extreme example of external inconsistency would be the "evidence" offered by Holocaust deniers that the Nazi Holocaust of the 1930s and 1940s never happened, which conflicts with a profound amount of historical data, eyewitness testimony, documentary films, and other authoritative evidence. Though that example is straightforward, others are less so. Sometimes those who offer evidence that seems externally inconsistent are not "wrong," but merely ahead of their time, as you saw in the discussion of scientific paradigm shifts in Chapter 1. The evidence Darwin offered for an evolutionary relationship between humans and other animals may not have seemed credible in the nineteenth century since it was at odds with the prevailing scientific opinion, but because of the intervening paradigm shift, Darwin's evidence seems much more credible today than does that of his opponents.

As noted earlier, critical thinking requires that we evaluate the arguments as well as the evidence, because sound evidence can be used as a basis for bad arguments.

Assess the Arguments

In evaluating arguments, it's important to be able to detect logical fallacies. What is a fallacy? *Merriam-Webster's Collegiate Dictionary* defines a fallacy as an "often plausible argument using false or invalid inference." In simpler language, a fallacious argument is one that seems convincing—often because it resonates with our values or prejudices—but that involves unsound reasoning. Watch for several kinds of fallacies: fallacies of false generalization, causal fallacies, and fallacies that involve emotional appeals or attacks.

Fallacies of False Generalization. Fallacies of false generalization can take many forms; they usually involve overgeneralizing. An example would be where someone extrapolates a generalization from a particular incident:

- Yoshi got an A on the exam. Asians have higher IQs than everyone else!
- Louise struck out six times in a row. All women are terrible athletes!
- When Jim was in France he asked the waiter for a "giraffe of wine" instead of a "carafe of wine." Americans are so dumb!

As these examples suggest, the process of overgeneralizing can lead to stereotypes, usually involving a rigid, simplistic attitude toward an entire group regardless of what the individual members of that group are actually like. Even with valid generalizations, it's important to allow for individual differences and exceptions.

One way of looking at the problem of overgeneralizing is to say it's a problem of an unrepresentative sample—the sample is too small or too biased to warrant general conclusions. It follows that if the sample is bigger and more representative, the conclusions could be warranted.

Note that the size of the sample alone is not the only variable, as the editors of the *Literary Digest* found out to their chagrin in a famous case from the 1930s. The magazine wanted to predict who was likely to win the 1936 presidential election—Franklin D. Roosevelt, the Democratic incumbent, or his Republican challenger, Alf Landon, who was governor of Kansas. A huge number of ballots (10 million) were mailed out, yielding a return of 2.3 million. Based on the large sample size and on the results obtained, the magazine didn't hesitate to predict in its October 31 issue that Landon would win the race. Yet Roosevelt won in a landslide, garnering 60.8 percent of the vote and sweeping forty-six of the forty-eight states. (The two exceptions were Maine and Vermont. The prevailing wisdom was that "as Maine goes, so goes the nation," but the 1936 election results led the Democratic Party chair to quip that "as Maine goes, so goes Vermont.")

What went wrong with the *Literary Digest* poll? The basic flaw was improper sampling. The magazine had made the mistake of limiting its sample to car and telephone owners and to its own subscribers or potential subscribers—all indicators of wealth in that period and thus of individuals likely to lean Republican. This humiliating experience badly damaged the credibility of the *Literary Digest*, and a few months later it ceased publication. One pollster who did get it right was George Gallup, an advertising executive who relied on a much smaller but more representative sample of 50,000 people. The soundness of Gallup's methods, as well as the accuracy of his prediction that Roosevelt would win (and that the *Literary Digest* would get it wrong), ushered in the age of scientific polling in presidential politics.

Fallacies of false generalization can also involve the problem of *false dilemma*: a simplistic, either-or assertion that doesn't allow for other alternatives. An example would be the expression "Love it or leave it!", sometimes hurled at critics or activists who call attention to problems in U.S. society. Obviously, those are not the only alternatives; a third choice would be to work to improve society.

Causal Fallacies. Flawed arguments not only involve fallacies of false generalization; they can also include causal fallacies. Causal arguments are those that attempt to show a cause-and-effect relationship between events, so causal fallacies occur when that relationship is not properly established. A common type of causal fallacy is known by the Latin term *post hoc, ergo propter hoc* ("After this, therefore because of it"), which involves confusion between correlation and causation. Some students take a good-luck charm with them or wear their favorite article of clothing when they take an important exam. Some athletes do similar things, performing arcane rituals during a big game. Maybe you've done these things yourself. If you got an A every time you took your good-luck charm to an exam, did the charm cause the good grade, or was there merely a correlation between the two events? If you hit a home run every time you scratched your head three times, closed one eye, then glanced at the sky, do you think that ritual caused the home run, or was the ritual merely correlated with the home run? In short, was the relationship between the two events just a coincidence? These examples are trivial, but the history of medicine is full of missteps resulting from this common type of causal fallacy. Scientist Max Cutler makes this point when he says that "medical literature has numerous examples of such fallacious conclusions. . . . Simply because one finds bullfrogs after a rain does not mean that it rained bullfrogs."[431] An implication is that a third cause is often being overlooked. If many older people tend to be depressed, is this because old age causes depression, or is there a third factor—like ageism, poverty, or the loss of loved ones—that causes the depression?

Another group of causal arguments is denoted by the term *slippery slope*. As the term implies, these arguments claim that if some action is taken, a whole series of undesirable consequences will follow ("If you miss one credit card or loan payment . . ."). In a political context, this line of thought is often called the *domino theory* ("If Vietnam falls to the communists, the Philippines will fall, then Hawai'i, then . . . ?"). In some cases these arguments can be accurate, but since there is no guarantee that the entire progression of undesirable events will unfold, I list them here as another category of causal fallacies.

Fallacies That Involve Emotional Appeals or Attacks. Fallacies aren't limited to faulty generalizations or causal errors. Other fallacies entail emotional appeals or attacks. Arguments that rely on these tactics are considered fallacious because they substitute emotional exchanges for a critical discussion of the issues. Common types of emotional appeals include appeals to pity and fear. Appeals to pity are frequently seen in the courtroom, where relatives of a crime victim attend a trial and may plead for a harsh sentence for the perpetrator during a sentencing hearing. Appeals to fear are common in the political arena; labels like *communist, Stalinist, Nazi,* and *fascist* have often been used to impugn candidates or causes and instill fear in voters.

As noted, personal attacks substitute for sound argument. It would be hard to find a better example than the attacks against Rachel Carson after she published her groundbreaking book *Silent Spring* (1962), ushering in the modern environmental movement.[432] As Carson's biographer, Linda Lear, notes, many of these attacks were gender-based: "Mixed in with all the other arguments was Carson's gender. . . . Her arguments were exaggerations born of hysteria at worst and an overly sensitive nature at best. Reason had been sacrificed to sentiment. Behind these charges was understandable resentment of Carson's aggressive attack on the scientific establishment and on a male-dominated technology. Among her other errors, Miss Carson had overstepped her place."[433] Part of *Silent Spring* was serialized in the *New Yorker* before the book was published, and the chemical industry and its supporters immediately went on the attack.[434] After reading the *New Yorker* installments, Ezra Taft Benson—former secretary of agriculture—is said to have asked in a letter to Dwight Eisenhower "why a spinster with no children was so concerned about genetics," then to have answered his own question by speculating that she was "probably a Communist."[435] Benson wasn't alone in attributing communist sympathies to Carson; another man who'd read the *New Yorker* articles declared in a letter to the magazine that

Miss Rachel Carson's reference to the selfishness of insecticide manufacturers probably reflects her Communist sympathies, like a lot of our writers these days.

We can live without birds and animals, but, as the current market slump shows, we cannot live without business.

As for insects, isn't it just like a woman to be scared to death of a few little bugs! As long as we have the H-bomb everything will be O.K. PS. She's probably a peace-nut too.[436]

At the beginning of this appendix I mentioned that an important feature of critical thinking is that it should be ethical. Personal attacks are not ethical. They can also backfire if readers or listeners decide that attackers resorted to the personal insults out of fear or weakness or incompetence.

As with the other strategies I've discussed, there are exceptions to the rule that appeals to emotion entail logical fallacies. Occasionally an appeal to fear, for example, may represent the most appropriate argument—say, when a utility company is warning people not to touch downed power lines or the police are trying to convince citizens not to confront an armed criminal.

The preceding paragraphs have given you tips on logical fallacies and other things to watch for, so you can eliminate information that seems unreliable or irrelevant and put more weight on information utilizing sound evidence and arguments. Once you've done this, you're ready for the final stages of the critical-thinking process.

Step 4: Draw the Conclusion That Makes the Most Sense to You

This step is the culmination of the previous three. It requires synthesizing the results of the previous steps, then adding your own perspective.

Draw a Well-Supported Conclusion

At this stage in the critical-thinking process, you should be ready to synthesize the information you've gathered and draw what seems the best-supported conclusion. This conclusion should be arrived at through careful consideration of all the evidence and arguments.

Make the Conclusion Consistent with Your Values and Goals

It's obviously not enough to arrive at a logical, well-grounded conclusion, because the conclusion you reach should be compatible with your own values, beliefs, and objectives. Your survey and analysis of a wide range of viewpoints should have given you a sound basis for constructing your perspective, which in many cases will have been enriched by the critical-thinking process.

Step 5: Remain Open to New Perspectives

The fact that you've successfully used critical-thinking tools to arrive at your conclusion doesn't mean this conclusion should be irrevocable. Chapter 10, on science, provided many examples of how people can come to see the "truth" differently over time. Your opportunity to rethink and change your beliefs is greater now than ever. John Stuart Mill (1806–1873), an influential British philosopher and economist, is said to have been the last person to know everything there was to know.[437] That idea would be ludicrous today, because "an avalanche of information and choices is made possible by burgeoning technological progress. Leading the way are developments in our ability to collect, store, retrieve, and communicate information. . . . Extensive cable and satellite systems provide one route for that information into the average home [and] the other major route is the personal computer."[438] Increasing personal mobility for many people in the twenty-first century—in terms of job or career path, choice of where to live, and travel opportunities—may also bring an unprecedented array of influences into your life.

This array of influences can help make you a better critical thinker if you remain flexible. As a critical thinker you should always be open to new experiences and insights, modifying your perspective as necessary to reflect your new understanding of the issues. This is the true meaning of "diving deep" as you search for truth: it's an ongoing quest that should be just as fluid and malleable as are the waters you're diving through.

Conclusion

This appendix has focused on the importance of critical thinking in everyday life. It has highlighted a simple, five-step approach in which you define a problem clearly, gather information and supporting evidence, evaluate the material you've gathered, draw the most appropriate conclusion, and keep an open mind in terms of revising your conclusion. There's no guarantee you can completely avoid the lies, bias, spin, scams, and fraud surrounding you. But by becoming a critical thinker, you'll stand a much better chance of being able to detect truth in a sea of deception.

Further Reading

There's a huge literature on critical thinking. For a popular, concise guide, see M. Neil Browne and Stuart M. Keeley, *Asking the Right Questions: A Guide to Critical Thinking*, 9th ed. (Upper Saddle River, NJ: Prentice Hall, 2009). For a more detailed introduction, see Brooke Noel Moore and Richard Parker, *Critical Thinking*, 9th ed. (New York: McGraw-Hill, 2008). A book that focuses on how to apply critical-thinking habits in every area of life is Richard Paul and Linda Elder, *Critical Thinking: Tools for Taking Charge of Your Learning and Your Life*, 2nd ed. (Upper Saddle River, NJ: Pearson Prentice Hall, 2006). Other aspects of critical thinking are covered in Carol Tavris and Elliott Aronson, *Mistakes Were Made (But Not by Me): Why We Justify Foolish Beliefs, Bad Decisions, and Hurtful Acts* (New York: Harcourt, 2007).

For practice in weighing conflicting viewpoints, Greenhaven Press's Opposing Viewpoints Series (www.gale.cengage.com/greenhaven) is a series of books on contentious issues ranging from abortion to genetic engineering to gun control. Each volume includes short articles debating various facets of the issue and provides a bibliography as well as other resources. Although aimed primarily at the high school market, these volumes are useful for adult audiences as well. For a website that promotes critical thinking by presenting the pros and cons of controversial issues, see www.procon.org.

On the importance of critical thinking in producing and interpreting statistics, see two books by Joel Best: *Damned Lies and Statistics: Untangling Numbers from the Media, Politicians, and Activists* (Berkeley: University of California Press, 2001), and *More Damned Lies and Statistics: How Numbers Confuse Public Issues* (Berkeley: University of California Press, 2004).

On anti-intellectualism, see Richard Hofstadter's Pulitzer Prize–winning book, *Anti-Intellectualism in American Life* (New York: Vintage, 1966). Susan Jacoby's *The Age of American Unreason* (New York: Pantheon Books, 2008) traces the dumbing down of America in the current era of infotainment and locates this anti-intellectual trend in a larger historical context.

On bullying and personal attacks (which can substitute for critical thinking) as well as civility, see P. M. Forni, *The Civility Solution: What to Do When People Are Rude* (New York: St. Martin's Press, 2008).

REFERENCES

Abagnale, Frank W. *The Art of the Steal: How to Protect Yourself and Your Business from Fraud—America's #1 Crime.* New York: Broadway Books, 2001.

Abagnale, Frank W. *Stealing Your Life: The Ultimate Identity Theft Prevention Plan.* New York: Broadway Books, 2007.

Abagnale, Frank W., with Stan Redding. *Catch Me If You Can: The Amazing True Story of the Youngest and Most Daring Con Man in the History of Fun and Profit!* New York: Broadway Books, [1980] 2002.

Abel, Richard L., and Philip S. C. Lewis, eds. *Lawyers in Society, Volume 2: The Civil Law World.* Berkeley: University of California Press, 1988.

Abeles, P. G. *Admit the Horse: A Political Thriller.* Rockville, MD: Oak Leaf Press, 2012.

Ackerman, Kenneth D. *Young J. Edgar: Hoover, the Red Scare, and the Assault on Civil Liberties.* New York: Carroll & Graf, 2007.

Albarelli, H. P., Jr. *A Terrible Mistake: The Murder of Frank Olson and the CIA's Secret Cold War Experiments.* Walterville, OR: Trine Day, 2009.

Albarelli, H. P., Jr. *Writing about the unspeakable (AIDS, the CIA and bio-warfare).* TVNewsLIES.org, April 12, 2010. http://tvnewslies.org/tvnl/index.php/editorial/guest-commentary/13873-writing-about-the-unspeakable-aids-and-bio-warfare.html.

Allport, Gordon W. *The Nature of Prejudice*. 25th anniv. ed. Reading, MA: Addison-Wesley, [1954] 1979.

American Bar Association. *Directory of lawyer disciplinary agencies 2011–12*. December 2011. http://www.americanbar.org/content/dam/aba/migrated/cpr/regulation/directory.authcheckdam.pdf.

American Bar Association. *Lawyer demographics*. 2011. http://www.americanbar.org/content/dam/aba/migrated/marketresearch/PublicDocuments/lawyer_demographics_2011.authcheckdam.pdf.

Anderson, Bonnie M. *News Flash: Journalism, Infotainment, and the Bottom-Line Business of Broadcast News*. San Francisco: Jossey-Bass, 2004.

Angell, Marcia. *The Truth about the Drug Companies: How They Deceive Us and What to Do about It*. New York: Random House, 2005.

Archibald, Kathy. Drug testing on animals is not beneficial. In David M. Haugen, ed., *Animal Experimentation, Opposing Viewpoints Series*, 157–164. Farmington Hills, MI: Greenhaven Press, 2007.

Arvedlund, Erin. *Too Good to Be True: The Rise and Fall of Bernie Madoff*. New York: Portfolio, 2009.

Auerbach, Jerold S. *Unequal Justice: Lawyers and Social Change in Modern America*. New York: Oxford University Press, 1976.

Austen, Ian. Canada takes steps to ban most plastic baby bottles. *New York Times*, April 19, 2008. http://www.nytimes.com/2008/04/19/business/worldbusiness/19plastic.html?ref=americas.

Baatz, Simon. *For the Thrill of It: Leopold, Loeb, and the Murder That Shocked Chicago*. New York: HarperCollins, 2008.

Bach, Steven. *Leni: The Life and Work of Leni Riefenstahl*. New York: Knopf, 2007.

Bachrach, Susan, and Steven Luckert. *State of Deception: The Power of Nazi Propaganda*. New York: Norton, 2009.

Bagdikian, Ben H. *The New Media Monopoly*. Rev. ed. Boston: Beacon Press, 2004.

Baird, Robert M., and Stuart E. Rosenbaum, eds. *Hatred, Bigotry, and Prejudice: Definitions, Causes, and Solutions.* Amherst, NY: Prometheus Books, 1999.

Balz, Dan, and Haynes Johnson. *The Battle for America 2008: The Story of an Extraordinary Election.* New York: Viking, 2009.

Beck, Eckardt C. The Love Canal tragedy. *EPA Journal,* January 1979. http://www.epa.gov/aboutepa/history/topics/lovecanal/01.html.

Bernard, Claude. *An Introduction to the Study of Experimental Medicine.* Trans. Henry Copley Green. New York: Macmillan, [1865] 1927.

Bernays, Edward L. *Biography of an Idea: Memoirs of Public Relations Counsel Edward L. Bernays.* New York: Simon & Schuster, 1965.

Bernays, Edward L. *Crystallizing Public Opinion.* New York: Boni & Liveright, 1923.

Bernays, Edward L. *Propaganda.* Brooklyn, NY: Ig Publishing, [1928] 2005.

Bernays, Edward L. *Public Relations.* Norman: University of Oklahoma Press, 1952.

Bernays, Edward L. *Take Your Place at the Peace Table.* New York: Gerent Press, 1945.

Berry, Sheila Martin. When experts lie. *Truth in Justice.* http://www.truthinjustice.org/expertslie.htm.

Best, Joel. *Damned Lies and Statistics: Untangling Numbers from the Media, Politicians, and Activists.* Berkeley: University of California Press, 2001.

Best, Joel. *More Damned Lies and Statistics: How Numbers Confuse Public Issues.* Berkeley: University of California Press, 2004.

Bilbo, Theodore G. Remarks delivered in the U.S. Senate, June 27, 1945. http://www.pierretristam.com/Bobst/07/wf071607.htm.

Bilbo, Theodore G. *Take Your Choice: Separation or Mongrelization.* Poplarville, MS: Dream House, 1947. http://www.archive.org/details/TakeYourChoice.

Blankenburg, Erhard, and Ulrike Schultz. German advocates: A highly regulated profession. In Richard L. Abel and Philip S. C. Lewis, eds., *Lawyers in Society, Volume 2: The Civil Law World*, 124–159. Berkeley: University of California Press, 1988.

Boehlert, Eric. *Bloggers on the Bus: How the Internet Changed Politics and the Press*. New York: Free Press, 2009.

Boigeol, Anne. The French bar: The difficulties of unifying a divided profession. In Richard L. Abel and Philip S. C. Lewis, eds., *Lawyers in Society, Volume 2: The Civil Law World*, 258–294. Berkeley: University of California Press, 1988.

Bok, Sissela. *Lying: Moral Choice in Public and Private Life*. Rev. ed. New York: Vintage, 1999.

Boller, Paul F., Jr. *Presidential Campaigns: From George Washington to George W. Bush*. 2nd ed. New York: Oxford University Press, 2004.

Borchard, Edwin. *Convicting the Innocent: Sixty-Five Actual Errors of Criminal Justice*. Garden City, NY: Garden City Publishing Company, 1932.

Bowers, Chris. Netroots demographics and diversity. *MyDD*, January 23, 2007. www.mydd.com/story/2007/1/23/133950/828.

Bowker, Gordon. *George Orwell*. London: Little, Brown, 2003.

Bowlby, Rachel. *Carried Away: The Invention of Modern Shopping*. New York: Columbia University Press, 2001.

Brandt, Allan M. *The Cigarette Century: The Rise, Fall, and Deadly Persistence of the Product That Defined America*. New York: Basic Books, 2007.

Bren, Linda. Frances Oldham Kelsey: FDA medical reviewer leaves her mark on history. *FDA Consumer Magazine*, March-April 2001.

Briggs, Asa, and Peter Burke. *A Social History of the Media: From Gutenberg to the Internet*. 3rd ed. Cambridge: Polity Press, 2009.

Brinkley, Alan. *Voices of Protest: Huey Long, Father Coughlin, and the Great Depression*. New York: Knopf, 1982.

Broad, William, and Nicholas Wade. *Betrayers of the Truth*. New York: Simon & Schuster, 1982.

Browne, M. Neil, and Stuart M. Keeley. *Asking the Right Questions: A Guide to Critical Thinking*. 9th ed. Upper Saddle River, NJ: Prentice Hall, 2009.

Brynner, Rock, and Trent Stephens. *Dark Remedy: The Impact of Thalidomide and Its Revival as a Vital Medicine.* New York: Perseus, 2001.

Buckingham, William, Jr. *Operation Ranch Hand: The Air Force and Herbicides in Southeast Asia, 1961–1971.* Washington, DC: U.S. Air Force, 1982.

Bundles, A'Lelia. *On Her Own Ground: The Life and Times of Madam C. J. Walker.* New York: Scribner, 2001.

Calfee, John E. The ghost of cigarette advertising past. *Regulation: The Cato Review of Business & Government* 20, no. 3 (1997): 38–45. *www.cato.org/pubs/regulation/regv20n3/reg20n3f.pdf.*

Callahan, David. *The Cheating Culture: Why More Americans Are Doing Wrong to Get Ahead.* Orlando, FL: Harcourt, 2004.

Callow, Simon. *Orson Welles: The Road to Xanadu.* New York: Viking, 1996.

Carson, Rachel. *Silent Spring.* Boston: Houghton Mifflin, 1962.

Carter, Dan T. *The Politics of Rage: George Wallace, the Origins of the New Conservatism, and the Transformation of American Politics.* New York: Simon & Schuster, 1995.

Chaffee, John. *Thinking Critically.* 9th ed. Boston: Heinle, 2007.

Changing the face of medicine: Dr. Frances Kathleen Oldham Kelsey. National Library of Medicine. 2003. *http://www.nlm.nih.gov/changingthefaceofmedicine/physicians/biography_182.html.*

Chin Yüeh-lin. Criticizing my idealistic bourgeois pedagogical ideology. *Peking Kuang Ming Jih Pao,* April 17, 1952. Included as an appendix to Robert Jay Lifton, *Thought Reform and the Psychology of Totalism: A Study of "Brainwashing" in China,* 473–484. New York: Norton, 1961. Reprint with a new preface, Chapel Hill: University of North Carolina Press, 1989.

Chow, Lena. Obama wins marketer of the year award. *City of Paris,* October 20, 2008. *www.cityofparis.us/obama-wins-marketer-of-the-year-award/.*

Cialdini, Robert B. *Influence: Science and Practice.* 5th ed. Boston: Pearson / Allyn and Bacon, 2009.

Clark, Stephen. *An ACORN by any other name still smells like an ACORN, critics say.* FOXNews.com, March 26, 2010. http://www.foxnews.com/politics/2010/03/25/similar-groups-acorns-place-republicans-foul/?test=latestnews.

Cocco, Marie. *Clinton campaign brought sexism out of hiding.* RealClearPolitics, May 13, 2008. www.realclearpolitics.com/articles/2008/05/clinton_campaign_brought_sexis.html.

Collins, Anne. *In the Sleep Room: The Story of the CIA Brainwashing Experiments in Canada.* Toronto: Lester & Orpen Dennys, 1988.

Collins, Denis. *Behaving Badly: Ethical Lessons from Enron.* Indianapolis: Dog Ear Publishing, 2006.

Committee on Un-American Activities, House of Representatives. *Communist Psychological Warfare (Brainwashing), Consultation with Edward Hunter, Author and Foreign Correspondent, March 13, 1958.* Washington, DC: Government Printing Office, 1958. http://www.crossroad.to/Quotes/globalism/Congress.htm.

Concern over canned foods: Our tests find wide range of bisphenol A in soups, juice, and more. Consumer Reports, December 2009, 54–55.

Condon, Richard. *The Manchurian Candidate.* New York: McGraw-Hill, 1959.

Cook, Fred J. *The Nightmare Decade: The Life and Times of Senator Joe McCarthy.* New York: Random House, 1971.

Cox, Stan. *Are your cell phone and laptop bad for your health?* AlterNet, July 31, 2007. www.alternet.org/story/58354/.

Cox, Stan. *Sick Planet: Corporate Food and Medicine.* London Pluto Press, 2008.

Creel, George. *How We Advertised America: The First Telling of the Amazing Story of the Committee on Public Information That Carried the Gospel of Americanism to Every Corner of the Globe.* New York: Arno Press, [1920] 1972.

Crichton, Robert. *The Great Impostor.* New York: Random House, 1959.

Crouse, Timothy. *The Boys on the Bus.* New York: Random House, 1973.

Cummins, Joseph. *Anything for a Vote: Dirty Tricks, Cheap Shots, and October Surprises in U.S. Presidential Campaigns.* Philadelphia: Quirk Books, 2007.

Day, Elizabeth. When one extraordinary life story is not enough. *The Observer*, February 15, 2009. www.guardian.co.uk/books/2009/feb/15/herman-rosenblat-oprah-winfrey-hoax.

De Beauvoir, Simone. *All Said and Done.* Trans. Patrick O'Brian. New York: Putnam, 1974.

Defining disinformation dispensers. Editorial. *Advertising Age*, October 20, 1986, 17.

Denton, Sally. *The Pink Lady: The Many Lives of Helen Gahagan Douglas.* New York: Bloomsbury Press, 2009.

Dionne, E. J., Jr. Biden admits plagiarism in school but says it was not "malevolent." *New York Times*, September 18, 1987, A1. www.nytimes.com/1987/09/18/us/biden-admits-plagiarism-in-school-but-says-it-was-not-malevolent.html.

Douglas, Helen Gahagan. *A Full Life.* Garden City, NY: Doubleday, 1982.

Doyle, James M. *True Witness: Cops, Courts, Science, and the Battle against Misidentification.* New York: Palgrave Macmillan, 2005.

Duffin, J., and C. R. R. Hayter. Baring the sole: The rise and fall of the shoe-fitting fluoroscope. *Isis* 91, no. 2 (2000): 260–282.

Edward R. Murrow: A report on Senator Joseph R. McCarthy. See It Now, CBS, March 9, 1954. Transcript. www.lib.berkeley.edu/MRC/murrowmccarthy.html.

Ekman, Paul. *Telling Lies: Clues to Deceit in the Marketplace, Politics, and Marriage.* Rev. ed. New York: Norton, 2009.

Ekman, Paul, with Mary Ann Mason Ekman and Tom Ekman. *Why Kids Lie: How Parents Can Encourage Truthfulness.* New York: Scribner's, 1989.

Ekman, Paul, and Maureen O'Sullivan. Who can catch a liar? *American Psychologist* 46, no. 9 (September 1991): 913–920.

Ellul, Jacques. *Propaganda: The Formation of Men's Attitudes.* Trans. Konrad Kellen and Jean Lerner. New York: Vintage Books, [1962] 1973.

Engdahl, F. William. *Seeds of Destruction: The Hidden Agenda of Genetic Manipulation.* Montreal: Global Research, 2007.

Engelhaupt, Erika. Happy birthday, Love Canal. *Chemical & Engineering News: Government & Policy* 86, no. 46 (November 17, 2008): 46–53. http://pubs.acs.org/cen/government/86/8646gov2.html.

Evanhoe, Ed. U.S. military Korean War statistics. *Korean-War.com.* 2000. http://www.korean-war.com/miakia.html.

Ewen, Stuart. *PR! A Social History of Spin.* New York: Basic Books, 1996.

Fagin, Dan, Marianne Lavelle, and the Center for Public Integrity. *Toxic Deception: How the Chemical Industry Manipulates Science, Bends the Law, and Endangers Your Health.* Monroe, ME: Common Courage Press, 1999.

Falk, Erika. *Women for President: Media Bias in Nine Campaigns.* 2nd ed. Urbana: University of Illinois Press, 2010.

Farnsworth, Stephen J., and S. Robert Lichter. *The Nightly News Nightmare: Media Coverage of U.S. Presidential Elections, 1988–2008,* 3rd ed. Lanham, MD: Rowman & Littlefield, 2011.

Farquhar, Michael. *A Treasury of Deception: Liars, Misleaders, Hoodwinkers, and the Extraordinary True Stories of History's Greatest Hoaxes, Fakes, and Frauds.* New York: Penguin, 2005.

Farrell, John A. *Clarence Darrow: Attorney for the Damned.* New York: Doubleday, 2011.

Federal Trade Commission. "I'm from the Government . . .": Sweepstakes scams feature con artists impersonating government officials. *FTC Consumer Alert,* May 2008. www.ftc.gov/bcp/edu/pubs/consumer/alerts/alt167.pdf.

Feldman, Marc D., and Charles V. Ford, with Toni Reinhold. *Patient or Pretender: Inside the Strange World of Factitious Disorders.* New York: Wiley, 1994.

Finlay, Anita. *Dirty Words on Clean Skin: Sexism and Sabotage, a Hillary Supporter's Rude Awakening.* Golden Middleway Books, 2012.

Finley, Keith M. *Delaying the Dream: Southern Senators and the Fight against Civil Rights, 1938–1965.* Baton Rouge: Louisiana State University Press, 2008.

FINRA Investor Education Foundation. *Fighting Fraud 101: Smart Tips for Older Investors.* Pamphlet. Washington, DC: SaveAndInvest.org, 2009.

Fischer, David. *Crist signs bill compensating man imprisoned for 24 years.* Associated Press, April 11, 2008. http://www.heraldtribune.com/article/20080411/NEWS/804110369/-1/rss01.

Fleegler, Robert L. *Theodore G. Bilbo and the decline of public racism, 1938–1947.* Journal of Mississippi History, spring 2006. http://www.mdah.state.ms.us/pubs/bilbo.pdf.

Ford, Charles V. *Lies! Lies!! Lies!!!: The Psychology of Deceit.* Washington, DC: American Psychiatric Press, 1996.

Forni, P. M. *The Civility Solution: What to Do When People Are Rude.* New York: St. Martin's Press, 2008.

Fox, Stephen. *The Mirror Makers: A History of American Advertising and Its Creators.* New York: Morrow, 1984.

Frame, Paul. *Shoe-fitting fluoroscope (ca. 1930–1940).* Oak Ridge Associated Universities. 2010. http://www.orau.org/ptp/collection/shoefittingfluor/shoe.htm.

Frances Oldham Kelsey. *National Women's Hall of Fame.* 2000. http://www.greatwomen.org/women-of-the-hall/search-the-hall/details/2/92-Kelsey.

Frankfurt, Harry G. *On Bullshit.* Princeton, NJ: Princeton University Press, 2005.

Freedman, David H. *Microchip technologies could make drug testing on animals unnecessary.* In David M. Haugen, ed., Animal Experimentation, Opposing Viewpoints Series, 165–172. Farmington Hills, MI: Greenhaven Press, 2007.

Freeman, Steven F., and Joel Bleifuss. *Was the 2004 Presidential Election Stolen? Exit Polls, Election Fraud, and the Official Count.* New York: Seven Stories Press, 2006.

Frey, James. *A Million Little Pieces.* New York: Doubleday, 2003.

Fried, Albert. *McCarthyism, the Great American Red Scare: A Documentary History.* Oxford: Oxford University Press, 1996.

Garrett, Brandon L. *Convicting the Innocent: Where Criminal Prosecutions Go Wrong.* Cambridge, MA: Harvard University Press, 2011.

George Wallace: Settin' the Woods on Fire. American Experience film series, PBS. 2000. www.pbs.org/wgbh/amex/wallace/filmmore/transcript/index.html. The "Wallace Quotes" page is available at http://www.pbs.org/wgbh/amex/wallace/sfeature/quotes.html.

Gibbs, Lois Marie. *Love Canal: The Story Continues . . .* Gabriola Island, BC: New Society Publishers, 1998.

Goldberg, Bernard. *A Slobbering Love Affair: The True (and Pathetic) Story of the Torrid Romance between Barack Obama and the Mainstream Media.* Washington, DC: Regnery, 2009.

Goodwin, A. J. H. *The curious story of the Piltdown fragments. South African Archaeological Bulletin* 8, no. 32 (December 1953): 103–105.

Governor Ryan declares moratorium on executions, will appoint commission to review capital punishment system. Illinois Government News Network (IGNN), press release, January 31, 2000. http://www.illinois.gov/pressreleases/showpressrelease.cfm?subjectid=3&recnum=359.

Graf, Joseph. *The audience for political blogs: New research on blog readership.* Project conducted by the Institute for Politics, Democracy & the Internet, George Washington University, October 2006. http://archive.knightdigitalmediacenter.org/resources/pdf/2007Election08-The%20Audience%20for%20Political%20Blogs.pdf

Greek, C. Ray, and Jean Swingle Greek. *Sacred Cows and Golden Geese: The Human Cost of Experiments on Animals.* New York: Continuum, 2000.

Greek, C. Ray, and Jean Swingle Greek. *Specious Science: How Genetics and Evolution Reveal Why Medical Research on Animals Harms Humans.* New York: Continuum, 2002.

Greenberg, David. *The write stuff? Why Biden's plagiarism shouldn't be forgotten. Slate.com,* August 25, 2008. http://www.slate.com/articles/news_and_politics/history_lesson/2008/08/the_write_stuff.html.

Griffith, Robert. *The Politics of Fear: Joseph R. McCarthy and the Senate.* Amherst: University of Massachusetts Press, 1970.

Grisham, John. *The Innocent Man: Murder and Injustice in a Small Town.* New York: Doubleday, 2006.

Groseclose, Tim. *Left Turn: How Liberal Media Bias Distorts the American Mind.* New York: St. Martin's Press, 2011.

Guerrini, Anita. *Experimenting with Humans and Animals: From Galen to Animal Rights.* Baltimore: Johns Hopkins University Press, 2003.

Hagen, Kimberly Sessions. *Bad blood: The Tuskegee Syphilis Study and legacy recruitment for experimental AIDS vaccines. In John P. Egan, ed., HIV/AIDS Education for Adults, New Directions for Adult and Continuing Education,* no. 105, 31–41. San Francisco: Jossey-Bass, spring 2005.

Halliday, Jon, and Bruce Cumings. *Korea: The Unknown War.* New York: Pantheon Books, 1988.

Harnett, Bertram. *Law, Lawyers, and Laymen: Making Sense of the American Legal System.* New York: Harcourt Brace Jovanovich, 1984.

Harris, Bev, with David Allen. *Black Box Voting: Ballot Tampering in the 21st Century.* Renton, WA: Talion, 2004.

Harter, Richard. *Piltdown man.* December 4, 2011. http://www.tiac.net/~cri_a/piltdown/piltdown.html.

Hassan, Steven. *Combatting Cult Mind Control.* Rochester, VT: Park Street Press, 1990.

Hastings, Deborah. *Adoption nightmares. Maine Sunday Telegram (from the Associated Press),* February 4, 2001, 1C, 6C.

Heiden, Konrad. *Introduction. Adolf Hitler, Mein Kampf,* trans. Ralph Manheim, xv–xxi. Boston: Houghton Mifflin, [vol. 1, 1925; vol. 2, 1927] 1943.

Heilemann, John, and Mark Halperin. *Game Change: Obama and the Clintons, McCain and Palin, and the Race of a Lifetime.* New York: Harper, 2010.

Henderson, Les. *Crimes of Persuasion: Schemes, Scams, Frauds.* 2nd ed. Azilda, ON: Coyote Ridge Publishing, 2003.

Henderson, Les. *Sweepstakes schemes, scams, frauds. Crimes of Persuasion.* 2011. *http://www.crimes-of-persuasion.com/Crimes/Telemarketing/Outbound/Major/Sweepstakes/sweepstakes.htm.*

Henriques, Diana B. *The Wizard of Lies: Bernie Madoff and the Death of Trust.* New York: Times Books / Henry Holt, 2011.

Herman, Arthur. *Joseph McCarthy: Reexamining the Life and Legacy of America's Most Hated Senator.* New York: Free Press, 2000.

Herman, Edward S., and Noam Chomsky. *Manufacturing Consent: The Political Economy of the Mass Media.* Rev. ed. New York: Pantheon Books, 2002.

Herman, Edward S., and Robert W. McChesney. *The Global Media: The New Missionaries of Corporate Capitalism.* London: Cassell, 1997.

Herrick, James A. *Critical Thinking: The Analysis of Arguments.* Scottsdale, AZ: Gorsuch Scarisbrick, 1991.

Higdon, Hal. *Leopold and Loeb: The Crime of the Century.* Urbana: University of Illinois Press, 1999. Originally published as *The Crime of the Century: The Leopold and Loeb Case.* New York: Putnam, 1975.

Hinkle, Lawrence E., and Harold G. Wolff. *Communist interrogation and indoctrination of "enemies of the state"—An analysis of methods used by the Communist state police.* AMA Archives of Neurology and Psychiatry 76 (August 1956): 115–174.

Hitchcock, Susan Tyler. *Frankenstein: A Cultural History.* New York: Norton, 2007.

Hitler, Adolf. *Mein Kampf.* Trans. Ralph Manheim. Boston: Houghton Mifflin, [1925, 1927] 1943.

Hofstadter, Richard. *Anti-Intellectualism in American Life.* New York: Vintage, 1966.

Holt, Penelope J. *The Apple: Based on the Herman Rosenblat Holocaust Love Story.* Ryebrook, NY: York House Press, 2009.

Hoobler, Dorothy, and Thomas Hoobler. *The Monsters: Mary Shelley and the Curse of Frankenstein.* New York: Little, Brown, 2006.

Hoover, J. Edgar. *Masters of Deceit: The Story of Communism in America and How to Fight It.* New York: Holt, 1958.

Hoover danced with Negro. Oelwein Daily Register (Oelwein, Iowa), October 18, 1928, 1.

Horowitz, Daniel. *Vance Packard and American Social Criticism.* Chapel Hill: University of North Carolina Press, 1994.

Hunter, Edward. *Brain-Washing in Red China: The Calculated Destruction of Men's Minds.* New York: Vanguard Press, 1951; 2nd ed., 1953.

Hunter, Edward. *Brainwashing: The Story of Men Who Defied It.* New York, Farrar, Straus and Cudahy, 1956.

Huxley, Aldous. *The final revolution.* In Aldous Huxley, Moksha: Writings on Psychedelics and the Visionary Experience, ed. Michael Horowitz and Cynthia Palmer, 163–173. Los Angeles: Tarcher, [1959] 1982.

Illinois commission announces nation's most comprehensive death penalty review; recommends sweeping changes to protect innocent, ensure fairness. Death Penalty Information Center (DPIC). 2002. http://www.deathpenaltyinfo.org/node/596.

Innocence Project. *Know the cases: Alan Crotzer.* 2012. http://www.innocenceproject.org/Content/Alan_Crotzer.php.

Innocence Project. *Understand the causes.* 2012. http://www.innocenceproject.org/understand/.

Innocence Project. *Understand the causes: Eyewitness misidentification.* 2012. http://www.innocenceproject.org/understand/Eyewitness-Misidentification.php.

Irvine, William. *Apes, Angels, and Victorians: The Story of Darwin, Huxley, and Evolution.* New York: McGraw-Hill, 1955.

Jackson, Brooks, and Kathleen Hall Jamieson. *unSpun: Finding Facts in a World of Disinformation.* New York: Random House, 2007.

Jacobson, Michael F., and Laurie Ann Mazur. *Marketing Madness: A Survival Guide for a Consumer Society.* Boulder, CO: Westview Press, 1995.

Jacoby, Susan. *The Age of American Unreason.* New York: Pantheon Books, 2008.

Jamieson, Kathleen Hall. *Dirty Politics: Deception, Distraction, and Democracy*. New York: Oxford University Press, 1992.

Johnson, David E., and Johnny R. Johnson. *A Funny Thing Happened on the Way to the White House: Foolhardiness, Folly, and Fraud in Presidential Elections, from Andrew Jackson to George W. Bush*. Rev. ed. Lanham, MD: Taylor Trade / Rowman & Littlefield, [1983] 2004.

Johnson, Haynes. *The Age of Anxiety: McCarthyism to Terrorism*. New York: Harcourt, 2005.

Joint Chiefs of Staff, U.S. Armed Forces. *Doctrine for Joint Psychological Operations*. Joint Publication 3-53, September 5, 2003. http://www.gwu.edu/~nsarchiv/NSAEBB/NSAEBB177/02_psyop-jp-3-53.pdf.

Jones, James H. *Bad Blood: The Tuskegee Syphilis Experiment*. Rev. ed. New York: Free Press, 1993.

Kaplan, David A. *The Accidental President: How 413 Lawyers, 9 Supreme Court Justices, and 5,963,110 (Give or Take a Few) Floridians Landed George W. Bush in the White House*. New York: William Morrow, 2001.

Kassirer, Jerome P. *On the Take: How Medicine's Complicity with Big Business Can Endanger Your Health*. New York: Oxford University Press, 2005.

Kelly, Denis G. *The Official Identity Theft Prevention Handbook: Everyone's Identity Has Already Been Stolen—Learn What You Can Do about It*. New York: Sterling & Ross, 2011.

Kershaw, Ian. *Hitler 1889–1936: Hubris*. New York: Norton, 1998.

Kilbourne, Jean. *Can't Buy My Love: How Advertising Changes the Way We Think and Feel*. New York: Free Press, 2000. Originally published as *Deadly Persuasion*.

Kingsolver, Barbara, with Steven L. Hopp and Camille Kingsolver. *Animal, Vegetable, Miracle: A Year of Food Life*. New York: HarperCollins, 2007.

Kirchheimer, Sid. *Scam-Proof Your Life: 377 Smart Ways to Protect You & Your Family from Ripoffs, Bogus Deals & Other Consumer Headaches*. New York: Sterling, 2007.

Kirtzman, Andrew. *Betrayal: The Life and Lies of Bernie Madoff.* New York: Harper, 2009.

Klein, Naomi. *The torture lab: Ewen Cameron, the CIA and the maniacal quest to erase and remake the human mind.* In Naomi Klein, *The Shock Doctrine: The Rise of Disaster Capitalism,* 25–48. New York: Metropolitan Books / Henry Holt, 2007.

Knopp, Guido. *Hitler's Women.* Trans. Angus McGeoch. New York: Routledge, [2001] 2003.

Köhn, Volker. *Theater des Westens' Berlin Cabaret–UFA Revue.* Stagebill, Kennedy Center, Washington, DC, May 1992, 29a.

Krimsky, Sheldon. *Science in the Private Interest: Has the Lure of Profits Corrupted Biomedical Research?* Lanham, MD: Rowman & Littlefield, 2003.

Kühl, Stefan. *The Nazi Connection: Eugenics, American Racism, and German National Socialism.* New York: Oxford University Press, 1994.

Kuhn, Thomas S. *The Structure of Scientific Revolutions.* 3rd ed. Chicago: University of Chicago Press, 1996.

Kumar, Krishan. *Politics and anti-utopia: George Orwell and Nineteen Eighty-Four.* In Krishan Kumar, *Utopia and Anti-Utopia in Modern Times,* 288–346. Oxford: Blackwell, 1987.

Lalich, Janja, and Madeleine Tobias. *Take Back Your Life: Recovering from Cults and Abusive Relationships.* 2nd ed. Berkeley, CA: Bay Street Publishing, 2006.

Lanford, Audri, and Jim Lanford. *Nigerian scam.* Internet ScamBusters #11. ScamBusters.org. www.scambusters.org/NigerianFee.html.

Layton, Deborah. *Seductive Poison: A Jonestown Survivor's Story of Life and Death in the Peoples Temple.* New York: Anchor, 1998.

Leamy, Elisabeth. *The Savvy Consumer: How to Avoid Scams and Ripoffs That Cost You Time and Money.* Herndon, VA: Capital Books, 2004.

Lear, Linda. *Rachel Carson's biography.* 1998. www.rachelcarson.org.

Lear, Linda. *Rachel Carson: Witness for Nature.* New York: Holt, 1997.

Lears, Jackson. *Fables of Abundance: A Cultural History of Advertising in America.* New York: Basic Books, 1995.

Lee, Martin A., and Bruce Shlain. *Acid Dreams: The CIA, LSD and the Sixties Rebellion.* New York: Grove Press, 1985.

Lee, Martin A., and Norman Solomon. *Unreliable Sources: A Guide to Detecting Bias in News Media.* New York: Lyle Stuart / Carol Publishing Group, 1998.

Lefkowitz, Bernard. *Our Guys: The Glen Ridge Rape and the Secret Life of the Perfect Suburb.* Berkeley: University of California Press, 1997.

Leonard, Tom. Holocaust survivor's love story exposed as fraud. *The Telegraph (UK),* December 28, 2008. http://www.telegraph.co.uk/news/worldnews/northamerica/usa/3998664/Holocaust-survivors-love-story-exposed-as-a-fraud.html.

Leopold, Nathan F. Jr. *Life Plus 99 Years.* Garden City, NY: Doubleday & Company, 1958.

Levin, Diane E., and Jean Kilbourne. *So Sexy So Soon: The New Sexualized Childhood and What Parents Can Do to Protect Their Kids.* New York: Ballantine Books, 2008.

Levin, Meyer. *Compulsion.* New York: Carroll & Graf, [1956] 1996.

Lewin, R. Do animals read minds, tell lies? *Science* 238, no. 4832 (December 4, 1987): 1350–1351.

Lewin, Roger. *Bones of Contention: Controversies in the Search for Human Origins.* New York: Simon & Schuster, 1987.

Liddy, G. Gordon. *Will.* 3rd ed. New York: St. Martin's Press, 1997.

Liebman, James S., Jeffrey Fagan, and Valerie West. *A Broken System: Error Rates in Capital Cases, 1973–1995.* New York: Columbia University School of Law, 2000. http://www2.law.columbia.edu/instructionalservices/liebman/index.html.

Lifton, Robert Jay. *The Nazi Doctors: Medical Killing and the Psychology of Genocide.* New York: Basic Books, 1986.

Lifton, Robert Jay. *Thought Reform and the Psychology of Totalism: A Study of "Brainwashing" in China.* New York: Norton, 1961. Reprinted with a new preface, Chapel Hill: University of North Carolina Press, 1989.

Linder, Douglas. *Famous American trials: Illinois v. Nathan Leopold and Richard Loeb, 1924.* University of Missouri at Kansas City Law

School, 1997. http://www.law.umkc.edu/faculty/projects/ftrials/leoploeb/leopold.htm.

Linder, Douglas. Famous trials: Trial of Galileo Galilei, 1633. University of Missouri at Kansas City Law School, 2002. www.law.umkc.edu/faculty/projects/ftrials/galileo/galileo.html.

Linn, Susan. Consuming Kids: The Hostile Takeover of Childhood. New York: New Press, 2004. Paperback edition published under the title Consuming Kids: Protecting Our Children from the Onslaught of Marketing & Advertising. New York: Anchor, 2005.

Lippmann, Walter. Public Opinion. New York: Macmillan, [1922] 1960.

Malone, Michael S. Media's presidential bias and decline. ABC News, October 24, 2008. http://abcnews.go.com/print?id=6099188.

Marchand, Roland. Advertising the American Dream: Making Way for Modernity, 1920–1940. Berkeley: University of California Press, 1985.

Marks, John. The Search for the "Manchurian Candidate": The CIA and Mind Control. Rev. ed. New York: Norton, [1979] 1991. The 1979 edition is available at http://www.druglibrary.org/schaffer/lsd/marks.htm.

Mauro, Tony. Lawyers' top topic: Public's perception. USA Today, August 10, 1993, 3A.

McCarthy, Joseph. Major Speeches and Debates of Senator Joe McCarthy Delivered in the United States Senate, 1950–1951. Washington, DC: Government Printing Office, 1951.

McChesney, Robert W., Russell Newman, and Ben Scott, eds. The Future of Media: Resistance and Reform in the 21st Century. New York: Seven Stories Press, 2005.

McDonald, Allan J., with James R. Hansen. Truth, Lies, and O-Rings: Inside the Space Shuttle Challenger Disaster. Gainesville: University Press of Florida, 2009.

Media Matters for America. Gender and ethnic diversity in prime-time cable news. July 2008. www.mediamatters.org/reports/diversity_report.

Media Report to Women. Industry statistics. March 2012. www.mediar-eporttowomen.com/statistics.htm.

Mid-Atlantic Innocence Project. Causes of wrongful convictions. 2010. http://www.exonerate.org/www.exonerate.org/about-2/causes-of-wrongful-convictions/.

Miller, David J., and Michel Hersen, eds. Research Fraud in the Behavioral and Biomedical Sciences. New York: Wiley, 1992.

Miller, Mark Crispin, ed. Loser Take All: Election Fraud and the Subversion of Democracy, 2000–2008. Brooklyn, NY: Ig Publishing, 2008.

A million little lies: Exposing James Frey's fiction addiction. The Smoking Gun, January 8, 2006. http://www.thesmokinggun.com/documents/celebrity/million-little-lies.

Mintz, Morton. Heroine of FDA keeps bad drug off market. Washington Post, July 15, 1962, A1.

Mitchell, Greg. Tricky Dick and the Pink Lady: Richard Nixon vs. Helen Gahagan Douglas—Sexual Politics and the Red Scare, 1950. New York: Random House, 1998.

Moore, Brooke Noel, and Richard Parker. Critical Thinking. 9th ed. New York: McGraw-Hill, 2008.

Morello, Karen Berger. The Invisible Bar: The Woman Lawyer in America, 1638 to the Present. New York: Random House, 1986.

Morgan, Chester M. Redneck Liberal: Theodore G. Bilbo and the New Deal. Baton Rouge: Louisiana State University Press, 1985.

Nader, Ralph, and Wesley J. Smith. No Contest: Corporate Lawyers and the Perversion of Justice in America. New York: Random House, 1996.

Nakashima, Ellen, and the Washington Post Political Staff. Deadlock: The Inside Story of America's Closest Election. New York: Public Affairs / Perseus Books Group, 2001.

The New Yorker Book of Lawyer Cartoons. New York: Knopf, 1994.

Nichols, John, and Robert W. McChesney. Tragedy and Farce: How the American Media Sell Wars, Spin Elections, and Destroy Democracy. New York: New Press, 2005.

Nietzsche, Friedrich. *Beyond Good and Evil*. Ed. R. J. Hollingdale and Michael Tanner. Trans. R. J. Hollingdale. New York: Penguin, [1886] 2003.

Nietzsche, Friedrich. *Thus Spoke Zarathustra: A Book for None and All*. Trans. Walter Kaufmann. New York: Penguin, [1883–1885] 1978.

Nixon, Richard M. "Checkers" speech, Los Angeles, September 23, 1952. In *American Rhetoric: Top 100 Speeches*. www.americanrhetoric. com/speeches/richardnixoncheckers.html.

Nolo. 50-state chart of small claims court dollar limits. 2012. http:// www.nolo.com/legal-encyclopedia/small-claims-suits-how-much-30031.html.

Oppenheimer, Jerry. *Madoff with the Money*. New York: Wiley, 2009.

Oppenheimer, Jerry. The making of Madoff. *Daily Beast*, August 1, 2009. www.thedailybeast.com/blogs-and-stories/2009-08-01/the-making-of-madoff/p/.

Origins of documentary film: Leni Riefenstahl. *Reel Life Stories: Documentary Film and Video Collections in the UC Berkeley Library's Media Resources Center*. http://www.lib.berkeley.edu/MRC/reel-life/riefenstahl.htm.

Orwell, George. *Animal Farm*. Foreword by Ann Patchett, preface by Russell Baker, introduction by C. M. Woodhouse. Centennial ed. New York: Plume [1946] 2003.

Orwell, George. *Nineteen Eighty-Four*. Foreword by Thomas Pynchon, afterword by Erich Fromm. Centennial ed. New York: Plume, [1949] 2003.

Orwell, Sonia, and Ian Angus, eds. *The Collected Essays, Journalism and Letters of George Orwell*. 4 vols. Harmondsworth: Penguin, 1970.

Oshinsky, David M. *A Conspiracy So Immense: The World of Joe McCarthy*. Oxford: Oxford University Press, 2005.

Owings, Alison. *Frauen: German Women Recall the Third Reich*. New Brunswick, NJ: Rutgers University Press, 1993.

Packard, Vance. *The Hidden Persuaders*. New York: David McKay Company, 1957.

Paczulla, Jutta. "Talking to India": George Orwell's work at the BBC, 1941–1943. *Canadian Journal of History* 42, no. 1 (spring-summer 2007). www.findarticles.com/p/articles/mi_qa3686/is_1_42/ai_n29367113.

Paglia, Camille. Obama's healthcare horror. *Salon.com,* August 12, 2009. http://www.salon.com/opinion/paglia/2009/08/12/town_halls/.

Parker, Karen F., Mari A. Dewees, and Michael L. Radelet. Racial bias and the conviction of the innocent. In Saundra D. Westervelt and John A. Humphrey, eds., *Wrongly Convicted: Perspectives on Failed Justice,* 114–131. New Brunswick, NJ: Rutgers University Press, 2001.

Parmet, Herbert S. *Eisenhower and the American Crusades.* New York: Macmillan, 1972.

Paul, Richard, and Linda Elder. *Critical Thinking: Tools for Taking Charge of Your Learning and Your Life.* 2nd ed. Upper Saddle River, NJ: Pearson Prentice Hall, 2006.

Peterson, Dale, and Jane Goodall. *Visions of Caliban: On Chimpanzees and People.* Rev. ed. Athens: University of Georgia Press, 2000.

Pietila, Antero. *Not in My Neighborhood: How Bigotry Shaped a Great American City.* Lanham, MD: Ivan R. Dee / Rowman & Littlefield, 2010.

Plutarch. *Life of Solon.* In *Plutarch's Lives,* vol. 1, trans. Bernadette Perrin. Loeb Classical Library. Cambridge, MA: Harvard University Press, 1982.

Pollan, Michael. *The Omnivore's Dilemma: A Natural History of Four Meals.* New York: Penguin Press, 2006.

Posner, Richard A. *The Little Book of Plagiarism.* New York: Pantheon Books, 2007.

Pratkanis, Anthony, and Elliot Aronson. *Age of Propaganda: The Everyday Use and Abuse of Persuasion.* Rev. ed. New York: W. H. Freeman / Holt, 2001.

Pratkanis, Anthony, and Doug Shadel. *Weapons of Fraud: A Source Book for Fraud Fighters.* Seattle: AARP Washington, 2005.

Press widely criticized, but trusted more than other information sources. Pew Research Center. September 22, 2011. http://www.people-press.org/2011/09/22/press-widely-criticized-but-trusted-more-than-other-institutions/.

Pringle, Peter. *Food, Inc.: Mendel to Monsanto—The Promises and Perils of the Biotech Harvest*. Rev. ed. New York: Simon & Schuster, 2005.

Quart, Alissa. *Branded: The Buying and Selling of Teenagers*. Cambridge, MA: Perseus, 2003.

Radelet, Michael L., and Hugo Adam Bedau. *Erroneous convictions and the death penalty*. In Saundra D. Westervelt and John A. Humphrey, eds., *Wrongly Convicted: Perspectives on Failed Justice*, 269–280. New Brunswick, NJ: Rutgers University Press, 2001.

Reagan, Ronald. *Address to the nation on the explosion of the Space Shuttle Challenger*. January 28, 1986. Public Papers of President Ronald W. Reagan, Ronald Reagan Presidential Library. http://www.reagan.utexas.edu/archives/speeches/1986/12886b.htm.

Redlich, Fritz. *Hitler: Diagnosis of a Destructive Prophet*. New York: Oxford University Press, 1999.

Reeves, Thomas C. *The Life and Times of Joe McCarthy: A Biography*. New York: Stein and Day, 1982.

Reporting a lawyer for ethics violations. Lawyers.com. 2012. http://legal-malpractice.lawyers.com/v2/Reporting-a-Lawyer-for-Ethics-Violations.html.

Reverby, Susan M. *Examining Tuskegee: The Infamous Syphilis Study and Its Legacy*. Chapel Hill: University of North Carolina Press, 2009.

Reverby, Susan M., ed. *Tuskegee's Truths: Rethinking the Tuskegee Syphilis Study*. Chapel Hill: University of North Carolina Press, 2000.

Rhode, Deborah L. *Access to Justice*. New York: Oxford University Press, 2004.

Rhode, Deborah L. *In the Interests of Justice: Reforming the Legal Profession*. New York: Oxford University Press, 2000.

Ricks, Thomas E. *Military plays up role of Zarqawi: Jordanian painted as foreign threat to Iraq's stability*. Washington Post, April 10, 2006. http://www.washingtonpost.com/wp-dyn/content/article/2006/04/09/AR2006040900890.html.

Riechers, Maggie. *Racism to redemption: The path of George Wallace.* Humanities 21, no. 2 (March-April 2000). www.neh.gov/news/humanities/2000-03/wallace.html.

Riefenstahl, Leni. *A Memoir.* New York: St. Martin's Press, 1992.

Rivers, Caryl. *Selling Anxiety: How the News Media Scare Women.* Hanover, NH: University Press of New England, 2007.

Robin, Marie-Monique. *The World According to Monsanto.* New York: New Press, 2010.

Robins, R. S., and J. M. Post. *Political Paranoia: The Psychopolitics of Hatred.* New Haven, CT: Yale University Press, 1997.

Rosenbaum, Ron. *Explaining Hitler: The Search for the Origins of His Evil.* New York: Random House, 1998.

Ross, Benjamin, and Steven Amter. *The Polluters: The Making of Our Chemically Altered Environment.* Oxford: Oxford University Press, 2010.

Ross, Brian. *The Madoff Chronicles: Inside the Secret World of Bernie and Ruth.* New York: Hyperion, 2009.

Roth, Andrew, and Jonathan Roth. *Devil's Advocates: The Unnatural History of Lawyers.* Ed. Barbara Repa. Berkeley, CA: Nolo Press, 1989.

Rubin, Aviel D. *Brave New Ballot: The Battle to Safeguard Democracy in the Age of Electronic Voting.* New York: Morgan Road Books, 2006.

Rudacille, Deborah. *The Scalpel and the Butterfly: The War between Animal Research and Animal Protection.* New York: Farrar, Straus and Giroux, 2000.

Rutherford, Paul. *Endless Propaganda: The Advertising of Public Goods.* Toronto: University of Toronto Press, 2000.

Scheck, Barry, Peter Neufeld, and Jim Dwyer. *Actual Innocence: Five Days to Execution and Other Dispatches from the Wrongly Convicted.* New York: Doubleday, 2000.

Schell, Orville, Jr. *Silent Vietnam: How we invented ecocide and killed a country.* Look Magazine, April 6, 1971, 55–58.

Schlosser, Eric. *Fast Food Nation: The Dark Side of the All-American Meal.* Rev. ed. New York: Mariner Books, 2012.

Schor, Juliet B. *Born to Buy: The Commercialized Child and the New Consumer Culture.* New York: Scribner, 2004.

Schudson, Michael. *Advertising, The Uneasy Persuasion: Its Dubious Impact on American Society.* New York: Basic Books: 1984.

Seal, Mark. *Madoff's world.* Vanity Fair, April 2009, 124–135, 166–173.

Shadel, Doug. *Outsmarting the Scam Artists: How to Protect Yourself from the Most Clever Cons.* Hoboken, NJ: AARP/Wiley, 2012.

Shelley, Mary. *Frankenstein, or the Modern Prometheus.* 3rd ed. Oxford: Oxford University Press, [1831] 1969.

Shenk, David. *Data Smog: Surviving the Information Glut.* San Francisco: HarperSanFrancisco, 1997.

Sifakis, Carl. *Hoaxes and Scams: A Compendium of Deceptions, Ruses, and Swindles.* New York: Facts On File, 1993.

Sigmund, Anna Maria. *Women of the Third Reich.* Richmond Hill, Ontario: NDE Publishing, [1998] 2000.

Signer, Michael. *Demagogue: The Fight to Save Democracy from Its Worst Enemies.* New York: Palgrave Macmillan, 2009.

Silver Lake Editors. *Scams & Swindles: Phishing, Spoofing, ID Theft, Nigerian Advance Schemes, Investment Frauds, False Sweethearts: How to Recognize and Avoid Financial Rip-Offs in the Internet Age.* Aberdeen, WA: Silver Lake Publishing, 2006.

Singer, Margaret Thaler. *Cults in Our Midst.* Rev. ed. San Francisco: Jossey-Bass, 2003.

Smith, David Livingstone. *Why We Lie: The Evolutionary Roots of Deception and the Unconscious Mind.* New York: St. Martin's Press, 2004.

Smith, Jeffrey M. *Genetic Roulette: The Documented Health Risks of Genetically Engineered Foods.* Fairfield, IA: Yes! Books, 2007.

Smith, Jeffrey M. *Seeds of Deception: Exposing Industry and Government Lies about the Safety of the Genetically Engineered Foods You're Eating.* Fairfield, IA: Yes! Books, 2003.

Smith, Jeffrey M. *Seeds of Deception by Jeffrey M. Smith: A 10-page summary.* 2003. www.wanttoknow.info/deception10pg.

Snow, Nancy. *Information War: American Propaganda, Free Speech, and Opinion Control Since 9/11.* New York: Seven Stories Press, 2003.

*Speaking of Research. Statistics. 2012. http://speakingofresearch.com/
facts/statistics/.*

Spencer, Frank. *The Piltdown Papers 1908–1955: The Correspondence
and Other Documents Relating to the Piltdown Forgery.* London:
Oxford University Press, 1990.

Stage, Sarah. *Female Complaints: Lydia Pinkham and the Business of
Women's Medicine.* New York: Norton, 1979.

Starr, Paul. *The Creation of the Media: Political Origins of Modern Communications.* New York: Basic Books, 2004.

Steel, Ronald. *Walter Lippmann and the American Century. Rev. ed.* New
Brunswick, NJ: Transaction, 1999.

Stewart, James B. *Tangled Webs: How False Statements Are Undermining America—From Martha Stewart to Bernie Madoff.* New York:
Penguin Press, 2011.

Stickley, Jim. *The Truth about Identity Theft.* Upper Saddle River, NJ: FT
Press / Pearson Education, 2008.

Stone, Irving. *Clarence Darrow for the Defense.* Garden City, NY: Doubleday, Doran & Company, 1941.

Strasser, Susan. *Satisfaction Guaranteed: The Making of the American
Mass Market. Rev. ed.* Washington, DC: Smithsonian Books, 2004.

Strong, Jonathan. *Zombie-like, "disbanded" ACORN coming back to life in
form of new groups. Daily Caller, April 1, 2010. http://dailycaller.
com/2010/04/01/zombie-like-disbanded-acorn-coming-back-to-
life-in-form-of-new-groups/.*

Sullivan, Walter. *"I wrote note, Loeb killed him," says Leopold in first interview. Chicago Herald and Examiner, June 2, 1924.*

Sunseri, Gina. *Enron victims look forward to justice at trial. ABC News,
January 30, 2006. www.abcnews.go.com/Business/LegalCenter/
story?id=1556334.*

Swint, Kerwin C. *Mudslingers: The Top 25 Negative Political Campaigns of
All Time.* Westport, CT: Praeger, 2006.

Talbot, Margaret. *The disconnected; attachment theory: The ultimate
experiment. New York Times Magazine, May 24, 1998, section 6, p. 24. http://www.nytimes.com/1998/05/24/magazine/*

the-disconnected-attachment-theory-the-ultimate-experiment. html?pagewanted=all&src=pm.

Tavris, Carol, and Elliot Aronson. *Mistakes Were Made (but Not by Me): Why We Justify Foolish Beliefs, Bad Decisions, and Hurtful Acts.* Orlando, FL: Harcourt, 2007.

Taylor, Kathleen. *Brainwashing: The Science of Thought Control.* Oxford: Oxford University Press, 2004.

Taylor, Philip M. *Munitions of the Mind: A History of Propaganda. 3rd ed.* Manchester: Manchester University Press, 2003.

Theodore, John. *Evil Summer: Babe Leopold, Dickie Loeb, and the Kidnap-Murder of Bobby Franks.* Carbondale: Southern Illinois University Press, 2007.

Thomas, Susan Gregory. *Buy, Buy Baby: How Consumer Culture Manipulates Parents and Harms Young Minds.* Boston: Houghton Mifflin, 2007.

Tocqueville, Alexis de. *Democracy in America.* Trans. Arthur Goldhammer. New York: Library of America, [1835, 1840] 2004.

Trimborn, Jürgen. *Leni Riefenstahl: A Life.* Trans. Edna McCown. New York: Faber & Faber, 2007.

Truth. Wikipedia. www.en.wikipedia.org/wiki/Truth.

Turow, Scott. *One L. Rev. ed.* New York: Farrar Straus Giroux, 1988.

Twain, Mark. *On the decay of the art of lying (1896).* Project Gutenberg, 2010. http://www.gutenberg.org/etext/2572.

Tye, Larry. *The Father of Spin: Edward L. Bernays and the Birth of Public Relations.* New York: Crown, 1998.

U.S. Department of Agriculture, Animal and Plant Health Inspection Service. *Annual Report Animal Usage by Fiscal Year. Fiscal Year: 2010, July 27, 2011.* http://www.aphis.usda.gov/animal_welfare/ efoia/downloads/2010_Animals_Used_In_Research.pdf.

Van Doren, Charles. *All the answers: The quiz-show scandals—and the aftermath.* New Yorker, July 28, 2008, 62–69. www.newyorker. com/reporting/2008/07/28/080728fa_fact_vandoren.

Van Gelder, Lawrence. *Margaret Truman Daniel, president's daughter and popular author, dies at 83.* New York Times, January

30, 2008. *www.nytimes.com/2008/01/30/nyregion/30daniel.html?pagewanted=all*.

Walsch, Neale Donald. *Conversations with God: An Uncommon Dialogue.* Charlottesville, VA: Hampton Roads Publishing Company, 1997.

Walt Disney goes to war. Life Magazine, August 31, 1942, 61–69.

Washington, Harriet A. *Medical Apartheid: The Dark History of Medical Experimentation on Black Americans from Colonial Times to the Present.* New York: Doubleday, 2006.

Watkins, Thayer. *Theodore G. Bilbo of Mississippi.* Department of Economics, San José State University. *http://www.applet-magic.com/bilbo.htm.*

Watson, Bruce. *Sacco and Vanzetti: The Men, the Murders, and the Judgment of Mankind.* New York: Viking, 2007.

Weber, Karl, ed. *Food, Inc.: How Industrial Food Is Making Us Sicker, Fatter, and Poorer—and What You Can Do about It.* New York: PublicAffairs / Perseus Books Group, 2009.

Weiner, J. S. *The Piltdown Forgery.* 50th anniv. ed. Ed. Chris Stringer. Oxford: Oxford University Press, 2003.

Weiner, Tim. *Legacy of Ashes: The History of the CIA.* New York: Doubleday, 2007.

Weingarten, Gene. *Cruel and unusual punishment. Washington Post Magazine,* March 23, 2008. *www.washingtonpost.com/wp-dyn/content/article/2008/03/18/AR2008031802463.html.*

Welch, David. *Propaganda and the German Cinema, 1933–1945.* Rev. ed. London: I. B. Tauris, 2001.

Welch, David. *The Third Reich: Politics and Propaganda.* 2nd ed. London: Routledge, 2002.

Wells, H. G. *The War of the Worlds.* New York: Popular Library, [1898] 1962.

Western Union. *Protect yourself from fraud.* 2012. *http://www.westernunion.com/WUCOMWEB/staticMid.do?method=load&pagename=fraudTips.*

Westervelt, Saundra D., and John A. Humphrey, eds. *Wrongly Convicted: Perspectives on Failed Justice.* New Brunswick, NJ: Rutgers University Press, 2001.

Wheaton, Ken. *Obama wins vote for marketer of the year. Advertising Age,* October 17, 2008. http://adage.com/campaigntrail/post?article_id=131811.

Wicker, Tom. *Shooting Star: The Brief Arc of Joe McCarthy.* Orlando, FL: Harcourt, 2006.

Wright, Richard. *Black Boy: A Record of Childhood and Youth.* New York: New American Library, [1945] 1951.

Zuckoff, Mitchell. *Ponzi's Scheme: The True Story of a Financial Legend.* New York: Random House, 2005.

NOTES

Introduction

1. Senator Alan Cranston (D-CA), eulogy delivered in the Senate on August 5, 1980, a few weeks after Douglas's death; in Helen Gahagan Douglas's memoir (published posthumously), *A Full Life* (Garden City, NY: Doubleday, 1982), 418–419 (quote on 418).

2. Douglas, *A Full Life*, 334.

3. Editorial, *Sacramento Bee*, July 2, 1980; quoted in Douglas, *A Full Life*, 419.

4. "Defining Disinformation Dispensers," editorial, *Advertising Age*, October 20, 1986, 17; quoted in David Shenk, *Data Smog: Surviving the Information Glut* (San Francisco: HarperSanFrancisco, 1997), 139.

5. Cathy Peterson; quoted in Gina Sunseri, "Enron Victims Look Forward to Justice at Trial," ABC News, January 30, 2006, www. abcnews.go.com/Business/LegalCenter/story?id=1556334.

6. Quoted in Mark Seal, "Madoff's World," *Vanity Fair*, April 2009, 124–135, 166–173 (quote on 134), www.vanityfair.com/politics/features/2009/04/madoff200904.

7. Jerry Oppenheimer, *Madoff with the Money* (New York: Wiley, 2009), 18; Erin Arvedlund, *Too Good to Be True: The Rise and Fall of Bernie Madoff* (New York: Portfolio, 2009), 3, 85, 249.

Chapter 1: Finding Truth

8. Frank W. Abagnale, *The Art of the Steal: How to Protect Yourself and Your Business from Fraud—America's #1 Crime* (New York: Broadway Books, 2001), 22.

9. The company is the Alibi Network (www.alibinetwork.com).

10. "Truth," *Wikipedia*, www.en.wikipedia.org/wiki/Truth.

11. For a list of dictionary definitions, see Dictionary.com, http://dictionary.reference.com/search?q=truth+&x=29&y=11.

12. See Douglas Linder, "Famous Trials: Trial of Galileo Galilei, 1633," University of Missouri at Kansas City Law School, 2002, www.law.umkc.edu/faculty/projects/ftrials/galileo/galileo.html.

13. Samuel Wilberforce; quoted in William Irvine, *Apes, Angels, and Victorians: The Story of Darwin, Huxley, and Evolution* (New York: McGraw-Hill, 1955), 5.

14. Thomas Henry Huxley; quoted in Irvine, *Apes, Angels, and Victorians*, 6.

15. Rachel Carson, *Silent Spring* (Boston: Houghton Mifflin, 1962).

16. Linda Lear, "Rachel Carson's Biography," 1998, www.rachelcarson.org. Lear's website—titled "The Life and Legacy of Rachel Carson" (www.rachelcarson.org)—provides other valuable resources besides the Carson biography. Also see Lear's prize-winning book, *Rachel Carson: Witness for Nature* (New York: Holt, 1997).

17. See Thomas S. Kuhn, *The Structure of Scientific Revolutions*, 3rd ed. (Chicago: University of Chicago Press, 1996).

18. Friedrich Nietzsche; quoted in Charles V. Ford, *Lies! Lies!! Lies!!!: The Psychology of Deceit* (Washington, DC: American Psychiatric Press, 1996), 87.

19. For more on the *Challenger* tragedy, see Allan J. McDonald with James R. Hansen, *Truth, Lies, and O-Rings: Inside the Space Shuttle* Challenger *Disaster* (Gainesville: University Press of Florida, 2009). McDonald, an engineer, was director of the Space Shuttle Solid Rocket Motor Project at Morton Thiokol at the time of

the disaster. He's widely regarded as a hero because he warned against the launch of the *Challenger* despite pressure to the contrary from both NASA and his own employer. He experienced retribution as a whistleblower but remained with Morton Thiokol so he could play a key role in the redesign of the solid rocket boosters.

20. Ronald Reagan, "Address to the Nation on the Explosion of the Space Shuttle Challenger," January 28, 1986; Public Papers of President Ronald W. Reagan, Ronald Reagan Presidential Library, ://www.reagan.utexas.edu/archives/speeches/1986/12886b.htm.

21. R. Lewin, "Do Animals Read Minds, Tell Lies?", *Science* 238, no. 4832 (December 4, 1987): 1350–1351. For other examples of deception among nonhuman species, see David Livingstone Smith, *Why We Lie: The Evolutionary Roots of Deception and the Unconscious Mind* (New York: St. Martin's Press, 2004), especially 29–49.

22. See Ford, *Lies! Lies!! Lies!!!*, 50.

23. Mark Twain, "On the Decay of the Art of Lying" (1896); Project Gutenberg, 2010, http://www.gutenberg.org/etext/2572.

24. See the entry titled "Barry, Dr. James, Male Impersonator" in Carl Sifakis, *Hoaxes and Scams: A Compendium of Deceptions, Ruses, and Swindles* (New York: Facts On File, 1993), 24.

25. Quoted in "Barry, Dr. James, Male Impersonator" in Sifakis, *Hoaxes and Scams*, 24.

26. See Robert Crichton, *The Great Impostor* (New York: Random House, 1959).

27. Ferdinand Waldo Demara Jr.; quoted in Crichton, *The Great Impostor*, 217. Elsewhere Crichton quotes Demara as saying that "I'm rotten. . . . Every bone in my body is rotten. I'm rotten through and through!" (p. 8), that he was the "excrement of the world" (p. 70), that he "reeked and stank" (p. 111), and that he was a "bum" (p. 112). Crichton speculates that Demara had "some of the classic background that might lead to impostoring. At an early age he lost his social status and all that went with it,

and many feel that he has been going through life in another guise trying to find it again" (p. 216). (Demara was raised in Lawrence, Massachusetts; when he was eleven, his father—the wealthy owner of a chain of movie theaters—lost everything in the Depression and they were reduced to poverty.)

28. Abagnale, *The Art of the Steal*, 6.

29. For the book version, see Frank W. Abagnale, with Stan Redding, *Catch Me If You Can: The Amazing True Story of the Youngest and Most Daring Con Man in the History of Fun and Profit!* (New York: Broadway Books, [1980] 2002). An interesting parallel between Demara's and Abagnale's lives is that as with Demara's family, the Abagnale family was reduced to near poverty when Frank W. Abagnale Sr. lost his business as the affluent owner of a New York stationery store. He had to give up a lavish home and two Cadillacs and survived as a postal clerk, exposing his family to the dramatic loss of status thought to fuel the exploits of impostors. In a revealing passage in his memoir, Abagnale Jr. says, for example, that "whenever I felt lonely, depressed, rejected or doubtful of my own worth, I'd dress up in my pilot's uniform and seek out a crowd. The uniform brought me respect and dignity" (Abagnale, *Catch Me If You Can*, 46).

30. Ford, *Lies! Lies!! Lies!!!*, 160. Munchausen syndrome is named for a German nobleman, Baron von Münchhausen (1720–1797), known for making up fantastic stories about his exploits. The term *Munchausen syndrome* was originally a catchall term for many types of con artists, impostors, and malingerers, then became restricted to people pretending to be ill. (The typical U.S. spelling omits one of the h's in Münchhausen's name.)

31. Ford, *Lies! Lies!! Lies!!!*, 164.

32. Marc D. Feldman and Charles V. Ford, with Toni Reinhold, *Patient or Pretender: Inside the Strange World of Factitious Disorders* (New York: Wiley, 1994), vii.

33. Harry G. Frankfurt, *On Bullshit* (Princeton, NJ: Princeton University Press, 2005).

34.   Frankfurt, *On Bullshit*, 38. Frankfurt acknowledges that the term *bull* in *bull session* and related terms could primarily denote the male gender, as the *Oxford English Dictionary's* definition of *bull session* suggests, but points out that these terms have a range of other implications as well (pp. 34–35).

35.   Frankfurt, *On Bullshit*, 52.

36.   Frankfurt, *On Bullshit*, 55–56.

37.   Ford, *Lies! Lies!! Lies!!!*, 76–77, 86.

38.   Carol Tavris and Elliot Aronson, *Mistakes Were Made (but Not by Me): Why We Justify Foolish Beliefs, Bad Decisions, and Hurtful Acts* (Orlando, FL: Harcourt, 2007).

39.   Tavris and Aronson, *Mistakes Were Made (but Not by Me)*, 2.

40.   Tavris and Aronson, *Mistakes Were Made (but Not by Me)*, 4.

41.   Richard A. Posner provides an excellent overview of plagiarism in his *The Little Book of Plagiarism* (New York: Pantheon Books, 2007).

42.   James Frey's *A Million Little Pieces* was published by Doubleday in 2003 to great critical acclaim. Its sales skyrocketed after Oprah Winfrey selected it for her book club. Then in January 2006, a website called The Smoking Gun published an exposé alleging that parts of the book were falsified; see "A Million Little Lies: Exposing James Frey's Fiction Addiction," The Smoking Gun, January 8, 2006, http://www.thesmokinggun.com/documents/celebrity/million-little-lies. In a highly publicized confrontation on her show on January 26, 2006, Winfrey lambasted Frey for having deceived her and others.

43.   Herman Rosenblat; quoted in Tom Leonard, "Holocaust Survivor's Love Story Exposed as Fraud," *The Telegraph* (UK), December 28, 2008, http://www.telegraph.co.uk/news/worldnews/northamerica/usa/3998664/Holocaust-survivors-love-story-exposed-as-a-fraud.html. Rosenblat's memoir was scheduled to be published by Berkley Books, an imprint of the Penguin Group, but publication was canceled after parts were shown to be fraudulent by the *New Republic* and other sources. A novel based on

Rosenblat's book has appeared; see Penelope J. Holt, *The Apple: Based on the Herman Rosenblat Holocaust Love Story* (Ryebrook, NY: York House Press, 2009). Ironically, Rosenblat didn't need to fabricate the memoir because his true story and his wife's are remarkable; see Elizabeth Day, "When One Extraordinary Life Story Is Not Enough," *The Observer*, February 15, 2009, www.guardian.co.uk/books/2009/feb/15/herman-rosenblat-oprah-winfrey-hoax.

44. Friedrich Nietzsche; quoted in Charles V. Ford, *Lies! Lies!! Lies!!!*, 173.

45. For a study comparing the skill of people in different occupations (law enforcement officers, Secret Service agents, judges, college students, and others) at detecting deception, see Paul Ekman and Maureen O'Sullivan, "Who Can Catch a Liar?", *American Psychologist* 46, no. 9 (September 1991): 913–920. Only the Secret Service excelled at this task; the performance of the other groups was at a chance level. Those who did best were attuned not only to verbal but to nonverbal cues and to "micro-expressions of emotions (very brief emotional lapses that are out of place)"—something the Secret Service had considerable practice at because of having to scan faces in crowds. Another intriguing explanation offered for the superior performance of Secret Service agents at detecting lies is that "their work in interrogating people has led them to believe that most people are telling the truth. This is in contrast to other law enforcement officers who believe that everybody lies to them" (Ford, *Lies! Lies!! Lies!!!*, 218–219).

46. Brooks Jackson and Kathleen Hall Jamieson, *unSpun: Finding Facts in a World of Disinformation* (New York: Random House, 2007), vii.

47. Jackson and Jamieson, *unSpun*, viii.

48. Simone de Beauvoir, *All Said and Done*, trans. Patrick O'Brian (New York: Putnam, 1974), 16.

49. For more on deception in childhood, see Ford, *Lies! Lies!! Lies!!!*, 69–86, 247–248.

50. On Leopold and Loeb as habitual liars, see Hal Higdon, *Leopold and Loeb: The Crime of the Century* (Urbana: University of Illinois Press, [1975] 1999), 202–203.

51. David Callahan, *The Cheating Culture: Why More Americans Are Doing Wrong to Get Ahead* (Orlando, FL: Harcourt, 2004), 262.

52. Callahan, *The Cheating Culture*, 263.

Chapter 2: Propaganda: From Nazism to Soft-Drink Ads and Soft Porn

53. Adolf Hitler; quoted in Steven Bach, *Leni: The Life and Work of Leni Riefenstahl* (New York: Knopf, 2007), 91. Bach discusses Riefenstahl's initial contact with Hitler and the commissioning of *Triumph of the Will* on pp. 90–93, 123–125, 131.

54. Frank Capra; quoted in "Origins of Documentary Film: Leni Riefenstahl," *Reel Life Stories: Documentary Film and Video Collections in the UC Berkeley Library's Media Resources Center*, http://www.lib.berkeley.edu/MRC/reellife/riefenstahl.htm.

55. Anthony Pratkanis and Elliot Aronson, *Age of Propaganda: The Everyday Use and Abuse of Persuasion*, rev. ed. (New York: W. H. Freeman / Holt, 2001), 11.

56. Josef Goebbels, March 28, 1933; quoted by Volker Köhn in "Theater des Westens' Berlin Cabaret–UFA Revue," *Stagebill*, Kennedy Center, Washington, DC, May 1992, 29a; also quoted in Michael F. Jacobson and Laurie Ann Mazur, *Marketing Madness: A Survival Guide for a Consumer Society* (Boulder, CO: Westview Press, 1995), 15.

57. George Orwell, *Nineteen Eighty-Four*, foreword by Thomas Pynchon, afterword by Erich Fromm, centennial ed. (New York: Plume, [1949] 2003), 53–54.

58. Cicero, *De inventione*; quoted in Pratkanis and Aronson, *Age of Propaganda*, 13–14.

59. Pratkanis and Aronson, *Age of Propaganda*, 14.

60. The committee was chaired by George Creel, a successful investigative journalist. Wilson chose Creel for that position because Creel came out of the Progressive tradition and so could presumably help win liberal support for the war. See George Creel, *How We Advertised America: The First Telling of the Amazing Story of the Committee on Public Information That Carried the Gospel of Americanism to Every Corner of the Globe* (New York: Arno Press, [1920] 1972).

61. See Larry Tye, *The Father of Spin: Edward L. Bernays and the Birth of Public Relations* (New York: Crown, 1998). On the relationship between Bernays and Sigmund Freud, see pp. 185–197 of Tye's book.

62. Edward L. Bernays, *Propaganda* (Brooklyn, NY: Ig Publishing, [1928] 2005), 37, 39–40.

63. Edward L. Bernays, *Public Relations* (Norman: University of Oklahoma Press, 1952), 74.

64. Bernays, *Public Relations*, 75.

65. Bernays, *Public Relations*, 75.

66. Stuart Ewen, *PR! A Social History of Spin* (New York: Basic Books, 1996), 108.

67. Inter-Allied Propaganda Commission, World War I propaganda leaflet; quoted in Ronald Steel, *Walter Lippmann and the American Century*, rev. ed. (New Brunswick, NJ: Transaction, 1999), 147–148.

68. Konrad Heiden, introduction to Adolf Hitler, *Mein Kampf*, trans. Ralph Manheim (Boston: Houghton Mifflin, [vol. 1, 1925; vol. 2, 1927] 1943), xv–xxi (quote on xv).

69. For example, Hitler says that in contrast to the ineffective propaganda efforts by the Germans and Austrians, "The war propaganda of the English and Americans was psychologically sound"; see Hitler, *Mein Kampf*, vol. 1, 181.

70. Pitman B. Potter, *American Political Science Review*, August 1945; quoted in Tye, *The Father of Spin*, 106. The 1943 English edition

of *Mein Kampf,* translated by Ralph Manheim, contains both volumes 1 and 2 (originally published in German in 1925 and 1927 respectively). Potter seems to be referring to Chapter 6 (titled "War Propaganda") in volume 1 and to Chapter 11 ("Propaganda and Organization") in volume 2 of *Mein Kampf.* For the book by Bernays that Potter is reviewing, see Edward L. Bernays, *Take Your Place at the Peace Table* (New York: Gerent Press, 1945).

71. Edward L. Bernays, *Crystallizing Public Opinion* (New York: Boni & Liveright, 1923).

72. Tye, *The Father of Spin,* 111.

73. "Walt Disney Goes to War," *Life* Magazine, August 31, 1942, 61–69 (especially 61).

74. J. Edgar Hoover, *Masters of Deceit: The Story of Communism in America and How to Fight It* (New York: Holt, 1958).

75. Pratkanis and Aronson, *Age of Propaganda,* 6.

76. Joint Chiefs of Staff, U.S. Armed Forces, *Doctrine for Joint Psychological Operations,* Joint Publication 3-53, September 5, 2003, http://www.gwu.edu/~nsarchiv/NSAEBB/NSAEBB177/02_psyop-jp-3-53.pdf, p. ix.

77. Col. James A. Treadwell; quoted in Thomas E. Ricks, "Military Plays Up Role of Zarqawi: Jordanian Painted as Foreign Threat to Iraq's Stability," *Washington Post,* April 10, 2006, http://www.washingtonpost.com/wp-dyn/content/article/2006/04/09/AR2006040900890.html.

78. Bernays, *Crystallizing Public Opinion,* 212.

79. Kathleen Taylor, *Brainwashing: The Science of Thought Control* (Oxford: Oxford University Press, 2004), 63.

80. Bernays, *Propaganda,* 37.

Chapter 3: Big Brother, Brainwashing, and You

81. George Orwell, *Nineteen Eighty-Four* (London: Secker and Warburg, 1949). For a reprint edition, see George Orwell, *Nineteen Eighty-Four,* foreword by Thomas Pynchon, afterword by Erich

Fromm, centennial ed. (New York: Plume, [1949] 2003). Edward Hunter elaborated on his views in many publications; see especially his books *Brain-Washing in Red China: The Calculated Destruction of Men's Minds* (New York: Vanguard Press, 1951; 2nd ed., 1953), and *Brainwashing: The Story of Men Who Defied It* (New York: Farrar, Straus and Cudahy, 1956).

82. Kathleen Taylor, *Brainwashing: The Science of Thought Control* (Oxford: Oxford University Press, 2004), 6.

83. Letter from George Orwell to his friend Rayner Heppenstall, November 1943; quoted in Jutta Paczulla, "'Talking to India': George Orwell's Work at the BBC, 1941–1943," *Canadian Journal of History* 42, no. 1 (spring-summer 2007), www.findarticles.com/p/articles/mi_qa3686/is_1_42/ai_n29367113.

84. Orwell, *Nineteen Eighty-Four,* part II, chap. IX (= chap. 1 of Goldstein's book); p. 219 of the Plume centennial edition.

85. Orwell, *Nineteen Eighty-Four,* part II, chap. IX (= chap. 1 of Goldstein's book); pp. 218, 220, of the Plume centennial edition.

86. As an example, see Krishan Kumar's chapter titled "Politics and Anti-Utopia: George Orwell and *Nineteen Eighty-Four,*" in his book *Utopia and Anti-Utopia in Modern Times,* 288–346 (Oxford: Blackwell, 1987).

87. George Orwell, letter to H. J. Willmett, May 18, 1944; in Sonia Orwell and Ian Angus, eds., *The Collected Essays, Journalism and Letters of George Orwell,* 4 vols. (Harmondsworth: Penguin, 1970) (for the quote, see vol. 3, 177).

88. See, for example, Jon Halliday and Bruce Cumings, *Korea: The Unknown War* (New York: Pantheon Books, 1988).

89. Ed Evanhoe, "U.S. Military Korean War Statistics," Korean-War.com, 2000, http://www.korean-war.com/miakia.html.

90. Robert Jay Lifton, *Thought Reform and the Psychology of Totalism: A Study of "Brainwashing" in China* (New York: Norton, 1961; reprint with a new preface, Chapel Hill: University of North Carolina Press, 1989), 6–7.

91. Chin Yüeh-lin, "Criticizing My Idealistic Bourgeois Pedagogical Ideology," Peking *Kuang Ming Jih Pao*, April 17, 1952; included as an appendix to Lifton, *Thought Reform and the Psychology of Totalism*, 473–484.

92. Chin Yüeh-lin; quoted in Lifton, *Thought Reform and the Psychology of Totalism*, 473, 475–476.

93. Chin Yüeh-lin; quoted in Lifton, *Thought Reform and the Psychology of Totalism*, 477.

94. Chin Yüeh-lin; quoted in Lifton, *Thought Reform and the Psychology of Totalism*, 483–484.

95. Nineteen-year-old Patty Hearst—the granddaughter of newspaper tycoon William Randolph Hearst—was kidnapped from the Berkeley apartment she shared with her boyfriend in February 1974. The kidnappers belonged to a leftist guerilla group called the Symbionese Liberation Army or SLA; they intended to exchange Hearst for jailed SLA members. That effort failed, and through physical coercion and indoctrination over the next year and a half, the SLA induced Hearst to join them in bank robberies and other illegal activities. She and other SLA members were arrested in San Francisco in September 1975. Despite being defended by noted attorney F. Lee Bailey and despite the testimony by Robert Jay Lifton and other experts that she showed classic signs of mind control, Hearst was convicted of bank robbery in March 1976. She was sentenced to thirty-five years in prison but served only twenty-two months; President Jimmy Carter commuted her sentence and she received a full pardon from President Bill Clinton.

96. Robert Jay Lifton, *The Nazi Doctors: Medical Killing and the Psychology of Genocide* (New York: Basic Books, 1986).

97. The results of this study originally appeared in a classified report; for an unclassified version, see Lawrence E. Hinkle and Harold G. Wolff, "Communist Interrogation and Indoctrination of 'Enemies of the State'—An Analysis of Methods Used by the Communist

State Police," *AMA Archives of Neurology and Psychiatry* 76 (August 1956): 115–174.

98. John Marks, *The Search for the "Manchurian Candidate": The CIA and Mind Control*, rev. ed. (New York: Norton, [1979] 1991). For the 1979 edition, see http://www.druglibrary.org/schaffer/lsd/marks.htm.

99. See Richard Condon, *The Manchurian Candidate* (New York: McGraw-Hill, 1959).

100. Marks, *The Search for the "Manchurian Candidate,"* 139.

101. Marks, *The Search for the "Manchurian Candidate,"* 138.

102. Marks, *The Search for the "Manchurian Candidate,"* 139.

103. Allen Dulles; quoted in Marks, *The Search for the "Manchurian Candidate,"* 139.

104. Marks, *The Search for the "Manchurian Candidate,"* 10.

105. Aldous Huxley, "The Final Revolution"; in Aldous Huxley, *Moksha: Writings on Psychedelics and the Visionary Experience*, ed. Michael Horowitz and Cynthia Palmer, 163–173 (Los Angeles: Tarcher, [1959] 1982) (quote on 171).

106. On the role of students and faculty at Harvard and other universities in testing LSD in CIA-sponsored experiments, see Marks, *The Search for the "Manchurian Candidate,"* 126–130. One of the best-known faculty members caught up in the emerging, CIA-sponsored drug culture was Harvard psychologist Timothy Leary (pp. 126–127). Marks argues that the CIA unintentionally played a major role in the spread of LSD around the country in the 1950s and 1960s (pp. 129–130). He writes that "no one could enter the world of psychedelics without first passing, unawares, through doors opened by the Agency. It would become a supreme irony that the CIA's enormous search for weapons among drugs—fueled by the hope that spies could, like Dr. Frankenstein, control life with genius and machines—would wind up helping to create the wandering, uncontrollable minds of the counterculture" (p. 130). Also see Martin A. Lee and Bruce Shlain, *Acid Dreams: The Complete Social History of LSD—the CIA, the Sixties, and Beyond*,

rev. ed. (New York: Grove Press, 1992); Don Lattin, *The Harvard Psychedelic Club: How Timothy Leary, Ram Dass, Huston Smith, and Andrew Weil Killed the Fifties and Ushered in a New Age for America* (New York: HarperOne, 2010); H. P. Albarelli Jr., *A Terrible Mistake: The Murder of Frank Olson and the CIA's Secret Cold War Experiments* (Walterville, OR: Trine Day, 2009), 299, 360–361.

107. Marks, *The Search for the "Manchurian Candidate,"* 79.

108. On the Japanese use of biological warfare in China, see Marks, *The Search for the "Manchurian Candidate,"* 82.

109. Marks, *The Search for the "Manchurian Candidate,"* 83.

110. In *A Terrible Mistake*, Albarelli speculates that Olson didn't jump but was pushed from his hotel window because he'd become a liability to the CIA. Albarelli theorizes that Olson had committed a security violation by talking indiscreetly with colleagues about an alleged CIA experiment gone awry in the southern French village of Pont-Saint-Esprit in 1951. In August 1951, an epidemic of psychotic symptoms (including delirium and hallucinations) as well as physical illness broke out in Pont-Saint-Esprit; several people died and others were injured or committed to asylums. Investigators have long suspected the outbreak was caused by bread contaminated by ergot (a fungus found in rye and other grains) or by mercury from fungicides, but Albarelli argues that it resulted from a CIA operation involving the aerosol spraying of the town and the contamination of its food supply with a potent form of LSD (p. 690). Shortly before his death, Olson apparently told his wife that he'd made a "terrible mistake" (p. 31) and expressed fear of the CIA. Albarelli took the title of his book from that phrase, hypothesizing that Olson's "mistake" was his indiscretion about the Pont-Saint-Esprit experiment (pp. 686–691).

111. Albarelli, *A Terrible Mistake*, 307.

112. H. P. Albarelli Jr., "Writing about the Unspeakable (AIDS, the CIA and Bio-Warfare)," TVNewsLIES.org, April 12, 2010,

http://tvnewslies.org/tvnl/index.php/editorial/guest-commentary/13873-writing-about-the-unspeakable-aids-and-bio-warfare.html.

113. Harriet A. Washington, *Medical Apartheid: The Dark History of Medical Experimentation on Black Americans from Colonial Times to the Present* (New York: Doubleday, 2006), 360–361.

114. Washington, *Medical Apartheid*, 361.

115. On Pelote's efforts to expose the mosquito experiments, see Washington, *Medical Apartheid*, 361–363, 381–383.

116. George White, letter to Sid Gottlieb, November 21, (probably) 1972; quoted in Marks, *The Search for the "Manchurian Candidate,"* 109. Marks discusses the safehouses on pp. 94–112; also see Albarelli, *A Terrible Mistake*, 385–391, 411–412, 574–579.

117. Marks, *The Search for the "Manchurian Candidate,"* 139–140.

118. The Canadian government funded Cameron's brainwashing research from 1961 to 1964, when he abruptly resigned to take a position in the United States. On Cameron's connection with the CIA, see Anne Collins, *In the Sleep Room: The Story of the CIA Brainwashing Experiments in Canada* (Toronto: Lester & Orpen Dennys, 1988), especially 137–140, 188–189, 256–257; Naomi Klein, *The Shock Doctrine: The Rise of Disaster Capitalism* (New York: Metropolitan Books / Henry Holt, 2007), 25–48.

119. Cameron had been part of a psychiatric team that evaluated Rudolf Hess's fitness to stand trial at Nuremberg. Hess was a high-level Nazi official—second in line to succeed Adolf Hitler after Hermann Göring—and had created a sensation when he commandeered a plane and flew solo to Scotland in 1942, apparently in the hope of negotiating a peace treaty with Prime Minister Winston Churchill. Though Hess had shown signs of mental illness while in British custody and subsequently, Cameron and his colleagues found him sane and fit to stand trial. Hess was sentenced to life imprisonment at Berlin's Spandau Prison; he was the last remaining prisoner there when he committed suicide in

1987. On Cameron's role at Nuremberg, see Collins, *In the Sleep Room*, 108–113.

120. Condon, *The Manchurian Candidate*, 183.

121. This characterization is by a member of an investigative team commissioned to review Cameron's work after his retirement from the Allan Memorial Institute; quoted in Marks, *The Search for the "Manchurian Candidate,"* 150.

122. Quoted in Marks, *The Search for the "Manchurian Candidate,"* 141.

123. Quoted in Marks, *The Search for the "Manchurian Candidate,"* 150.

124. Albarelli, *A Terrible Mistake*, 191.

125. On food, politics, and Pavlov's dog, see Robert B. Cialdini, *Influence: Science and Practice*, 5th ed. (Boston: Pearson / Allyn and Bacon, 2009), 163–165.

126. Anthony Pratkanis and Elliot Aronson, *Age of Propaganda: The Everyday Use and Abuse of Persuasion*, rev. ed. (New York: W. H. Freeman / Holt, 2001), 305; Margaret Thaler Singer, *Cults in Our Midst*, rev. ed. (San Francisco: Jossey-Bass, 2003).

127. For more discussion, see Taylor, *Brainwashing*, 167–186, 213–218, 250–252.

128. Taylor, *Brainwashing*, 143–145.

129. Marks, *The Search for the "Manchurian Candidate,"* 228.

130. Marks, *The Search for the "Manchurian Candidate,"* 229.

131. Marks, *The Search for the "Manchurian Candidate,"* 229.

Chapter 4: The Brave New World of Advertising

132. Vance Packard, *The Hidden Persuaders* (New York: David McKay Company, 1957).

133. Packard, *The Hidden Persuaders*, 3.

134. Packard, *The Hidden Persuaders*, 5.

135. For the photo of the correspondence room, see Sarah Stage, *Female Complaints: Lydia Pinkham and the Business of Women's*

Medicine (New York: Norton, 1979), 153. Stage discusses the controversies surrounding the tombstone photo and the handling of the correspondence on pp. 163–165.

136. The following passage is typical: "If everyone went around pricing, and chemically tasting before purchasing, the dozens of soaps or fabrics or brands of bread which are for sale, economic life would be hopelessly jammed. To avoid such confusion, society consents to have its choice narrowed to ideas and objects brought to its attention through *propaganda* of all kinds" (Edward L. Bernays, *Propaganda* (Brooklyn, NY: Ig Publishing, [1928] 2005), 39; italics added).

137. Larry Tye, *The Father of Spin: Edward L. Bernays and the Birth of Public Relations* (New York: Crown, 1998), 197.

138. Quoted in Tye, *The Father of Spin*, 56.

139. Tye, *The Father of Spin*, 23.

140. On this campaign to turn women into smokers, see Tye, *The Father of Spin*, 23–38; Allan M. Brandt, *The Cigarette Century: The Rise, Fall, and Deadly Persistence of the Product That Defined America* (New York: Basic Books, 2007), 82–88.

141. Robert W. McChesney, *The Problem of the Media: U.S. Communication Politics in the Twenty-First Century* (New York: Monthly Review Press, 2004), 167.

142. McChesney, *The Problem of the Media*, 138. McChesney includes a good discussion of the trend toward hypercommercialism, with useful examples and references (pp. 138–174).

143. Packard, *The Hidden Persuaders*, 74. I've summarized this list of eight items from pp. 72–83 of Packard's book.

144. Packard, *The Hidden Persuaders*, 77.

145. Packard, *The Hidden Persuaders*, 81.

146. See the discussion of the Marlboro campaign on pp. 95–97 of *The Hidden Persuaders*.

147. Packard, *The Hidden Persuaders*, 93.

148. Packard, *The Hidden Persuaders*, 116–117.

149. Packard, *The Hidden Persuaders*, 266.

150. See Susan Gregory Thomas, *Buy, Buy Baby: How Consumer Culture Manipulates Parents and Harms Young Minds* (Boston: Houghton Mifflin, 2007).

151. Quoted in McChesney, *The Problem of the Media*, 161–162.

152. McChesney, *The Problem of the Media*, 166–167.

153. Edward L. Bernays, *Public Relations* (Norman: University of Oklahoma Press, 1952), 339. This quote appears in a chapter titled "How American Business Can Sell the American Way of Life to the American People" (pp. 335–345).

154. Quoted in John E. Calfee, "The Ghost of Cigarette Advertising Past," *Regulation: The Cato Review of Business & Government* 20, no. 3 (1997): 38–45, www.cato.org/pubs/regulation/regv20n3/reg20n3f.pdf. This article provides a good overview of the regulation of tobacco advertising—and of the ingenious efforts of the tobacco companies to put their products in the best light despite mounting health concerns. Also see Brandt, *The Cigarette Century*.

155. Senior editor at *Adweek* magazine; quoted in Michael F. Jacobson and Laurie Ann Mazur, *Marketing Madness: A Survival Guide for a Consumer Society* (Boulder, CO: Westview Press, 1995), 82.

Chapter 5: Media Bias and What You Can Do about It

156. Quoted in David E. Johnson and Johnny R. Johnson, *A Funny Thing Happened on the Way to the White House: Foolhardiness, Folly, and Fraud in Presidential Elections, from Andrew Jackson to George W. Bush*, rev. ed. (Lanham, MD: Taylor Trade / Rowman & Littlefield, [1983] 2004), 138.

157. John Nichols and Robert W. McChesney, *Tragedy and Farce: How the American Media Sell Wars, Spin Elections, and Destroy Democracy* (New York: New Press, 2005), 126.

158. Nichols and McChesney, *Tragedy and Farce*, 126.

159. Martin A. Lee and Norman Solomon, *Unreliable Sources: A Guide to Detecting Bias in News Media* (New York: Lyle Stuart / Carol Publishing Group, 1998), 332.

160. Richard Paul and Linda Elder, *Critical Thinking: Tools for Taking Charge of Your Learning and Your Life*, 2nd ed. (Upper Saddle River, NJ: Pearson Prentice Hall, 2006), 270.

161. For more detail, see Bruce Watson, *Sacco and Vanzetti: The Men, the Murders, and the Judgment of Mankind* (New York: Viking, 2007).

162. Bartolomeo Vanzetti, in the *New York World*, May 13, 1927, 15; quoted in Watson, *Sacco and Vanzetti*, 304–305. Watson notes that Vanzetti's "impromptu soliloquy became immortal" (p. 304).

163. Hoover was appointed to head the Bureau of Investigation in 1924; it was renamed the Federal Bureau of Investigation in 1935. On Hoover and the Palmer Raids, see Kenneth D. Ackerman, *Young J. Edgar: Hoover, the Red Scare, and the Assault on Civil Liberties* (New York: Carroll & Graf, 2007).

164. Ben H. Bagdikian, *The New Media Monopoly*, rev. ed. (Boston: Beacon Press, 2004), xv.

165. Bagdikian, *The New Media Monopoly*, xvii.

166. Bagdikian, *The New Media Monopoly*, xvi–xvii.

167. Admiral William Leahy; quoted in William Buckingham Jr., *Operation Ranch Hand: The Air Force and Herbicides in Southeast Asia, 1961–1971* (Washington, DC: U.S. Air Force, 1982), 82.

168. Edward S. Herman and Noam Chomsky, *Manufacturing Consent: The Political Economy of the Mass Media*, rev. ed. (New York: Pantheon Books, 2002), xxxi.

169. Herman and Chomsky, *Manufacturing Consent*, xxxii.

170. Orville Schell Jr., "Silent Vietnam: How We Invented Ecocide and Killed a Country," *Look* Magazine, April 6, 1971, 55–58.

171. Herman and Chomsky, *Manufacturing Consent*, xxxi–xxxii.

172. Deborah Hastings, "Adoption Nightmares," *Maine Sunday Telegram* (from the Associated Press), February 4, 2001, 1C, 6C

(quote on 6C). I've also based my account of the Venhaus and Whatcott cases below on this article.

173. Barbara Holtan, who directs adoptions for Tressler Lutheran Services; quoted in Hastings, "Adoption Nightmares," 6C.

174. Caryl Rivers, *Selling Anxiety: How the News Media Scare Women* (Hanover, NH: University Press of New England, 2007), 52–53.

175. Margaret Talbot, "The Disconnected; Attachment Theory: The Ultimate Experiment," *New York Times Magazine*, May 24, 1998, section 6, p. 24, http://www.nytimes.com/1998/05/24/magazine/the-disconnected-attachment-theory-the-ultimate-experiment.html?pagewanted=all&src=pm.

176. Talbot, "The Disconnected."

177. Rivers, *Selling Anxiety*, 53.

178. Lee and Solomon, *Unreliable Sources*, 229.

179. In his *Bloggers on the Bus: How the Internet Changed Politics and the Press* (New York: Free Press, 2009), Eric Boehlert offers this account of the origin of blogging: "Blogging's semiofficial birth date is December 23, 1997, when the online diarist and computer programmer Jorn Barger decided to keep a daily log of links to favorite items he read as he surfed the Internet. These were articles and posts about his intellectual pursuits, which included politics, culture, books, and technology. The online roundup was dubbed a 'weblog,' quickly shortened to 'blog.' By 2008 more than 100 million blogs populated the Internet worldwide" (p. 48). On a related issue of terminology, Boehlert notes that while *blogosphere* and *netroots* are often used interchangeably, technically the blogosphere is a subcategory of the larger netroots community, which encompasses other online sources besides blogs (p. 48).

180. Boehlert, *Bloggers on the Bus*, xvi. For the book on which Boehlert modeled his book, see Timothy Crouse, *The Boys on the Bus* (New York: Random House, 1973).

181. Boehlert, *Bloggers on the Bus*, 120–121. Also see Marie Cocco, "Clinton Campaign Brought Sexism out of Hiding," RealClearPolitics,

May 13, 2008, www.realclearpolitics.com/articles/2008/05/clinton_
campaign_brought_sexis.html.

182. Jarhead5536, Daily Kos; quoted in Boehlert, *Bloggers on the Bus*,
122–123.

183. Armando Llorens-Sar; quoted in Boehlert, *Bloggers on the Bus*, 128.

184. Boehlert, *Bloggers on the Bus*, 149.

185. On the predominantly white and male composition of most
areas of the media, see Media Report to Women, "Industry Statistics," March 2012, www.mediareporttowomen.com/statistics.
htm; Media Matters for America, "Gender and Ethnic Diversity
in Prime-Time Cable News," July 2008, www.mediamatters.org/
reports/diversity_report; Chris Bowers, "Netroots Demographics and Diversity," MyDD, January 23, 2007, www.mydd.com/
story/2007/1/23/133950/828; Joseph Graf, Institute for Politics,
Democracy & the Internet, George Washington University, "The
Audience for Political Blogs: New Research on Blog Readership,"
October 2006, http://archive.knightdigitalmediacenter.org/
resources/pdf/2007Election08-The%20Audience%20for%20
Political%20Blogs.pdf

186. For more on the fake-pregnancy story, see Boehlert, *Bloggers on
the Bus*, 232–243.

187. Gene Weingarten, "Cruel and Unusual Punishment," *Washington Post Magazine*, March 23, 2008, www.washingtonpost.com/
wp-dyn/content/article/2008/03/18/AR2008031802463.html.

188. Weingarten, "Cruel and Unusual Punishment."

189. Dan Balz and Haynes Johnson, *The Battle for America 2008: The
Story of an Extraordinary Election* (New York: Viking, 2009), 385.

190. Balz and Johnson, *The Battle for America 2008*, 385.

191. Balz and Johnson, *The Battle for America 2008*, 385–386.

192. "Press Widely Criticized, but Trusted More Than Other Information Sources," Pew Research Center, September 22, 2011, http://
www.people-press.org/2011/09/22/press-widely-criticized-but-
trusted-more-than-other-institutions/.

193. Nichols and McChesney, *Tragedy and Farce*, 182.

194. Nichols and McChesney, *Tragedy and Farce*, 186.

195. Paul and Elder, *Critical Thinking*, 271. (I've shortened Paul and Elder's list slightly.)

196. Robert W. McChesney, Russell Newman, and Ben Scott, eds., *The Future of Media: Resistance and Reform in the 21st Century* (New York: Seven Stories Press, 2005), 303–371.

Chapter 6: Truth and Lies in Politics

197. The flap copy I've quoted is reprinted on the back flap of George Orwell, *Nineteen Eighty-Four*, foreword by Thomas Pynchon, afterword by Erich Fromm, centennial ed. (New York: Plume, [1949] 2003).

198. In Orwell's *Nineteen Eighty-Four*, the population is relentlessly indoctrinated by the Two Minutes Hate, a diatribe against Emmanuel Goldstein and other enemies of the Party: "The next moment a hideous, grinding screech, as of some monstrous machine running without oil, burst from the big telescreen at the end of the room. It was a noise that set one's teeth on edge and bristled the hair at the back of one's neck. The Hate had started. . . . The program of the Two Minutes Hate varied from day to day, but there was none in which Goldstein was not the principal figure. He was the primal traitor, the earliest defiler of the Party's purity" (Orwell, *Nineteen Eighty-Four*, 11–12).

199. Charges of fundraising and lobbying irregularities have been leveled against many U.S. politicians. Certain policies and practices followed by both Democratic and Republican administrations have been criticized as "totalitarian." For example, Salon.com columnist Camille Paglia had this to say about information-gathering practices attributed to the Obama administration: "The ethical collapse of the left was nowhere more evident than in the near total silence of liberal media and Web sites at the Obama administration's outrageous solicitation to private citizens to report unacceptable 'casual conversations' to the White House.

If Republicans had done this, there would have been an angry explosion by Democrats from coast to coast. I was stunned at the failure of liberals to see the blatant totalitarianism in this incident, which the president should have immediately denounced. His failure to do so implicates him in it" (Camille Paglia, "Obama's Healthcare Horror," Salon.com, August 12, 2009, http://www.salon.com/opinion/paglia/2009/08/12/town_halls/).

200. Quoted in David E. Johnson and Johnny R. Johnson, *A Funny Thing Happened on the Way to the White House: Foolhardiness, Folly, and Fraud in Presidential Elections, from Andrew Jackson to George W. Bush*, rev. ed. (Lanham, MD: Taylor Trade / Rowman & Littlefield, [1983] 2004), 5.

201. Johnson and Johnson, *A Funny Thing Happened on the Way to the White House*, 5.

202. The candidates' wives were even slower to begin campaigning. The first candidate's wife to take part in a presidential campaign was Eleanor Roosevelt, who made a speech on behalf of Franklin D. Roosevelt's vice presidential choice, Henry Wallace, at the 1940 Democratic convention. Jackie Kennedy was a popular campaign asset when she appeared with her husband, John F. Kennedy, on the campaign trail, and she occasionally made short remarks. But the first candidate's wife to take to the campaign trail herself was Lady Bird Johnson, who went on a four-day trip in the South in 1964 to win support for the efforts of her husband, Lyndon B. Johnson, on behalf of civil rights (Paul F. Boller Jr., *Presidential Campaigns: From George Washington to George W. Bush*, 2nd ed. (New York: Oxford University Press, 2004), 416).

203. Edward L. Bernays, *Public Relations* (Norman: University of Oklahoma Press, 1952), 67.

204. The Association of National Advertisers named Obama the winner at its October 2008 conference. See Lena Chow, "Obama Wins Marketer of the Year Award," City of Paris, October 20, 2008, www.cityofparis.us/obama-wins-marketer-of-the-year-award/;

Ken Wheaton, "Obama Wins Vote for Marketer of the Year," *Advertising Age*, October 17, 2008, http://adage.com/campaign-trail/post?article_id=131811.

205. Kathleen Hall Jamieson, *Dirty Politics: Deception, Distraction, and Democracy* (New York: Oxford University Press, 1992), 55–56.

206. Anthony Pratkanis and Elliot Aronson, *Age of Propaganda: The Everyday Use and Abuse of Persuasion*, rev. ed. (New York: W. H. Freeman / Holt, 2001), 66.

207. Jamieson, *Dirty Politics*, 170.

208. President Harry S. Truman; quoted in Lawrence Van Gelder, "Margaret Truman Daniel, President's Daughter and Popular Author, Dies at 83," *New York Times*, January 30, 2008, www.nytimes.com/2008/01/30/nyregion/30daniel.html?pagewanted=all.

209. Richard M. Nixon, "Checkers" speech, Los Angeles, September 23, 1952; in *American Rhetoric: Top 100 Speeches*, www.americanrhetoric.com/speeches/richardnixoncheckers.html.

210. James A. Farley; quoted in Larry Tye, *The Father of Spin: Edward L. Bernays and the Birth of Public Relations* (New York: Crown, 1998), 86.

211. Helen Gahagan Douglas, *A Full Life* (Garden City, NY: Doubleday, 1982), 332.

212. Neale Donald Walsch, *Conversations with God: An Uncommon Dialogue*, book 2 (Charlottesville, VA: Hampton Roads Publishing Company, 1997), 133.

213. Charles V. Ford, *Lies! Lies!! Lies!!!: The Psychology of Deceit* (Washington, DC: American Psychiatric Press, 1996), 11.

214. Ford, *Lies! Lies!! Lies!!!*, 11; also see E. J. Dionne Jr., "Biden Admits Plagiarism in School but Says It Was Not 'Malevolent,'" *New York Times*, September 18, 1987, A1, www.nytimes.com/1987/09/18/us/biden-admits-plagiarism-in-school-but-says-it-was-not-malevolent.html.

215. David Greenberg, "The Write Stuff? Why Biden's Plagiarism Shouldn't Be Forgotten," Slate.com, August 25, 2008, http://www.

slate.com/articles/news_and_politics/history_lesson/2008/08/
the_write_stuff.html.

216. Ford, *Lies! Lies!! Lies!!!*, 11, 99–101, 123.

217. Richard A. Posner, *The Little Book of Plagiarism* (New York: Pantheon Books, 2007), 37.

218. Ford, *Lies! Lies!! Lies!!!*, 123.

219. Ford, *Lies! Lies!! Lies!!!*, 124.

220. Ford, *Lies! Lies!! Lies!!!*, 124.

221. Jamieson, *Dirty Politics*, 74.

222. Joseph Cummins, *Anything for a Vote: Dirty Tricks, Cheap Shots, and October Surprises in U.S. Presidential Campaigns* (Philadelphia: Quirk Books, 2007), 179.

223. Sally Denton, *The Pink Lady: The Many Lives of Helen Gahagan Douglas* (New York: Bloomsbury Press, 2009), 173.

224. Mitchell, *Tricky Dick and the Pink Lady: Richard Nixon vs. Helen Gahagan Douglas—Sexual Politics and the Red Scare, 1950* (New York: Random House, 1998), 26.

225. Douglas, *A Full Life*, 402.

226. Mitchell, *Tricky Dick and the Pink Lady*, 4.

227. Statement attributed to George Smathers; from the Claude Pepper Museum, quoted in Kerwin C. Swint, *Mudslingers: The Top 25 Negative Political Campaigns of All Time* (Westport, CT: Praeger, 2006), 47.

228. Douglas considered the Pink Sheet the "single most damaging piece of literature" Nixon used against her (*A Full Life*, 315). Some sources say Nixon distributed only 50,000 copies, but according to Douglas, the flyer was so successful that a second printing of 500,000 was ordered a few days later (p. 315).

229. Douglas, *A Full Life*, 91.

230. Mitchell, *Tricky Dick and the Pink Lady*, 14.

231. Kyle Palmer, *Los Angeles Times*, September 10, 1950; quoted in Denton, *The Pink Lady*, 163.

232. Richard Nixon, quoted in Swint, *Mudslingers*, 170; for a slightly different version, see Mitchell, *Tricky Dick and the Pink Lady*,

165. Part of the quote is also in Douglas, *A Full Life*, 311. Nixon's close aides later revealed the duplicity in these remarks when they described his prejudice against women; one colleague characterized him as having "a total scorn for female mentality" and a second said he regarded women as "an extra appendage, a different species" (Mitchell, *Tricky Dick and the Pink Lady*, 66).

233. Denton, *The Pink Lady*, 157.

234. Douglas, *A Full Life*, 334.

235. Jimmy Carter; quoted in Denton, *The Pink Lady*, 189.

236. Senator Alan Cranston (D-CA), eulogy delivered in the Senate on August 5, 1980, a few weeks after Douglas's death; in Douglas, *A Full Life*, 418–419 (quote on 418). In a 1976 interview, Douglas's friend Philip Noel-Baker—an influential British politician, pacifist, and Nobel laureate—speculated that "if Helen had stayed in the House of Representatives, she would have been the presidential candidate, and the first woman president of the United States. I think she would have had an enormous influence on American public life, on the position of women in every country in the world, and on the success of the United Nations. That's another of the ifs of history" (quoted in Denton, *The Pink Lady*, 189).

237. Douglas, *A Full Life*, 341.

238. Douglas, *A Full Life*, 336.

239. George Wallace, inaugural address as governor of Alabama, January 14, 1963; quoted in Dan T. Carter, *The Politics of Rage: George Wallace, the Origins of the New Conservatism, and the Transformation of American Politics* (New York: Simon & Schuster, 1995), 11.

240. Carter, *The Politics of Rage*, 150.

241. George Wallace, quoted in Carter, *The Politics of Rage*, 96; this quote is also included in "Wallace Quotes," *George Wallace: Settin' the Woods on Fire*, American Experience film series, PBS, 2000, http://www.pbs.org/wgbh/amex/wallace/sfeature/quotes.html. For an article on the film *George Wallace: Settin' the Woods*

on Fire that puts the quote in the context of Wallace's "Faustian bargain" to advance his political career by exploiting racism, see Maggie Riechers, "Racism to Redemption: The Path of George Wallace," *Humanities* 21, no. 2 (March-April 2000), www.neh.gov/news/humanities/2000-03/wallace.html. Some sources give a different version of Wallace's comment, quoting him as saying he'd been "outsegged [outsegregated]" by his opponent and that he would "never be outsegged again."

242. George Wallace, quoted in *George Wallace: Settin' the Woods on Fire*; the quote is also included in Riechers, "Racism to Redemption."

243. Swint, *Mudslingers*, 226.

244. George Wallace; quoted in Carter, *The Politics of Rage*, 391.

245. George Wallace; quoted in Carter, *The Politics of Rage*, 391.

246. Carter, *The Politics of Rage*, 384–385, 387–389, 392.

247. Albert Brewer, CBS interview; quoted in Carter, *The Politics of Rage*, 395. The election statistics in this paragraph are from Swint, *Mudslingers*, 227, 230.

248. Carter, *The Politics of Rage*, 459–462.

249. Quoted in David A. Kaplan, *The Accidental President: How 413 Lawyers, 9 Supreme Court Justices, and 5,963,110 (Give or Take a Few) Floridians Landed George W. Bush in the White House* (New York: William Morrow, 2001), 28–29.

250. Alexis de Tocqueville, *Democracy in America*; quoted in Kaplan, *The Accidental President*, 46.

251. The phrase "nine scorpions in a bottle" has been attributed to Justice Oliver Wendell Holmes Jr., who served on the Supreme Court between 1902 and 1932; quoted in Kaplan, *The Accidental President*, 241–242.

252. Mark Russell; quoted in Boller, *Presidential Campaigns*, 411.

253. Steven F. Freeman and Joel Bleifuss, *Was the 2004 Presidential Election Stolen? Exit Polls, Election Fraud, and the Official Count* (New York: Seven Stories Press, 2006), 177.

254. Freeman and Bleifuss, *Was the 2004 Presidential Election Stolen?*, 177.

255. Freeman and Bleifuss, *Was the 2004 Presidential Election Stolen?*, xi–xiii.

256. On voting-machine fraud and other types of election fraud in 2004, see especially Freeman and Bleifuss, *Was the 2004 Presidential Election Stolen?*, 1–31, 55–83. For their calculations of the margin by which Kerry won, see pp. 173–175.

257. Freeman and Bleifuss, *Was the 2004 Presidential Election Stolen?*, 191.

258. Stephen Clark, "An ACORN by Any Other Name Still Smells Like an ACORN, Critics Say," FOXNews.com, March 26, 2010, http://www.foxnews.com/politics/2010/03/25/similar-groups-acorns-place-republicans-foul/?test=latestnews; Jonathan Strong, "Zombie-Like, 'Disbanded' ACORN Coming Back to Life in Form of New Groups," Daily Caller, April 1, 2010, http://dailycaller.com/2010/04/01/zombie-like-disbanded-acorn-coming-back-to-life-in-form-of-new-groups/.

Chapter 7: Bigots and Demagogues

259. Gordon W. Allport, *The Nature of Prejudice*, 25th anniv. ed. (Reading, MA: Addison-Wesley, [1954] 1979), 419–420.

260. Carol Tavris and Elliot Aronson, *Mistakes Were Made (but Not by Me): Why We Justify Foolish Beliefs, Bad Decisions, and Hurtful Acts* (Orlando, FL: Harcourt, 2007), 60.

261. Tavris and Aronson, *Mistakes Were Made (but Not by Me)*, 65.

262. Ian Kershaw, *Hitler 1889–1936: Hubris* (New York: Norton, 1998), 11.

263. Kershaw, *Hitler 1889–1936*, 13.

264. Fritz Redlich, *Hitler: Diagnosis of a Destructive Prophet* (New York: Oxford University Press, 1999), 16.

265. Adolf Hitler, *Mein Kampf*, trans. Ralph Manheim (Boston: Houghton Mifflin, [1925, 1927] 1943). On the book's composition and publishing history, see Konrad Heiden's introduction (pp. xv–xxi of the English translation just cited).

266. Kershaw, *Hitler 1889–1936*, 73.

267. Erich Ludendorff; quoted in "Talk: Erich Ludendorff," Wikiquote, http://en.wikiquote.org/wiki/Talk:Erich_Ludendorff.

268. Kershaw, *Hitler 1889–1936*, 12.

269. Redlich, *Hitler*, 283–284.

270. Redlich, *Hitler*, 78. For more, see Redlich's discussion on pp. 79–85, as well as the discussion of these and other women in Anna Maria Sigmund, *Women of the Third Reich* (Richmond Hill, Ontario: NDE Publishing, [1998] 2000), and Guido Knopp, *Hitler's Women*, trans. Angus McGeoch (New York: Routledge, [2001] 2003).

271. Keith M. Finley, *Delaying the Dream: Southern Senators and the Fight against Civil Rights, 1938–1965* (Baton Rouge: Louisiana State University Press, 2008), 44.

272. Bilbo's early years are hard to reconstruct from published sources; for the details of his educational background I've relied on Chester M. Morgan, *Redneck Liberal: Theodore G. Bilbo and the New Deal* (Baton Rouge: Louisiana State University Press, 1985), 27–29.

273. Thayer Watkins, "Theodore G. Bilbo of Mississippi," Department of Economics, San José State University, http://www.applet-magic.com/bilbo.htm.

274. Fred Sullens, *Jackson Daily News*; quoted in Watkins, "Theodore G. Bilbo of Mississippi."

275. "Hoover Danced with Negro," *Oelwein Daily Register* (Oelwein, Iowa), October 18, 1928, 1. The incident is mentioned more generally in Morgan, *Redneck Liberal*, 42–43.

276. *The New Republic*, September 17, 1930.

277. For a view of the university controversy more sympathetic to Bilbo, see Morgan, *Redneck Liberal*, 44–46.

278. This mixture of political views is reflected in the title of Morgan's *Redneck Liberal*. See his book for more discussion of Bilbo's cultural background and politics, especially pp. 232–253 and the references cited there.

279.   Theodore G. Bilbo; quoted in Robert L. Fleegler, "Theodore G. Bilbo and the Decline of Public Racism, 1938–1947," *Journal of Mississippi History*, spring 2006, http://www.mdah.state.ms.us/pubs/bilbo.pdf.

280.   Remarks delivered by Senator Theodore G. Bilbo in the U.S. Senate, June 27, 1945, http://www.pierretristam.com/Bobst/07/wf071607.htm. Also see Richard Wright, *Black Boy: A Record of Childhood and Youth* (New York: New American Library, [1945] 1951).

281.   Theodore G. Bilbo, *Take Your Choice: Separation or Mongreliza-tion* (Poplarville, MS: Dream House, 1947), http://www.archive.org/details/TakeYourChoice.

282.   Bilbo, preface to *Take Your Choice*.

283.   Arthur Herman, *Joseph McCarthy: Reexamining the Life and Legacy of America's Most Hated Senator* (New York: Free Press, 2000), 30.

284.   For more discussion of McCarthy's war record, see Herman, *Joseph McCarthy*, 30–34.

285.   Herman, *Joseph McCarthy*, 51.

286.   Thomas C. Reeves, *The Life and Times of Joe McCarthy: A Biography* (New York: Stein and Day, 1982), 185. Reeves describes McCarthy's role in the Malmédy case on pp. 161–185.

287.   Joseph McCarthy, speech to the Republican Women's Club of Wheeling, West Virginia, February 9, 1950; quoted in Robert Griffith, *The Politics of Fear: Joseph R. McCarthy and the Senate* (Amherst: University of Massachusetts Press, 1970), 49.

288.   Griffith, *The Politics of Fear*, 127–129; Fred J. Cook, *The Nightmare Decade: The Life and Times of Senator Joe McCarthy* (New York: Random House, 1971), 312.

289.   Joseph McCarthy, *Major Speeches and Debates of Senator Joe McCarthy Delivered in the United States Senate, 1950–1951* (Washington, DC: Government Printing Office, 1951), 215.

290.   Joseph McCarthy; quoted in David M. Oshinsky, *A Conspiracy So Immense: The World of Joe McCarthy* (Oxford: Oxford University Press, 2005), 194.

291. Albert Fried, *McCarthyism, the Great American Red Scare: A Documentary History* (Oxford: Oxford University Press, 1996), 179.

292. Dwight Eisenhower; in Herbert S. Parmet, *Eisenhower and the American Crusades* (New York: Macmillan, 1972), 248, 337, 577.

293. Joseph McCarthy; quoted in Reeves, *The Life and Times of Joe McCarthy*, 203.

294. Joseph Welch; quoted in Griffith, *The Politics of Fear*, 259.

295. Haynes Johnson, *The Age of Anxiety: McCarthyism to Terrorism* (New York: Harcourt, 2005), 250.

296. Allport, *The Nature of Prejudice*, 415.

297. Redlich, *Hitler*, 69.

298. P. M. Forni, *The Civility Solution: What to Do When People Are Rude* (New York: St. Martin's Press, 2008), 79.

Chapter 8: The Legal Web

299. Scott Turow, *One L*, rev. ed. (New York: Farrar Straus Giroux, 1988), 306.

300. Turow, *One L*, 306.

301. Tony Mauro, "Lawyers' Top Topic: Public's Perception," *USA Today*, August 10, 1993, 3A.

302. Andrew Roth and Jonathan Roth, *Devil's Advocates: The Unnatural History of Lawyers*, ed. Barbara Repa (Berkeley, CA: Nolo Press, 1989), 157.

303. Erhard Blankenburg and Ulrike Schultz, "German Advocates: A Highly Regulated Profession," 124–159 (especially 126), and Anne Boigeol, "The French Bar: The Difficulties of Unifying a Divided Profession," 258–294 (especially 272), both in Richard L. Abel and Philip S. C. Lewis, eds., *Lawyers in Society, Volume 2: The Civil Law World* (Berkeley: University of California Press, 1988).

304. Anacharsis; quoted in Plutarch, *Life of Solon* 5.2, in *Plutarch's Lives*, vol. 1, trans. Bernadette Perrin, Loeb Classical Library

(Cambridge, MA: Harvard University Press, 1982), 415. The Scythians were a nomadic people who flourished between the eighth and third centuries BCE in Eurasia.

305. Irving Stone, *Clarence Darrow for the Defense* (Garden City, NY: Doubleday, Doran & Company, 1941).

306. Stone, *Clarence Darrow for the Defense*, 384–385.

307. Some sources disagree about the ages at which Leopold and Loeb entered and graduated from college and whether they were the youngest graduates ever of their alma maters. I've followed the discussion in Simon Baatz, *For the Thrill of It: Leopold, Loeb, and the Murder That Shocked Chicago* (New York: HarperCollins, 2008), 40–53. Baatz says Loeb "graduated from University High [adjacent to the University of Chicago and founded by the University of Chicago philosophy professor John Dewey] in June 1919, just a few days past his fourteenth birthday" (p. 40). Loeb entered the University of Chicago in the fall of 1919, spent two years there, then became bored living at home and attending that familiar campus, so he transferred to the University of Michigan at Ann Arbor for his junior and senior years. He graduated in June 1923, a few weeks before his eighteenth birthday, making him "the youngest graduate in the history of the University of Michigan" (p. 50). Leopold, who was six months older than Loeb, entered the University of Chicago in the fall of 1920, accompanied Loeb (with whom he had become infatuated) to the University of Michigan in September 1921, then returned to Chicago a year later after Loeb ostensibly ended their friendship. (Loeb was trying to join a fraternity and was told that his friendship with a "suspected homosexual" like Leopold would "torpedo his chances"; Baatz, *For the Thrill of It*, 47.) Leopold had an outstanding record at the University of Chicago in 1922–1923—taking languages like Sanskrit, Greek, Latin, and Russian and being elected to Phi Beta Kappa—and graduated in March 1923, a year ahead of his classmates. The two young men became reacquainted in September 1923 at the University of Chicago, where Leopold had entered law school and Loeb was doing

graduate work in history. Their reacquaintance was fateful; it gave Loeb the accomplice he needed for the "perfect crime" he dreamed of committing (p. 53). The young ages at which the two murderers attended college were probably also fateful, because a major theme brought out by psychiatrists during the trial was Leopold and Loeb's immaturity and low self-esteem, compensated for by grandiosity. Loeb in particular seemed to have had an inferiority complex, resulting partly from his inability to cope with the demands of college in his early teens (Baatz, *For the Thrill of It*, 263–264). Interestingly, Leopold speculated in his memoir—written after he had been in prison more than thirty years—that "the only fundamental characteristic in which I believe that criminals may differ significantly from the general population is in their emotional immaturity" (Nathan F. Leopold Jr., *Life Plus 99 Years* (Garden City, NY: Doubleday & Company, 1958), 198).

308.   Stone, *Clarence Darrow for the Defense*, 385–386.

309.   In the early twentieth century, Nietzsche's philosophy swept through the U.S. academic community, so the idea of superman and related concepts from Nietzsche's *Thus Spoke Zarathustra* (1883–1885), *Beyond Good and Evil* (1886), and other works would have been hotly debated during Leopold's student years. See Friedrich Nietzsche, *Thus Spoke Zarathustra: A Book for None and All*, trans. Walter Kaufmann (New York: Penguin, 1978); Friedrich Nietzsche, *Beyond Good and Evil*, ed. R. J. Hollingdale and Michael Tanner, trans. R. J. Hollingdale (New York: Penguin, 2003). Years later, in the aftermath of World War II, Leopold told a fellow inmate named Gene Lovitz in the Stateville Penitentiary in Illinois that he had first learned about Nietzsche from Jack London's novel *The Sea-Wolf* (Hal Higdon, *Leopold and Loeb: The Crime of the Century* (Urbana: University of Illinois Press, [1975] 1999), 305). Lovitz was apparently less enamored of Nietzsche than Leopold was; Lovitz later said he told the Jewish and homosexual Leopold that "his [Nietzsche's] precious

superman theories would have put you in the ovens" (quoted in Higdon, *Leopold and Loeb*, 306).

310. Stone, *Clarence Darrow for the Defense*, 388.

311. Stone, *Clarence Darrow for the Defense*, 388.

312. William Alanson White, psychiatrist testifying for the defense in *People of the State of Illinois vs. Nathan Leopold and Richard Loeb*, Trial Transcript, fol. 1342; quoted in Baatz, *For the Thrill of It*, 311.

313. Richard A. Loeb to Clarence Darrow; quoted in Stone, *Clarence Darrow for the Defense*, 399. Nathan Leopold made a similar comment to a *Chicago Herald and Examiner* reporter named Walter Sullivan in the immediate aftermath of the crime. After telling Sullivan that he committed the crime to see what it was like to kill someone, he explained that intellectual curiosity is "highly commendable, no matter what extreme pain or injury it may inflict upon others. A 6-year-old-boy is justified in pulling the wings from a fly, if by so doing he learns that without wings the fly is helpless" (Walter Sullivan, "'I Wrote Note, Loeb Killed Him,' Says Leopold in First Interview," *Chicago Herald and Examiner*, June 2, 1924; quoted in Baatz, *For the Thrill of It*, 148).

314. Joseph G. Schwab, 1974; quoted in Higdon, *Leopold and Loeb*, 301.

315. Alexis de Tocqueville, *Democracy in America*, trans. Arthur Goldhammer (New York: Library of America, [1835, 1840] 2004).

316. Tocqueville, *Democracy in America*, vol. 1, part 2, chap. 8, p. 311.

317. Jerold S. Auerbach, *Unequal Justice: Lawyers and Social Change in Modern America* (New York: Oxford University Press, 1976), 21.

318. Roth and Roth, *Devil's Advocates*, 162. They draw on Bertram Harnett, *Law, Lawyers, and Laymen: Making Sense of the American Legal System* (New York: Harcourt Brace Jovanovich, 1984), 37.

319. American Bar Association, "Lawyer Demographics," 2011, http://www.americanbar.org/content/dam/aba/migrated/marketresearch/PublicDocuments/lawyer_demographics_2011.authcheckdam.pdf; Deborah L. Rhode, *In the Interests of Justice: Reforming the Legal Profession* (New York: Oxford University Press, 2000), 118. For a discussion of the issues surrounding the high number of lawyers and lawsuits in the United States, see Chapter 5 of Rhode's book, titled "Too Much Law/ Too Little Justice: Too Much Rhetoric/Too Little Reform" (pp. 117–141).

320. Bernard Lefkowitz, *Our Guys: The Glen Ridge Rape and the Secret Life of the Perfect Suburb* (Berkeley: University of California Press, 1997). For Lefkowitz's description of Glen Ridge as a "picture-perfect" suburb, see pp. 11–12.

321. Lefkowitz, *Our Guys*, 171.

322. Lefkowitz, *Our Guys*, 310.

323. Lefkowitz, *Our Guys*, 418.

324. Lefkowitz, *Our Guys*, 420, 424–425.

325. Quoted in Rhode, *In the Interests of Justice*, 102.

326. Quoted in Rhode, *In the Interests of Justice*, 102.

327. Quoted in Rhode, *In the Interests of Justice*, 102.

328. Rhode, *In the Interests of Justice*, 102.

329. On women's entry into the legal profession in the United States, see Karen Berger Morello, *The Invisible Bar: The Woman Lawyer in America, 1638 to the Present* (New York: Random House, 1986).

330. Clarence Darrow; quoted in Morello, *The Invisible Bar*, x.

331. "Governor Ryan Declares Moratorium on Executions, Will Appoint Commission to Review Capital Punishment System," Illinois Government News Network (IGNN), press release, January 31, 2000, http://www.illinois.gov/pressreleases/showpressrelease.cfm?subjectid=3&recnum=359.

332. George Ryan; quoted in "Governor Ryan Declares Moratorium on Executions." On Anthony Porter, see Michael L. Radelet and Hugo

Adam Bedau, "Erroneous Convictions and the Death Penalty," in Saundra D. Westervelt and John A. Humphrey, eds., *Wrongly Convicted: Perspectives on Failed Justice*, 269–280 (New Brunswick, NJ: Rutgers University Press, 2001) (especially 269–271).

333. "Illinois Commission Announces Nation's Most Comprehensive Death Penalty Review; Recommends Sweeping Changes to Protect Innocent, Ensure Fairness," Death Penalty Information Center (DPIC), 2002, http://www.deathpenaltyinfo.org/node/596.

334. Edwin Borchard, *Convicting the Innocent: Sixty-Five Actual Errors of Criminal Justice* (Garden City, NY: Garden City Publishing Company, 1932).

335. Karen F. Parker, Mari A. Dewees, and Michael L. Radelet, "Racial Bias and the Conviction of the Innocent," in Saundra D. Westervelt and John A. Humphrey, eds., *Wrongly Convicted: Perspectives on Failed Justice*, 114–131 (New Brunswick, NJ: Rutgers University Press, 2001).

336. Innocence Project, "Know the Cases: Alan Crotzer," 2012, http://www.innocenceproject.org/Content/Alan_Crotzer.php; David Fischer, "Crist Signs Bill Compensating Man Imprisoned for 24 Years," Associated Press, April 11, 2008, http://www.heraldtribune.com/article/20080411/NEWS/804110369/-1/rss01.

337. The main Innocence Project website (www.innocenceproject.org) provides extensive resources, including case profiles, factual information on the problem of wrongful convictions, and links to affiliated organizations. Many of the affiliated organizations also provide valuable resources. For example, the "Additional Sources" page of the Mid-Atlantic Innocence Project's website (http://www.exonerate.org/about-2/additional-sources/) lists books, reports, films, and other sources of information on the topic of wrongful convictions.

338. For a landmark study done by the Columbia University School of Law at the behest of the U.S. Senate and Department of Justice, see James S. Liebman, Jeffrey Fagan, and Valerie West, *A Broken System: Error Rates in Capital Cases, 1973–1995* (New

York: Columbia University School of Law, 2000), http://www2. law.columbia.edu/instructionalservices/liebman/index.html.

339. Brandon L. Garrett, *Convicting the Innocent: Where Criminal Prosecutions Go Wrong* (Cambridge, MA: Harvard University Press, 2011), 231.

340. For more on the causes of wrongful convictions, see Innocence Project, "Understand the Causes," 2012, http://www.innocenceproject.org/understand/; Mid-Atlantic Innocence Project, "Causes of Wrongful Convictions," 2010, http://www.exonerate.org/www.exonerate.org/about-2/causes-of-wrongful-convictions/.

341. Innocence Project, "Understand the Causes: Eyewitness Misidentification," 2012, http://www.innocenceproject.org/understand/Eyewitness-Misidentification.php.

342. Sheila Martin Berry, "When Experts Lie," Truth in Justice, http://www.truthinjustice.org/expertslie.htm.

343. For more on Fred Zain, see Barry Scheck, Peter Neufeld, and Jim Dwyer, *Actual Innocence: Five Days to Execution and Other Dispatches from the Wrongly Convicted* (New York: Doubleday, 2000), 109–125; Garrett, *Convicting the Innocent*, 92, 252–254; Berry, "When Experts Lie."

344. Richard Ofshe, a social psychologist and expert on false confessions; quoted in Carol Tavris and Elliot Aronson, *Mistakes Were Made (but Not by Me): Why We Justify Foolish Beliefs, Bad Decisions, and Hurtful Acts* (Orlando, FL: Harcourt, 2007), 130.

345. Nolo, "50-State Chart of Small Claims Court Dollar Limits," 2012, http://www.nolo.com/legal-encyclopedia/small-claims-suits-how-much-30031.html. Check your state's website for the most up-to-date information—not only on the jurisdictional limit but on other rules that may affect your case.

346. On the difficulty of filing complaints and taking disciplinary action against lawyers, see Rhode, *In the Interests of Justice*, 158–168.

347.   For lists of these offices together with contact information, see American Bar Association, "Directory of Lawyer Disciplinary Agencies 2011–12," December 2011, http://www.american-bar.org/content/dam/aba/migrated/cpr/regulation/directory.authcheckdam.pdf; "Reporting a Lawyer for Ethics Violations," Lawyers.com, 2012, http://legal-malpractice.lawyers.com/v2/Reporting-a-Lawyer-for-Ethics-Violations.html.

Chapter 9: Fighting Scams

348.   Deputy U.S. Marshal Barry Golden; quoted in Jerry Oppenheimer, *Madoff with the Money* (New York: Wiley, 2009), 177.

349.   Erin Arvedlund, *Too Good to Be True: The Rise and Fall of Bernie Madoff* (New York: Portfolio, 2009), 78–79, 171–172. Arvedlund says "the premises of Madoff's advisory business were off-limits to most employees from the broker-dealer side. Generally, the hotshot traders on eighteen and nineteen and the people working on seventeen didn't mix or socialize much" (p. 171). To reinforce this separation, Madoff hired many nonnative speakers of English on the seventeenth floor (p. 79).

350.   Doug Kass, Seabreeze Partners hedge fund, Palm Beach, Florida; quoted in Arvedlund, *Too Good to Be True*, 80.

351.   Donald Trump is quoted in Mark Seal, "Madoff's World," *Vanity Fair*, April 2009, 124–135, 166–173 (quote on 168).

352.   On Madoff's compulsiveness, see Oppenheimer, *Madoff with the Money*, 26, 125–126, 162, 180, 200–201; Jerry Oppenheimer, "The Making of Madoff," Daily Beast, August 1, 2009, www.thedailybeast.com/blogs-and-stories/2009-08-01/the-making-of-madoff/p/; Seal, "Madoff's World," 135.

353.   Julia Fenwick; quoted in Oppenheimer, *Madoff with the Money*, 180.

354.   Arvedlund, *Too Good to Be True*, 23–24.

355.   Oppenheimer, *Madoff with the Money*, 25–26.

356. Simon Callow, *Orson Welles: The Road to Xanadu* (New York: Viking, 1996), 404.

357. Dorothy Thompson; quoted in Carl Sifakis, *Hoaxes and Scams: A Compendium of Deceptions, Ruses, and Swindles* (New York: Facts On File, 1993); entry titled "Men from Mars Panic: Orson Welles' Radio Scare," 172–174 (quote on 173–174).

358. Callow, *Orson Welles*, 400–402.

359. Charles Van Doren describes the experience in "All the Answers: The Quiz-Show Scandals—and the Aftermath," *New Yorker*, July 28, 2008, 62–69, www.newyorker.com/reporting/2008/07/28/080728fa_fact_vandoren.

360. For more on religious Ponzi schemes, see Doug Shadel, *Outsmarting the Scam Artists: How to Protect Yourself from the Most Clever Cons* (Hoboken, NJ: AARP/Wiley, 2012), 63–75.

361. Sara Needleman (a pseudonym); quoted in Shadel, *Outsmarting the Scam Artists*, 117.

362. Frank W. Abagnale, *The Art of the Steal: How to Protect Yourself and Your Business from Fraud—America's #1 Crime* (New York: Broadway Books, 2001), 212–213.

363. Silver Lake Editors, *Scams & Swindles: Phishing, Spoofing, ID Theft, Nigerian Advance Schemes, Investment Frauds, False Sweethearts: How to Recognize and Avoid Financial Rip-Offs in the Internet Age* (Aberdeen, WA: Silver Lake Publishing, 2006), 25.

364. For these and other examples of counterfeiting, see Abagnale, *The Art of the Steal*, 167–185.

365. For example, according to a National Consumers League survey, 92 percent of adults had received a letter or postcard notifying them that they were entitled to "free prizes." Nearly a third took the bait, and less than a fifth of those individuals were able to claim their prize without paying a fee or making a purchase (Les Henderson, "Sweepstakes Schemes, Scams, Frauds," Crimes of Persuasion, 2011, http://www.crimes-of-persuasion.com/Crimes/Telemarketing/Outbound/Major/Sweepstakes/sweepstakes.htm).

366. The items in the list are quoted from Henderson, "Sweepstakes Schemes, Scams, Frauds."

367. Henderson, "Sweepstakes Schemes, Scams, Frauds."

368. FINRA Investor Education Foundation, *Fighting Fraud 101: Smart Tips for Older Investors*, pamphlet (Washington, DC: SaveAndInvest.org, 2009), 1.

369. Sara Needleman; quoted in Shadel, *Outsmarting the Scam Artists*, 121.

370. Henderson, *Crimes of Persuasion*, 388.

371. Henderson, *Crimes of Persuasion*, 388.

372. Shadel, *Outsmarting the Scam Artists*, 137–144.

373. Quoted in Anthony Pratkanis and Doug Shadel, *Weapons of Fraud: A Source Book for Fraud Fighters* (Seattle: AARP Washington, 2005), 13–14.

374. Ed Joseph (a pseudonym); quoted in Shadel, *Outsmarting the Scam Artists*, 33.

375. and Shadel, *Weapons of Fraud*, 161–162.

376. Shadel, *Outsmarting the Scam Artists*, 156.

377. Western Union, "Protect Yourself from Fraud," 2012, http://www.westernunion.com/WUCOMWEB/staticMid.do?method=load&pagename=fraudTips.

378. Federal Trade Commission, "'I'm from the Government. . .': Sweepstakes Scams Feature Con Artists Impersonating Government Officials," *FTC Consumer Alert*, May 2008, *www.ftc.gov/bcp/edu/pubs/consumer/alerts/alt167.pdf.*

379. Jim Stickley, *The Truth about Identity Theft* (Upper Saddle River, NJ: FT Press / Pearson Education, 2008), 157, 169.

380. Abagnale, *The Art of the Steal*, 218–219.

Chapter 10: Science: Not Always "Scientific"

381. On these and other examples of scientific fraud, see William Broad and Nicholas Wade, *Betrayers of the Truth* (New York: Simon & Schuster, 1982); David J. Miller and Michel Hersen,

eds., *Research Fraud in the Behavioral and Biomedical Sciences* (New York: Wiley, 1992).

382. A. J. H. Goodwin, "The Curious Story of the Piltdown Fragments," *South African Archaeological Bulletin* 8, no. 32 (December 1953): 103–105 (the suffragist incident is mentioned on p. 103).

383. Frances Oldham Kelsey; quoted in Linda Bren, "Frances Oldham Kelsey: FDA Medical Reviewer Leaves Her Mark on History," *FDA Consumer* Magazine, March-April 2001.

384. See, for example, Morton Mintz, "Heroine of FDA Keeps Bad Drug Off Market," *Washington Post*, July 15, 1962, A1.

385. James H. Jones, *Bad Blood: The Tuskegee Syphilis Experiment*, rev. ed. (New York: Free Press, 1993). The title of Jones's book comes from the diagnosis given to the participants in the study, whose official title was the Tuskegee Study of Untreated Syphilis in the Negro Male. The men were told they were being treated for "bad blood," a local phrase with a range of meanings that could include syphilis but could also include lesser conditions like anemia or fatigue.

386. The study not only included the 399 men known to have syphilis, but also a control group of 201 men who didn't have the disease. On the withholding of penicillin, see Jones, *Bad Blood*, 7–9, 178–180.

387. *St. Louis Post-Dispatch*, July 30, 1972, 2D; quoted in Jones, *Bad Blood*, 9.

388. James B. Lucas, assistant chief of the Venereal Disease Branch, U.S. Public Health Service, "An Analysis of the Current Status of the Tuskegee Study," memo, September 10, 1970, TF-CDC; quoted in Jones, *Bad Blood*, 202.

389. Deborah Rudacille, *The Scalpel and the Butterfly: The War between Animal Research and Animal Protection* (New York: Farrar, Straus and Giroux, 2000), 96–97.

390. Kimberly Sessions Hagen, "Bad Blood: The Tuskegee Syphilis Study and Legacy Recruitment for Experimental AIDS Vac-

cines," in John P. Egan, ed., *HIV/AIDS Education for Adults*, New Directions for Adult and Continuing Education, no. 105, 31–41 (San Francisco: Jossey-Bass, spring 2005) (quote on 31).

391. Hagen, "Bad Blood," 31.

392. Hagen, "Bad Blood," 31; italics in the original.

393. Lois Marie Gibbs, *Love Canal: The Story Continues...* (Gabriola Island, BC: New Society Publishers, 1998), 21.

394. Gibbs, *Love Canal*, 22.

395. Eckardt C. Beck, Administrator of EPA Region 2, 1977–1979; his recollections appear in his article "The Love Canal Tragedy," *EPA Journal*, January 1979, http://www.epa.gov/aboutepa/history/topics/lovecanal/01.html.

396. Gibbs, *Love Canal*, 205.

397. Gibbs, *Love Canal*, 205.

398. Gibbs, *Love Canal*, 216.

399. Jeffrey M. Smith, *Seeds of Deception: Exposing Industry and Government Lies about the Safety of the Genetically Engineered Foods You're Eating* (Fairfield, IA: Yes! Books, 2003); Jeffrey M. Smith, *Genetic Roulette: The Documented Health Risks of Genetically Engineered Foods* (Fairfield, IA: Yes! Books, 2007). A ten-page summary of *Seeds of Deception* is available at www.wanttoknow.info/deception10pg; for material related to *Genetic Roulette*, go to www.seedsofdeception.com.

400. Jeffrey M. Smith, "*Seeds of Deception* by Jeffrey M. Smith: A 10-Page Summary," 2003, www.wanttoknow.info/deception10pg. For more detailed examples of animals that avoid eating GM foods, see pp. 45 (geese), 76 (cows), 106 (cows and hogs), 126 (squirrels, elk, deer, raccoons, and mice), and 157 (rats) of Smith's book *Seeds of Deception*.

401. Stan Cox, "Are Your Cell Phone and Laptop Bad for Your Health?", AlterNet, July 31, 2007, www.alternet.org/story/58354/.

402. Cox, "Are Your Cell Phone and Laptop Bad for Your Health?"

403. For more on Teflon and other industrial chemicals, see Stan Cox, *Sick Planet: Corporate Food and Medicine* (London: Pluto

Press, 2008), 134–153. He mentions the death of pet birds on p. 137.

404. Ian Austen, "Canada Takes Steps to Ban Most Plastic Baby Bottles," *New York Times*, April 19, 2008, http://www.nytimes.com/2008/04/19/business/worldbusiness/19plastic.html?ref=americas.

405. For example, critics of D. Ewen Cameron—whose unethical brainwashing experiments are discussed in Chapter 3—have argued that "if one word had to be chosen as a comment on [his] career...hubris is the one" (Anne Collins, *In the Sleep Room: The Story of the CIA Brainwashing Experiments in Canada* (Toronto: Lester & Orpen Dennys, 1988), 203).

406. Mary Shelley, introduction to *Frankenstein, or the Modern Prometheus*, 3rd ed. (Oxford: Oxford University Press, [1831] 1969), 8. Though *Frankenstein* was originally published in 1818, most contemporary editions—including the Oxford edition—are based on the third edition of 1831, which was heavily revised by Mary Shelley.

407. Shelley, *Frankenstein*, 9.

408. Claude Bernard, *An Introduction to the Study of Experimental Medicine*, trans. Henry Copley Green (New York: Macmillan, [1865] 1927). For a good account of the early history of vivisection in Europe and the United States—as well as of the emergence of the antivivisection movement—see Rudacille, *The Scalpel and the Butterfly*, 17–79.

409. On Kingsford, see Rudacille, *The Scalpel and the Butterfly*, 30–49, and the references cited there.

410. Anna Kingsford, August 20, 1879; quoted in Rudacille, *The Scalpel and the Butterfly*, 35.

411. Anna Kingsford; quoted in Rudacille, *The Scalpel and the Butterfly*, 35–36.

412. Edward Maitland; quoted in Rudacille, *The Scalpel and the Butterfly*, 48.

413. Antivivisection organizations included the Pennsylvania Society for the Prevention of Cruelty to Animals (founded in 1867), American Antivivisection Society (1883), New England Antivivisection Society (1895), Antivivisection Society of Maryland (1898), Vivisection Reform Society (1903), Society for the Prevention of Abuse in Animal Experimentation (1907), California Antivivisection Society (1908), Vivisection Investigation League (1912), and others. For a discussion of why women usually spearheaded these organizations, see Rudacille, *The Scalpel and the Butterfly*, 50–54.

414. Jane Goodall; in Dale Peterson and Jane Goodall, *Visions of Caliban: On Chimpanzees and People*, rev. ed. (Athens: University of Georgia Press, 2000), 280.

415. Jane Goodall; in Peterson and Goodall, *Visions of Caliban*, 278.

416. For discussion, see C. Ray Greek and Jean Swingle Greek, *Sacred Cows and Golden Geese: The Human Cost of Experiments on Animals* (New York: Continuum, 2000), especially 28–32.

417. Kathy Archibald, "Drug Testing on Animals Is Not Beneficial," in David M. Haugen, ed., *Animal Experimentation*, Opposing Viewpoints Series, 157–164 (Farmington Hills, MI: Greenhaven Press, 2007) (quote on 158–160).

418. James Schardein; quoted in Archibald, "Drug Testing on Animals Is Not Beneficial," 160. Also see Greek and Greek, *Sacred Cows and Golden Geese*, 44–48.

419. On microchip technologies and the promise they hold for replacing animal tests, see David H. Freedman, "Microchip Technologies Could Make Drug Testing on Animals Unnecessary," in David M. Haugen, ed., *Animal Experimentation*, Opposing Viewpoints Series, 165–172 (Farmington Hills, MI: Greenhaven Press, 2007).

420. Carol Tavris and Elliot Aronson, *Mistakes Were Made (but Not by Me): Why We Justify Foolish Beliefs, Bad Decisions, and Hurtful Acts* (Orlando, FL: Harcourt, 2007), 48–49.

421. "Concern over Canned Foods: Our Tests Find Wide Range of Bisphenol A in Soups, Juice, and More," *Consumer Reports*, December 2009, 54–55 (quote on 55).

422. Karl Weber, ed., *Food, Inc.: How Industrial Food Is Making Us Sicker, Fatter, and Poorer—and What You Can Do about It* (New York: PublicAffairs / Perseus Books Group, 2009).

Conclusion

423. Editorial, *Sacramento Bee*, July 2, 1980; quoted in Helen Gahagan Douglas, *A Full Life* (Garden City, NY: Doubleday, 1982), 419.

Appendix

424. Anthony Pratkanis and Elliot Aronson, *Age of Propaganda: The Everyday Use and Abuse of Persuasion*, rev. ed. (New York: W. H. Freeman / Holt, 2001), 356.

425. For some examples, see Brooke Noel Moore and Richard Parker, *Critical Thinking*, 9th ed. (New York: McGraw-Hill, 2008); M. Neil Browne and Stuart M. Keeley, *Asking the Right Questions: A Guide to Critical Thinking*, 9th ed. (Upper Saddle River, NJ: Prentice Hall, 2009); John Chaffee, *Thinking Critically*, 9th ed. (Boston: Heinle, 2007).

426. See the box titled "FactCheck.org's Guide to Testing Evidence" in Brooks Jackson and Kathleen Hall Jamieson, *unSpun: Finding Facts in a World of Disinformation* (New York: Random House, 2007), 121–122 (quote on 121). Jackson and Jamieson are the founders of FactCheck.org.

427. Paul Frame, "Shoe-Fitting Fluoroscope (ca. 1930–1940)," Oak Ridge Associated Universities, 2010, http://www.orau.org/ptp/collection/shoefittingfluor/shoe.htm.

428. Quoted in Frame, "Shoe-Fitting Fluoroscope (ca. 1930–1940)." On the shoe-fitting machines, also see J. Duffin and C. R. R. Hay-

ter, "Baring the Sole: The Rise and Fall of the Shoe-Fitting Fluoroscope," *Isis* 91, no. 2 (2000): 260–282.

429. Frame, "Shoe-Fitting Fluoroscope (ca. 1930–1940)."

430. James A. Herrick, *Critical Thinking: The Analysis of Arguments* (Scottsdale, AZ: Gorsuch Scarisbrick, 1991), 42.

431. Max Cutler, 1954; quoted in Allan M. Brandt, *The Cigarette Century: The Rise, Fall, and Deadly Persistence of the Product That Defined America* (New York: Basic Books, 2007), 130.

432. Rachel Carson, *Silent Spring* (Boston: Houghton Mifflin, 1962).

433. Linda Lear, *Rachel Carson: Witness for Nature* (New York: Holt, 1997), 430.

434. Excerpts from *Silent Spring* appeared in the "Reporter at Large" column of the *New Yorker* in the issues dated June 16, 23, and 30, 1962. The official publication date of the book version published by Houghton Mifflin was September 27, 1962.

435. Ezra Taft Benson; quoted in Lear, *Rachel Carson*, 429.

436. The letter is from H. Davidson, San Francisco, June 29, 1962, originally published in the *New Yorker*, February 20 and 27, 1995, 18; quoted in Lear, *Rachel Carson*, 409. Lear explains that "the P.S. was not included in the anniversary edition, but Carson quotes it in her speech to the National Parks Association" (p. 567n43).

437. Robert B. Cialdini, *Influence: Science and Practice*, 5th ed. (Boston: Pearson / Allyn and Bacon, 2009), 230.

438. Cialdini, *Influence*, 230.

INDEX

CPSIA information can be obtained at www.ICGtesting.com
Printed in the USA
LVOW11s1735110815

449697LV00003B/513/P

9 781469 980683